W9-BIS-906

Challenging Time Series

Challenging Time Series

Limits to Knowledge, Inertia and Caprice

T.D. Stanley
*Professor of Economics and Business,
Hendrix College, Conway, AR 72032, USA*

Edward Elgar

Cheltenham, UK · Northampton, MA, USA

Published by
Edward Elgar Publishing Limited
Glensanda House
Montpellier Parade
Cheltenham
Glos GL50 1UA
UK

Edward Elgar Publishing, Inc.
136 West Street
Suite 202
Northampton
Massachusetts 01060
USA

A catalogue record for this book
is available from the British Library

Library of Congress Cataloguing in Publication Data

Stanley, T. D., 1950–
    Challenging time series : limits to knowledge, inertia and caprice
/ T. D. Stanley.
    Includes bibliographical references and index.
    1. Time–series analysis.   I. Title.
HA30.3.S7   2000
519.5'5—dc21   99–41928
                                                                      CIP

ISBN 1 84064 143 6

Contents

Figures

Tables

Preface

There are obvious patterns routinely found in our most important measures of the world's economies: GDP, prices, inflation, consumer spending, stock market prices . . . for which conventional economic theory has no explanation. This book demonstrates the explanatory power of the behavior inertia hypothesis in a wide variety of applications and develops an epistemological and methodological rationale for its structure and antecedence. My framework postulates that inertia and randomness (or 'caprice') are the most important (but not the only) factors in representing and forecasting many economic time series. The resulting statistical models are simple and widely accessible to students, business economists and financial analysts.

This research is a synthesis of many applied econometric studies and the philosophical inquiry into the appropriate methods for economic science. My approach is derived from widely accepted tenets of contemporary philosophy of science that constitute fundamental and inescapable constraints to human knowledge. Several epistemological constraints are identified, and their import to economic behavior and econometric methodology are discussed. My theory is derived from epistemological considerations but leads to practical economic models that are well corroborated by actual economic data and events.

The scope of this inquiry is broad. Philosophy of science begets methodology and economic theory; economic data and experiments corroborate theory and methodology. Thus, I beg the reader's patience. This work integrates well-known patterns in economic time series data to well-accepted theses of contemporary philosophy of science. And, along the way, a philosophical and empirical case is made for a new econometric methodology that is amply illustrated through econometric applications.

The breadth of this project makes it unusually difficult to fully acknowledge all those who have made significant contributions. At the risk of important omissions, I must acknowledge the gracious efforts of a few. First, I would like to thank my students and the College. Hendrix College is the Platonic ideal of a small, liberal arts college. I especially appreciate the encouragement and of the Dean of the College, Dr. John Churchill, and my

Department Chair, Stephen Kerr. Although there are considerable start-up costs associated with involving undergraduate students in genuine research, the long-term returns are quite high. Several chapters of this book began as joint research projects capably conducted by the students of my Economic Research class. In particular, I wish to thank Tami Araiza for her studious attention to 'An Empirical Critique of the Lucas Critique', Chapter 8, Laura Frets for her careful and professional leadership in conducting the experiments reported in Chapter 10, 'The Trouble with Testing: Bubbles, Inertia, and Experience in Experimental Asset Markets', and Natalie Brooks for her perseverance and excellent assistance with Chapter 9, 'Meta-Analysis of Ricardian Equivalence: New Wine in Old Bottles'.

Furthermore, I would like to acknowledge the support of Hendrix College, Conway, and Wolfson College, Cambridge, for my sabbatical leave. This book began while on sabbatical at Cambridge, and I greatly benefited from Tony Lawson's Workshop on Realism and the discussions with his students and numerous visiting scholars.

Versions of several chapters have appeared previously in academic journals. I am very grateful to the editors and publishers of the *Southern Economic Journal*, the *Journal of Post-Keynesian Economics*, the *Journal of Economic Issues*, and the *Journal of Socio-Economics* for their permission to include this research. A special thanks goes to Richard Hattwick, editor of the *Journal of Socio-Economics*, for his gracious support of my research and for his series idea, 'in search of behavioral economic man'. This book represents my tentative answer to a few of the more general characteristics that constitute 'behavioral economic man'.

Finally, I would be remiss if I did not recognize the invaluable support and encouragement of my wife, Ann Robinson, and my best friend, Stephen B. Jarrell. Without their wise advice and active assistance, this book could not have been written. Thanks greatly one and all. Needless to say, any error or omission is solely my responsibility.

1. Introduction

Might it be possible to suggest that, just as in the case of the history of physics, once stochastic concepts are admitted into the field, one progressively discovers that the damage to deterministic world view is not so easily localized? And that, just perhaps, the more that we find out, the more meaningless the paradigm of constrained optimization becomes?

– Mirowski (1989a, p.235)

ISSUES AT STAKE

It is often asserted that economic science is predictive. Our textbooks are full of such claims. Predictive success, in fact, is given the central role in what serves as the conventional methodology of orthodox economics– Friedman's 'methodology of positive economics'. According to this popular view, theories rise or fall based upon their records of predictive success (Friedman, 1953, Boland, 1979, Stanley, 1985). And certainly, the majority of economists would agree with the view expressed by Christ (1951) that, 'The ultimate test of an econometric model... comes with checking its predictions' (Armstrong, 1984, p.19). With such importance placed upon prediction, why do economic models predict so poorly?

Specifically, why do naive time series methods typically outperform theoretically well-supported, macroeconomic forecasting models? After decades of distinguished development, what explains the meager record of successful econometric accomplishments? Although most economists dismiss this 'econometric puzzle' and choose instead to believe that econometric methods produce accurate short term forecasts, much empirical evidence and the current practice of econometrics clearly demonstrate the superiority of simple atheoretical, time series techniques (Armstrong, 1984, Makridakis and Hibon, 1984, Cooper, 1972, Naylor *et al.*, 1972).

Contemporary topics such as nonstationarity, unit roots and cointegration push this puzzle center stage. As a result, macroeconomists and econometricians find themselves in the awkward position of embracing *ad hoc* statistical models that have no orthodox theoretical foundation. The

1

challenge confronting orthodox and heterodox economics alike is to discover a genuine explanation of economic time series that does not resort to *ad hoc* rationalizations. It is a central purpose of this book to show how the simple behavioral dynamics of inertia and caprice can explain many of the recent empirical economic puzzles and provide an alternative, general theory of economic phenomena. I will argue that the theory advanced here is more general than conventional economic theory and possesses greater explanatory power, making conventional theory a limiting case. The behavioral inertia hypothesis represents a progressive problem shift for economics.

'Ten years ago it was conventional to think of mainstream economics as being in a state of crisis. Now such talk is rejected' (Dow, 1997, p. 85). Evidence of crisis, or its equivalent, is found in the renewed interest in methodology and a long list of books with titles such as: *Economics in Disarray, Why Economics is not yet a Science, Dangerous Currents: the State of Economics, The Crisis in Economic Theory,* and *The Death of Economics.* The most fundamental of economic theories, the rationality postulate with its attendant equilibrium theory, has been pushed past the point of negative net returns, and the mainstream is retreating (Blaug, 1980, Malinvaud, 1991, Baumol, 1991, Stiglitz, 1991, Hahn, 1991, Mayer, 1993).[1] The psychological literature on preference reversals and related phenomena has decisively shown rationality to be untenable, or at least its reliance on transitivity (Lichtenstein and Slovic, 1971, Machina, 1987, Tversky *et al.*, 1990, Hausman, 1992). 'Putting the arguments together, we see a denial of the fundamental principle of mainstream theory construction, *i.e.*, the principle of axiomatic, closed-system, mathematically-expressed theory which yields equilibrium solutions' (Dow, 1997, p.84). Apparently, 'the war is over, and the victors have lost' (March, 1992). 'Crisis or not, there can be little doubt that the confidence acquired by economists during the post-war period has been severely shaken' (Pheby, 1988, p. ix).

In contrast to the orthodox, static, 'Newtonian' conception of economic science, the approach offered here focuses on the inherently stochastic and habitual nature of economic behavior. This stochastic behavior – termed 'caprice', following Dostoevsky – cannot be conveniently tacked onto the end of deterministic systems of equations and assumed to be randomly and independently distributed. Rather, the evolution of economic systems and the process of human learning involve dynamic components of inertia and caprice (or habit and innovation, if you prefer). 'Caprice' is part of our fundamental economic nature, and it leads to a more dynamic conception of economic theory.

My approach follows in the tradition of behavioral and institutional economics by not forcing economic behavior into the straightjacket of neoclassical maximization. Why should economists *constrain* man to *maximize*? It is my thesis that inertia and caprice define a useful framework in which to study the dynamic aspects of economic phenomena, especially as observed in economic and financial time series data. In the following chapters, the behavioral inertia hypothesis (BIH) is shown to solve many of the empirical/theoretical puzzles that define the modern economic malaise and its symptoms.

CAVEAT

> Economists who are strong advocates of one type of economics, be it mathematical formalism or institutionally grounded economics, sometimes dismiss the other type of work with the words: 'this is not economics'. There is no reason why they should be allowed to thus practice lexicography without a license.
>
> – Mayer (1993, p.52)

This book is not intended to be a personal assault on mainstream economists, although some will no doubt feel that it is. Some of my best friends, most capable students, and brilliant teachers are orthodox economists. Rather, I wish to offer and test an alternative unconventional theory for a few of the more puzzling features of economic time series. The researcher who advances an alternative theory is thereby obligated to differentiate his approach sharply from the *monopolistic* competition of orthodoxy. However, therein lies a dilemma.

Catch-22

The discipline of economics places the would-be unconventional economist between Scylla and Charybdis. If he or she is not openly critical of the deficiencies of modern orthodoxy, then the alternative theory is dismissed for not being derived explicitly from individual utility maximization or the related ruling methodology.[2] Omission of conventional theory or the latest econometric fashion is taken as evidence of poor scholarship rather than an intelligent response to fatally flawed economic theory and econometric practice.

If the offered criticism is less than comprehensive, some specific utility function or approach will be suggested to circumvent the stated deficiencies. In this way, the would-be unconventional economist is prohibited from conducting alternative research unless an exhaustive critique of individual utility maximization is first given. However, stating such an exhaustive critique succeeds only in making mainstream economists more defensive, dismissing the critic as an outsider, 'one of those'. One reviewer of this book serves as an illustration, 'What is the use of heaping insults on mainstream economists after one hundred years of abuse from Marxists economists?' My purpose of criticizing neoclassical orthodoxy is to be entitled to practice unconventional economics.

Fortunately, this catch-22 is not a genuine dilemma, such as the econometric dilemma of pretesting or accepting misspecification, but rather an artificial construction to trap the unfaithful. The solution, of course, is quite simple. The unconventional economist should offer his or her theory, marshal the relevant empirical evidence and be permitted to do so. As eloquently expressed by the famous plea for pluralism, signed by the most respected members of the profession and published in the *American Economic Review* a few years ago,

> We the undersigned are concerned with the threat to economic science posed by intellectual monopoly. Economists today enforce a monopoly of method or core assumptions, often defended on no better ground that it constitutes the 'mainstream'. Economists will advocate free competition, but will not practice it in the marketplace of ideas.

So what is the best way forward? I do not wish to attempt a comprehensive critique of mainstream economics because it would be counterproductive and likely to distract from the genuine purpose of this research. Let me simply say that I do not believe that economic agents behave as if they maximize utility or any other objective function. They do not know the dimensions of the relevant optimization problem, let alone the prices or the critical parameters of the many underpinning distributions when some version of imperfect information is assumed. It is my view that epistemological constraints shape the behavior of economic agents – see Chapters 3, 4 and.5.

Anticipating Mainstream Criticism: A Modest Proposal

> For many years I have argued against intellectual fashions in the sciences, and even more against intellectual fashions in philosophy. . . . Today it has become fashionable in the sciences to appeal to the specialized knowledge and authority of expert, . . . For just as the fashionable thinker is a prisoner of his fashion, the expert is a prisoner of his specialization.
>
> –Popper (1994, p. ix)

Mainstream economists will likely be troubled by much of this book. To them, BIH will appear to be pulled 'out-of-the-blue'. It was not. Rather, it was derived from the epistemological constraints discussed in Chapters 3 and 4 and from my econometric experience during the 1970s when the importance of first differences was manifest. The sense that BIH is pulled out of the air reflects the fact that it is not derived from individual utility maximization, but it is possible to do – see the Appendix of Chapter 3.

The mainstream economist is also likely to be underwhelmed by the absence of mathematical rigor. This too is no oversight. Like Thomas Mayer's 'Truth versus Precision', I believe that there is a misallocation of limited research resources to mathematical rigor at the expense of empirical progress. Mayer (1993) identifies the weakness of mainstream's formalist bias as the 'principle of the strongest link', which is defined as the 'procedure of focusing attention on the strongest part of an argument and then attributing its strength to the entire argument' (p. 57). Such a principle is invalid and misdirects research away from important empirical inquiry.

Following Barrett (1958), the related faith in the rigor of the latest econometric tool may be termed the 'illusion of technique'. Chapter 5 argues that the important problems confronting contemporary econometric methodology cannot be solved by any technique, no matter how rigorously derived. The empirical studies found in Chapters 6-10 illustrate how common problems of econometric applications are the result of model misspecification not the omission of the latest full-information or nonparametric estimation technique. Hence, the focus of these empirical studies is upon the specification testing of simple, yet robust, models and estimation techniques.

My theory, BIH, is merely the first filter with which to sift understanding from chaotic economic time series. Not to employ such a filter is likely to mistake spurious correlation for genuine explanation. However, BIH is but a simple theory, not a Theory. It is not meant to be a grand covering law that explains all microeconomic and macroeconomic phenomena. Rather, due in part to the law of large numbers, it explains a few of our more important economic time series and related phenomena.

IGNORANCE AS INERTIA AND CAPRICE

Perfect information, or its equivalent, is critical to orthodox economic theory. How can economic agents be expected to make choices that maximize utility or profits if they are not fully aware of the alternatives and all of their consequences? Latsis (1976), for example, considered perfect information an essential part of the theory of the firm, assigning it to the

Lakatosian 'hard core' and thereby protecting it from any criticism. Likewise, Friedman (1953) conditioned his 'maximization-of-returns hypothesis' upon the presumption of 'full knowledge'.   Nor does the economics of information escape such an onerous epistemological burden. For example, 'rational expectations' requires at least as much 'full knowledge' – perfect information of the central tendency of the underlying distributions and knowledge of the 'correct' theory of the relevant economic processes.   But how do economic agents acquire the information they so obviously need?   What can any of us know about the world around us, and how do we gain such knowledge?   Human learning, which is shaped by epistemological constraints, induces a degree of inertia (or habit) into economic choices and behavior.

As widely accepted by philosophers, there exists no justifiable inductive method.   That is, there is no means to make valid generalizations on the basis of individual instances of some phenomenon, no matter how frequently or accurately observed.   Neither can past observation warrant a prediction of future events about which we cannot have direct experience. More than two centuries ago, David Hume provided a critique of naïve empiricism that stands to the present day (Chapter 3).   Without induction, how can we learn from experience?   But learn we must, if we are to survive and thrive.   Hume believed that custom and habit, based on repeated observation, is the only reasonable basis of action, though it is not logically justifiable.   Custom and habit alone prevent one from falling into the abyss of dysfunctional skepticism, as did Hume, that is endemic in our post-modern world.   Neither can our most advanced sciences escape the consequences of Hume's problem of induction.   Without some persistence, we would have no effective means to criticize economic theories and therefore no way to learn from our mistakes.

Thus, inertia or habit is necessary for 'rational' behavior.   Because knowledge and ignorance are prior to maximizing behavior (whether returns, profit, or utility), so is inertia.   However, a society (or economic theory) which operates solely upon inertia and habit (or the 'ruling' conventional paradigm) would quickly become sterile and degenerating. Genuine progress requires something more; it requires 'caprice'.

Intelligent economic agents have the option of conforming to their own simple-minded preferences – or not.   Free will undermines the conventional notions of rational determinism, creating uncertainty, and perhaps caprice, in all economic behavior and phenomena – Dostoevsky's uncertainty principle (Chapter 4).   Dostoevsky's uncertainty principle refers to the necessity of some minimal level of uncertainty in a free economy, analogous to Heisenberg's uncertainty principle in physics.   Intelligent economic agents, possessing free will, force economic theory to contain a degree of uncertainty. This random or capricious behavior has evolutionary value. Evolution teaches that characteristics are inherited from one generation to the next with 'blind' variations that, once in a great while, lead to improvements and are retained (Campbell, 1987). Together, inertia and caprice provide the core of an evolutionary theory of economic phenomena and a progressive epistemology.

THEORY: THE BEHAVIORAL INERTIA HYPOTHESIS

There could be no fairer destiny for any . . . theory than it should point the way to a more comprehensive theory in which it lives on, as a limiting case.
— A. Einstein

Change, error, and the stochastic behavior of the economic system are the more important aspects to model correctly. Because error terms are the source of the derived statistical properties, expedient econometric practice attends closely to how these errors are interrelated through time and throughout the system. Treating stochastic economic behavior in an *ad hoc* and instrumental manner is the cause of the poor predictive success of econometrics. Hence, my remedy is to fix on the stochastic and changing elements of the economic landscape. Caprice, in this context, represents the interesting force in the economy, and it should be modelled explicitly. If we are to predict or explain economic phenomena, we must first understand how caprice ripples through the economy.

In the absence of socio-economic forces for change, inertia will keep the economy moving at a constant rate. As in Newtonian physics, such inertia is fundamental to the dynamic behavior of the economy. Simple inertia (or habit) in economic behavior generates discernible time patterns. Together, these two forces form the behavioral inertia hypothesis (BIH) and may be used to derive a multivariate, first order autoregressive model in first differences (*d*),

$$dY_t = \alpha_0 (1 - \rho) + \rho \, dY_{t-1} + X_t \beta + \varepsilon_t \qquad (1.1)$$

where X_t is a vector of variables, usually expressed in first differences, that causes changes in the phenomenon of interest, Y_t. Chapters 2, 6, 7 and 9 present empirical applications.

This framework does not preclude conventional economic theory. In fact, neoclassical theory may be seen as a limiting case of BIH. In general as $dY \to 0$, so goes uncertainty, and maximization becomes a reasonable objective. Under these circumstances, conventional economic theory may be used to guide the empirical scientist in choosing X_t. The acceptance of BIH does not necessarily entail the rejection of the past century of economic development. Such lessons may be used to inform the researcher's specification of X_t and incorporated into the above relationship.

EMPIRICAL SUPPORT

When applied to the US GNP time series (Chapter 2), this simple model explains GNP's well-established, stable structure. Specifically, unlike conventional economics, BIH easily resolves several empirical 'paradoxes' involving GNP identified by Rose (1986). Rose notes that conventional macroeconomics cannot explain GNP's unit root, its low order of autoregressivity (AR(2) or ARIMA(1,1,0)), why GNP's time series representation is simpler than its components, or why both quarterly and annual series have the same ARIMA(1,1,0) representation.[3]

When applied to the 'consumption puzzle' (Chapter 6), BIH again gives an agreeable interpretation for many accepted empirical regularities concerning aggregate consumption expenditures. Essentially, the consumption puzzle is the observed difference between estimated long run and short run marginal propensities to consume (MPC) or between average propensity to consume and the MPC. It was the impetus for the development of the permanent income and the life-cycle theories of consumption. BIH provides a statistically adequate explanation of consumption expenditures, which can be demonstrated to improve upon more conventional econometric models. It explains how and where more conventional approaches fail. The behavioral inertia hypothesis resolves the consumption puzzle without recourse to the permanent income hypothesis or life-cycle theories, and BIH augurs the ubiquitous autocorrelations found in most economic time series. Finally, BIH predicts the last consumer recession, 1990-1991, quite accurately (mean absolute percent error = 0.6%) as well as other exceptional periods, the Second World War and its aftermath. BIH compares favorably with the better-known error correction models (ECM), and anticipates which ECM representations will be weak and which ones will appear well supported by the data. However, when compared directly with one another, the restrictions imposed by BIH are accepted by the data while ECM's restrictions are not (Chapter 6).

Habit and random selections are sufficient to explain the empirical regularities found in the aggregate consumption expenditures. This resolution of the consumption puzzle is independent of orthodox utility theory. Individual utility maximization and hence conventional consumer theory are unnecessary; thus irrelevant. Habit and randomness are sufficient to explain observed consumer behavior, so why demand more? If, as economic rhetoric repeatedly asserts, the simplicity of an explanation has value, then the behavioral inertia hypothesis is the clear choice and consumer theory may be freed from the unnecessary constraint of individual utility maximization.

BIH also explains the apparent support for the Lucas critique (Chapter 8). Recall that Lucas questions the ability of empirical economics to correctly model, test, or predict the economy based on his interpretation of rational expectations theory. Although most studies ostensibly find support for the Lucas critique, a meta-analysis reveals how the apparent applicability of the Lucas critique may be attributed to misspecification (i.e., not including lags and/or differences in an econometric model) and the manner in which expectations are treated. When models with questionable specification are discounted, empirical support for the Lucas critique vanishes. If proper model specification is given sufficient attention (Chapter 5), econometrics can escape this threat to its validity, and inertia can explain the mixed empirical support found for the Lucas critique.

In a second meta-analysis of an empirical economic literature, strong and statistically significant evidence against Ricardian equivalence is revealed (Chapter 9). Here too, the use of differences and lags in an econometric model is found to be a key aspect of the reported tests of Ricardian equivalence. In spite of great ambiguity reported in the literature about the empirical validity of the Ricardian equivalence theorem (RET), our meta-analysis uncovers and corroborates evidence against RET in striking ways. A study's degrees of freedom and its proper econometric specification increase the likelihood of rejecting RET. Furthermore, when Ricardian equivalence is embedded in BIH, Ricardian equivalence is rejected.

In a series of experiments regarding the formation of 'rational bubbles' (Chapter 10), inertia explains both the observed *irrationality* of the asset's price and the failure of conventional econometric tests to detect gross departures from market rationality. When market traders value assets according to the heuristic: 'an asset is worth what someone has paid for it', irrational expectations and market price can appear 'rational'. In these experiments, prices are determined not on the basis of the 'fundamentals' (in fact, they are sometimes negatively correlated with the fundamentals) but by inertia. Worse, conventional econometric tests are often insensitive to the difference.

Finally, BIH is also used to explain movements in prices and inflation (Chapter 7). BIH is corroborated by consumer prices, 1929–1996, and serves as a falsifying hypothesis for conventional theory, the 'expectations–augmented Phillips curve'. Behavioral inertia explains the well-known historical episodes of non-decelerating unemployment during the Great Depression, the high unemployment of Western Europe since the 1980s, and the currently falling (1997–1998) US unemployment and inflation rates. Inflation depends on the change in unemployment, not its level. Thus, all levels of the unemployment rate are NAIRU (non-accelerating inflation rates of unemployment), overturning orthodox views of macroeconomic policy, whether new classical or old Keynesian. BIH provides a useful framework in which to examine economic phenomena and to understand the successes and failures of previous empirical studies.

EPISTEMOLOGICAL CONSTRAINT AND ECONOMETRIC METHODOLOGY

Although in conflict with conventional optimization theory, BIH does have considerable philosophical and methodological support. Because economic behavior must be based on information held by *human* economic agents, limits on human knowledge are the most fundamental constraints. Such epistemological constraints are prior to 'rational' behavior and equilibrium. Behavioral inertia is not *ad hoc* nor is it an afterthought used to make one's statistics look good. It is a basic aspect of economic behavior. Models of rational choice assume a given set of knowledge available to the decision-maker. Any limitation to the agent's knowledge must be explicitly incorporated into the decision model; otherwise, derived behavior will not, in fact, be optimal or 'rational'. Just as the budget constraint casts a distinct silhouette for consumer theory (specifically, the dependence of demand on prices and income), epistemological constraints shape economic behavior. Because there are constraints to human knowledge, there are inertia and caprice in economic behavior.

Complementing inertia, Dostoevsky's uncertainty principle and the econometric consequence of the Duhem–Quine thesis guarantee a role for randomness or caprice in econometric models. If economics is to learn from its empirical database, such stochasticism must be made an explicit part of economic theorizing. The Duhem–Quine thesis or its econometric shadow, the pretest/specification dilemma, can explain much of the historic difficulty in empirically refuting economic theory. The Duhem–Quine thesis (DQ) contends that one can never be sure which specific hypothesis is responsible for a given empirical refutation. Rather, it is the entire theoretical system, and perhaps all of science itself, that is implicated by the empirical record (Duhem, 1906, Quine, 1953). The Duhem–Quine thesis allows dogmatic defenders to deflect empirical criticism indefinitely. However, these methodological limitations need not render econometrics empirically impotent. Witness the natural sciences. Although they too suffer from the methodological problems associated with the Duhem–Quine thesis, the critical attitude of the natural sciences has sometimes permitted effective empirical criticism.

In econometrics, the Duhem–Quine thesis is manifested as the pretest/specification dilemma. If we do not test the proper statistical specification of an econometric model, conventional inference is suspect because the necessary assumptions of these models are routinely violated in practice. If, on the other horn, we do test our model's specification, we introduce unknown distortions into conventional estimates and inferences (i.e., pretest bias). It has been forthrightly acknowledged that there is no econometric solution to this dilemma (Darnell and Evans, 1990, pp. 70–73) nor, would I argue, can there be. This econometric dilemma is a reflection of deeper philosophical limitations and will not yield to a technical solution no matter how elaborate or adroitly executed. The pretest/specification dilemma may be managed only by methodological decision.

The recognition of these limitations forms the basis of a reasonable empirical methodology (Chapter 5). Against the conventional economic view, my approach allows people to be intelligent, capable of genuine learning and innovation. Contrary to the orthodox view, the behavior of economic agents is dominated by inertia and caprice.

SUMMARY

Much of this book is devoted to demonstrating the power of inertia and caprice in explaining specific, empirical economic phenomena. In addition to aggregate consumption expenditures and GNP, BIH is applied to inflation, the effects of deficit spending, and experimental market pricing. In contrast to the orthodox approach, the behavioral inertia hypothesis explains:

- why economic time series frequently contain unit roots
- the surprising simplicity of economic time series models
- the prevalence and importance of hysteresis
- common violations to the sunk cost rule
- why conventional econometric models so often contain autocorrelated residuals.

BIH gives structure and a theoretical understanding to the common, but *ad hoc*, practice of adding lags indiscriminately in applied econometrics. Because the behavioral inertia hypothesis captures the underlying dynamic structure of economic time series, it has material implications for policy and practice. If policy makers and business economists wish to understand and forecast those economic statistics that are so closely followed by government and the media, then their models must make some accommodation for this dynamic structure. The BIH provides a simple, systematic, and logical framework for the study of economic time series, one that has considerable empirical support.

NOTES

1 Elsewhere, I have argued that rationality 'theory' is not theory at all (Stanley, 1986b). Orthodox economists treat rationality or individual utility maximization as a central part of their methodology. That is, all economic explanations must employ the rationality postulate if they are to be regarded as legitimate.

2 Because orthodox economists treat individual utility maximization as their accepted methodology, I am not sanguine about convincing them to use an alternative theory through either rational or empirical argument. Mainstream economists and their critics are speaking on different levels of discourse for contrary purposes, as if they are using different languages. Thus, critics and defenders have little chance of convincing one another, and debates can persist indefinitely (e.g., the 'assumptions debate') (Stanley, 1986b). Contrary to Kuhn (1962), alternative paradigms need not be incommensurable, in spite of the fact that many economists and some scientists choose not to understand their opposition.

3 AR(p) represents an autoregressive time series model of the form: $Y_t = \alpha_1 Y_{t-1} + \alpha_2 Y_{t-2} + \ldots + \alpha_p Y_{t-p} + u_t$. ARIMA are autoregressive, integrated, moving average models. The moving average portion allows for a lag structure in the error terms, and integration refers to the number of times the data is differenced before being modelled.

2. Empirical Paradox and the Behavioral Inertia Hypothesis[*]

> If chance will have me king,
> why, chance may crown me,
> Without my stir . . . .
> Come what come may,
> Time and the hour runs through the roughest day.
>
> – Shakespeare, the Scottish play

Nineteenth century political economy was dominated by the deductive or *a priori* method (Blaug, 1992, Hausman, 1992, Stanley, 1982). General laws were discovered by introspection. For example, the laws of diminishing marginal utility and diminishing returns were thought to be obvious truths in little need of empirical validation. From such laws and assumptions of convenience, empirical and policy implications were deduced. If experience verifies the deduced predictions or implications, great confidence is placed on the general law (Friedman, 1953). If, on the other hand, observation is in conflict with the deduced predictions, the deficiency is attributed to the *ceteris paribus* clause (or 'disturbing causes') which is omnipresent in the nonexperimental science of economics. The philosopher Daniel Hausman (1992) claims that the practice of twentieth century economics is also consistent with this deductive method and further that such a method is advantageous.

> At one time, economists believed that economic theories were obvious facts of experience, that *casual* introspection was sufficient to establish the theory of value and maximization, and that economic principles could be known *a priori* (Knight, 1940) (Mises, 1949 and 1960) (Robbins, 1962). I wish that I could accurately report that those days are long gone – that economists have progressed far beyond their deductive, aprioristic roots. Unfortunately, this methodological perspective was dominant less than fifty years ago when our elder statesmen were trained, and it still colors and shapes the debate. Its influence upon contemporary economics is stronger than is usually perceived or freely admitted. – Stanley (1991)

13

Let us for the moment suppose that the method *a priori* is correct.[1] What is a better example of an intuitively obvious generalization about economic behavior than the law of inertia? That is, people are habitual in their economic actions and choices. Casual introspection reveals no economic law more clearly.[2] Habit plays a significant role in our routine economic decisions, consumption choices, occupational pursuits and chosen investment alternatives long after these decisions are optimal, or sensible, and in the face of changing economic conditions. Economic inertia is as obvious and as accurate a description of economic behavior as any economic 'law', so called.

To illustrate the importance of habit in economic behavior, consider the old economic adage, 'never make decisions on the basis of sunk costs'. People (especially undergraduate economic students) routinely break this obvious corollary to economic optimization. Exceptions to this rule are well known and frequently observed. An example is the college upper-classman who remains in school long after the expected future benefits of continuing his education sink below the current net costs of school. The observed persistence attributed to 'sunk cost' may be seen as nothing more than inertia or habit. However, orthodox economics implies that only opportunity costs should be considered if one is optimizing. Frequent violations to this sunk cost rule are problematic to neoclassical economics; however, they are an obvious implication of the view developed below, the behavioral inertia hypothesis.

In this chapter, a general model of economic time series is developed and used to explain observed economic time series paradoxes. In the following chapter, Chapter 3, more detailed reasons are given for the prevalence of inertia in economic behavior. Because there are fundamental limits to human knowledge, the behavior of economic agents will be largely habitual. The second major economic force explored in this book, caprice, loosely defined as anything that might cause behavior to change, is discussed in greater detail in Chapter 4. Below a simple, dynamic framework is offered and used to solve well-known puzzles in macroeconomic time series data.

AN ECONOMETRIC PUZZLE

Inertia produces highly autocorrelated time series in which random events have lasting effects. Such series make it easy to draw incorrect inferences about causal processes. . . . In forecasting, simplicity usually works better than complexity. Complex forecasting methods mistake random noise for information.

– Pant and Starbuck (1990, p.433)

The central problem with conventional econometrics is that it is often reduced to *ad hoc* empiricism. Stochastic economic behavior is treated completely separate and independent from the economic theory. It is as if there are two distinct worlds. One is a world of abstract, deductive, deterministic theory; the other is a world of realistic, inductive, stochastic disturbances required to test economic theories. Aside from this *ad hoc* empiricism, conventional econometric practice is associated with many other routine problems, ranging from the biases associated with specification errors and specification searches to the near impotence of econometrics in the testing of any economic theory (Chapter 5). Such a neat separation of deterministic theory from stochastic econometric errors allows defenders of a theory to blame the statistical model for any unfortunate empirical embarrassment. This stochastic quarantine serves to inoculate economic theory from both empirical falsification and improvement.

An important symptom of the problem of traditional econometric practice is its poor predictive performance as compared to very simple time series models. For example, naive models such as:

$$Y_t = \alpha_0 + \alpha_1 Y_{t-1} + \varepsilon_t \tag{2.1}$$

often predict more accurately than sophisticated econometric models associated with well-accepted theories. The inadequacy of the conventional econometric approach has been widely discussed in the literature – see, for example, Makridakis and Hibon (1984) and Armstrong (1984) for reviews. Since the 1980s, 'it has become increasingly necessary to introduce Y_{t-1} in some *ad hoc* way to generate any kind of "meaningful" result' (Foster, 1987, p.242).[3] 'Commonly, research workers find themselves having to include lagged variables in their estimated equations, even though the original theoretical model could not account for them' (Spanos, 1986, p.660). As a consequence of these limitations, the practice of econometrics has itself changed. Times series analysis has become part of the standard econometric repertoire. However, the use of these techniques leads to problems of their own.

Making matters worse, it is now accepted wisdom that many economic data sets have 'unit roots' and are therefore nonstationary (Nelson and Plosser, 1982). A unit root occurs when the first order autoregression coefficient is one, e.g., $\alpha_1 = 1$ in equation (2.1). The limiting distributions of nonstationary time series do not possess finite moments (means and variances), invalidating everything that was once taught about classical statistical inferences (Hendry, 1986). One problem, as shown by Granger and Newbold (1975), is that 'spurious regressions' are often found when two variables are in fact unrelated, but nonstationary. Two unrelated economic time series may appear highly correlated by conventional statistical measures when each is moving according to its own inertia and random variation. These phenomena serve only to confirm the concern expressed by Leamer and Leonard (1983).

> Empirical results reported in economic journals are selected from a large set of estimated models. Journals, through their editorial policies, engage in some selection, which in turn stimulates extensive model searching and prescreening by prospective authors. Since this process is well known to professional readers, the reported results are widely regarded to overstate the precision of the estimates, and probably to distort them as well. As a consequence, statistical analyses are either discounted or completely ignored. (p.306)

How many of the 'significant results' reported in the journals are little more than these 'spurious regressions' and other, equally serious, statistical artifacts (Stanley, 1989)?

Some econometricians have advanced 'cointegration' in the hopes of preserving a large portion of the traditional econometric methods and results (Hendry, 1986, Granger, 1986, Hall, 1986, Stock, 1988). Two variables are said to be 'cointegrated' if they are integrated to the same degree and if the difference between one and a linear function of the other is stationary.[4] Integration, in turn, refers to the number of times a series must be differenced (i.e., $Y_t - Y_{t-1}$) in order to achieve stationarity– i.e., constant mean and covariance structure. Now, if two cointegrated variables, X_t and Y_t, are regressed,

$$Y_t = \beta_0 + \beta_1 X_t + \varepsilon_t \qquad (2.2)$$

the ordinary least squares estimates (OLS) of β_0 and β_1 become 'super consistent', converging faster to the true parameter values than conventionally expected (Stock, 1988). This, of course, is the good news. The bad news is that these same estimators are biased in small samples and, thus, in all actual applications. Cointegration has been found in many economic variables (Granger, 1986, Hall, 1986), and it can help in those areas rich in data. Nevertheless, in practice, considerable problems will remain. First, it appears that the rate of convergence for cointegrated variables is not as rapid in practice as theory would lead us to believe (Banerjee *et al.*, 1986). Secondly, important small sample biases will remain. In fact, the famous 'consumption puzzle' (between short and long run marginal propensities to consume (MPCs) or between the APC and MPC) and Friedman's permanent income hypothesis can be explained by this small sample bias of the cointegrated variables, consumption and income (Stock, 1988).[5] 'Contrary to popular belief, the concept of "cointegration" does not offer any easy short-cuts in the construction and estimation of dynamic time series models in economics' (Muscatelli and Hurn, 1992, p.35).

Even if the idea of cointegrated variables were to succeed in restoring many of the past econometric results and methods, what has already been learned of the time series properties of economic variables poses a significant puzzle for empirical economics. In particular, Rose (1986) identifies four 'paradoxes' in the GNP time series. 'However, the fact that GNP (and many other macroeconomic time-series) likely does have a unit root even though there is no theoretical reason to expect it, surely constitutes an intriguing paradox for macroeconomists' (Rose, 1986, p.139). GNP's unit root is the first of Rose's paradoxes. Second is GNP's low order of the autoregressivity – AR(1) or AR(2). If GNP is truly a dynamic process affected by past values of money, interest, government policy, etc., then a more complex time series structure would be expected. Third, the simplicity of GNP's times series model is even more striking when compared to the greater complexity of its components – investment, consumption, and government expenditures. Lastly, Rose notices that both the quarterly GNP and the annual GNP series can be described by the same ARIMA(1,1,0) model – why? The unexplained simplicity that Rose finds in the GNP series may be found in many other economic time series as well (Nelson and Plosser, 1982). Conventional econometrics and macroeconomics does not explain these empirical regularities. This Rose paradox is symptomatic of a larger 'econometric puzzle'.

Why do most economic time series exhibit simple, nonstationary regularities? How are these time series properties generated? How may they be explained? Regardless, it is becoming clear that the traditional econometric approach does not work. One might even speculate on whether a Kuhnian crisis is currently under way in econometrics. Recall that according to Kuhn's view of science a paradigm is in 'crisis' when the ruling approach repeatedly fails to explain some empirical anomaly (Kuhn, 1962). Eventually, crisis leads to the overthrow of the ruling paradigm, and a new scientific tradition begins. Clearly, there are all the ingredients for a crisis within econometrics, and practice is changing. The extent to which this crisis is recognized and resolved will say a great deal about how 'scientific' econometricians perceive their discipline. If not orthodox econometrics, what does work?[6]

BEHAVIORAL INERTIA HYPOTHESIS

> The only difference between a caprice and a lifelong passion is that the caprice
> lasts a little longer.
>
> – Oscar Wilde

Change, error, and the stochastic behavior of an economic system are the
more important aspects to model correctly. Because error terms are the
source of all derived statistical properties, prudent econometric practice
attends closely to how these errors are interrelated through time and
throughout the system. Treating stochastic economic behavior in an *ad hoc*
and instrumental manner is the cause of the poor predictive success of
econometrics. Hence, my remedy is to fix on the stochastic and changing
elements of the economic landscape. Caprice, in this context, represents the
only interesting force in the economy, and it should be modelled explicitly.
If we are to predict or explain economic phenomena, we must first
understand how caprice ripples through the economy. Toward this end, the
following basic time series model of economic caprice is offered.

First, times series phenomena may be defined to be the function of two
basic factors, inertia and caprice.

$$Y_t = f(Y_{t-1}, C_t) \tag{2.3}$$

where:

Y_t is the economic phenomenon of interest
Y_{t-1} is the previous value of Y
C_t is everything else that may cause Y_t to change – the caprice.

In the absence of socio-economic forces for change, inertia will keep the
economy moving at the same rate. Operationalizing this definition gives[7]

$$Y_t = \alpha_0 + \alpha_1 Y_{t-1} + C_t \tag{2.4}$$

Normally, α_1 will be equal or close to one and α_0 will be zero since C_t is
meant to capture change. Equation (2.4) is a general linear relation that
allows for time trends and stationary, as well as nonstationary,
autoregressive processes.

The real trick, of course, is to correctly model the caprice. In general,
caprice can be usefully modelled as

$$C_t = X_t \beta + \rho C_{t-1} + \varepsilon_t \tag{2.5}$$

where:

X_t is a 1xk vector of explanatory variables

β is a kx1 vector of regression coefficients

ε_t is the truly random, irreducibly stochastic part of this
   phenomenon

ρ is the autoregression coefficient for caprice, a measure of its
   persistence.

Together, these two forces form the behavioral inertia hypothesis (BIH). The term ρC_{t-1}, above, allows caprice to be 'trendy', permitting change and innovation to exhibit inertia and some persistence of its own. When some economic agents are slower to adjust than others to modified economic circumstances, the effect of an innovation may persist. Or, if a random (or 'blind') variation is found advantageous (or fashionable), it will likely be imitated.

Some readers will, no doubt, consider the above framework without theoretical foundation. However, BIH borrows its dynamics from elementary physics. Inertia in physical systems implies that the present velocity of an object is related to its past velocity and the product of its acceleration and time, $v_t = v_0 + at$ (assuming constant acceleration). Or if we observe velocity each period of time, $v_t = v_{t-1} + a$. In economics, income, production, consumption expenditures, etc. may be considered analogous to velocity because they are measured as rates over time. Acceleration of an object, in turn, depends upon the forces acting on it (recall that $F = ma$).

Like physical scientists, empirical economists need to specify the relevant economic 'forces' if they are to explain time series movements. Because socio-economic forces often exhibit time persistence, that is, they are neither instantaneous nor serially uncorrelated, BIH permits some inertia in these forces. Specific economic forces tend to build and subside as the tide. 'Very few phenomena arise, grow, wane, or disappear with great rapidity. Most phenomena, even fads and fashions, rise gradually and wane gradually over several years' (Pant and Starbuck, 1990, p.433). If the observational period is shorter than the ebb and flow of the typical disturbing force, its effect will be autocorrelated over time.

The effect on velocity for such variable forces is: $dv_t = v_t - v_{t-1} = \int kF(t)dt$ evaluated between t and $t-1$, where k is a constant and $F(t)$ is the force at time t. Note that such an effect is proportional to the area under a graph of $F(t)$ between $t-1$ and t. As long as $F(t)$ is a smooth and continuous relation which rises and falls slower than the observation period, areas will be clearly correlated over time. If we were to know perfectly all the determinants of the forces that affect any given economic phenomenon, the autoregressive nature of these forces could be safely ignored because their structure could be explicitly modelled. However, in all actual econometric applications, some determinants remain unknown, unmeasured, and purely random, causing the likely autocorrelation of residual caprice.

This inertia in economic caprice, expressed by ρC_{t-1} in equation (2.5), is the simplest way to model time-dependence. Equation (2.5) also allows for entirely random forces to affect economic behavior, ε_t, and those which follow predictably from more conventional economic considerations, $X_t\beta$. Needless to say, the actual change of any economic data would be subjected to institutional resistance and human limitations. Such resistance to the full force of change (i.e., inertia) is likely to follow the familiar partial adjustment process, $(C_t - C_{t-1}) = \delta(C^*_t - C_{t-1})$. When the current impulse for change, C^*_t – conventionally called the 'desired' or 'optimal' level – is dependent on X_t and a purely random caprice, equation (2.5) results. That is, a partially adjusting caprice exhibits a lagged response.

Orthodox treatments also use partial adjustment mechanisms and related lags, so what's the difference? The difference is merely the matter of one derivative. Conventional analysis partially adjusts the level of consumption, investment, etc. to some optimal or equilibrium level. BIH, in contrast, postulates that it is their rates of change that partially adjust.

When combined with (2.4), equation (2.5) becomes

$$Y_t = \alpha_0 + \alpha_1 Y_{t-1} + X_t \beta + \rho C_{t-1} + \varepsilon_t \tag{2.6}$$

By substituting $C_{t-1} = Y_{t-1} - \alpha_0 + \alpha_1 Y_{t-2}$ from (2.4), we obtain

$$Y_t = \alpha_0(1-\rho) + (\alpha_1 + \rho)Y_{t-1} - \rho\alpha_1 Y_{t-2} + X_t\beta + \varepsilon_t$$

or $\tag{2.7}$

$$Y_t = \delta_0 + \delta_1 Y_{t-1} + \delta_2 Y_{t-2} + X_t \beta + \varepsilon_t$$

Equation (2.7) is a compact form of BIH and clearly illustrates the dependence of Y_t on its past values (Y_{t-1} and Y_{t-2}) and the current values of the explanatory variables. Such dependence creates persistence in macroeconomic phenomena; that is, hysteresis both general and specific (Katzner, 1993). This equation is an ordinary regression model where all the usual assumptions should hold, except of course stationarity. Applications of BIH usually involve a restricted version of the above equation ($\alpha_1 = 1$) where all variables are in first differences. Models of first differences are an economical way to obtain stationarity and avoid obvious specification problems. This chapter uses both versions of the behavioral inertia model because Rose (1986) focuses on an AR(2) model of GNP.

Notice further that there is nothing else in this model that precludes traditional econometric analysis. The explanatory variables X_t can be derived from orthodox economic theory, or any other theory, in a conventional or heterodox manner. BIH does not pretend to be an entirely comprehensively and fully specified theory of all economic time series. No economic theory is. Admittedly, inertia and randomness, alone, are insufficient to specify some economic series fully – for example, inflation (Chapter 7). Nonetheless they are sufficient to provide an adequate empirical explanation of the well-known puzzles of consumption (Chapter 6) and GNP, below. BIH provides a dynamic structure that explains how changes in the economic environment affect many time series. However, it does not completely identify nor restrict all the potential causes.

Such flexibility may be regarded as either a strength or a weakness. Widely accepted conventional theories such as the natural rate hypothesis or the Keynesian consumption function may be added, giving BIH a more conventional basis for $X_t \beta$. However, conventional critics may view such flexibility as an implicit admission that there is no 'theory' here at all. Again, BIH is not meant to explain the entire causal structure of all economic time series. It merely identifies a necessary filter with which to explore and test alternative causal mechanisms of economic phenomena. Even the discipline's most general and most venerated theory, individual utility maximization, is not sufficient, not by a long shot, to specify the entire causal structure of all, or any, economic time series. However, this fact is unlikely to dissuade orthodox economists from demanding that unconventional approaches satisfy standards that their theories cannot. It is my view that individual utility maximization does not provide an explanation of any empirical phenomenon. Only after many auxiliary hypotheses are added does it refer to actual phenomena (Chapter 5). And, I would argue that it is the auxiliary hypotheses that have empirical content, rather than individual utility maximization.

Aside from the issues surrounding nonstationarity, the only potential econometric problem is that the presence of lagged values of the dependent variable causes the conventional estimators to be biased (Malinvaud, 1966). However, this is not usually seen as a serious problem (Theil, 1971), and, in any case, autoregressive models are consistently estimated by OLS (ordinary least squares).

What is truly interesting is how well this basic model of caprice explains the econometric puzzle and Rose's paradoxes. To illustrate the remarkable consistency of this behavioral approach with the times series properties of US GNP, the model is first simplified – $\alpha_1 = 1$ and $\beta = 0$.[8] That is, assume that there is no inertial decay and that the effects of explanatory variables are negligible. In this case, BIH becomes,

$$Y_t = \alpha_0(1-\rho) + (\alpha_1 + \rho)Y_{t\text{-}1} - \rho\alpha_1 Y_{t\text{-}2} + \varepsilon_t \qquad (2.8)$$

or

$$dY_t = \alpha_0(1-\rho) + \rho dY_{t\text{-}1} + \varepsilon_t \qquad (2.9)$$

Where $dY_t = Y_t - Y_{t\text{-}2}$. This is an autoregressive model of order two, AR(2), the same form that provides the basis of Rose's paradoxes. According to Blanchard (1981) and quoted by Rose (1986), 'One of the few undisputed facts in macroeconomics is that output is hump shaped... nearly equivalently, output is well characterized by the following AR(2):

$$y_t = 1.34\,y_{t\text{-}1} - 0.42\,y_{t\text{-}2} + \varepsilon_t \;\;' \qquad (2.10)$$
$$\;\;(16.4) \quad (-5.21)$$

(p.137), where y_t above is the detrended logarithm of real quarterly GNP, and t-statistics are in parentheses. Not only does our behavioral model have the correct form, but also the linear restriction implied by (2.8) that the AR coefficients sum to one (i.e., $1+\rho-\rho = 1$) seems to be confirmed by these empirical estimates.

To test the implied structure of BIH more formally, Blanchard's analysis may be updated using annual US data, 1929–1991 – see Figure 2.1. For GNP expressed as the natural logarithm of real (1982) dollars, we find

$$\ln \hat{Y}_t = .1184 + 1.52 \ln Y_{t\text{-}1} - .54 \ln Y_{t\text{-}2} \quad R^2 = .993 \qquad (2.11)$$
$$\;\;(14.53) \quad\quad (-5.12)$$

ln, of course, denotes natural logarithms and the numbers in parentheses are t-values. The restriction derived from BIH, $\delta_1 + \delta_2 = 1$ (where δ_1 and δ_2 are the 'true', or population, autoregression coefficients), implies that there is a well-defined relation among the differences in GNP – recall equation (2.9). Regressing these differences in logarithms yields:

$$d\ln \hat{Y}_t = .0154 + .53\,d\ln Y_{t\text{-}1} \qquad R^2 = .299 \qquad (2.12)$$
$$\;\;(5.01)$$

See Figure 2.1. Using equation (2.12), BIH's restrictions ($\delta_1 + \delta_2 = 1$), and therefore its dynamic structure, are clearly accepted ($F_{1,58} = 1.62$).[9] Because the dependent variable is different in equation (2.12), R^2 may give the erroneous impression that difference models fit the data poorly. The standard errors of the estimate, however, are virtually the same whether the model is fitted in the form of first differences or levels, doubly lagged.

Thus, the empirical structure of GNP time series provides a clear corroboration of BIH.

Figure 2.1: Actual and Predicted GNP

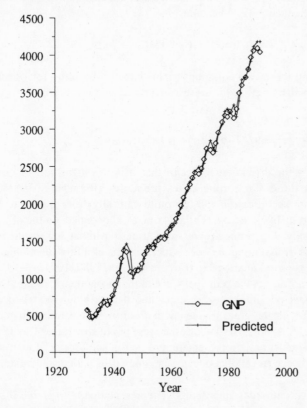

Other aspects of the empirical data lend further support to this basic model of behavioral dynamics. For instance, Rose reports that GNP may also be modelled as an integrated, first order, autoregessive model, ARIMA(1,1,0). And, again the specification of the model defined by (2.4) and (2.5) implies this time series property. Equation (2.9) is, by definition, ARIMA(1,1,0) with autoregression coefficient ρ.

An interesting extension to this basic model is to allow for 'friction' or inertial decay. If the force of habit (or, inertia) decays at a constant rate, $(1-\alpha_1)$, equation (2.4) becomes

$$Y_t = \alpha_0 \ Y_{t-1}^{\alpha_1} C_t$$

or   (2.13)

$$lnY_t = ln\alpha_0 + \alpha_1 lnY_{t-1} + lnC_t$$

If then caprice experiences the same type of exponential decay, a simple version of equation (2.5) becomes

$$C_t = C_{t-1}^{\rho}\varepsilon_t \qquad \text{or} \qquad lnC_t = \rho \ lnC_{t-1} + ln \ \varepsilon_t \tag{2.14}$$

Combining these two equations yields exactly the same relationships as previously discussed and it is estimated by equation (2.11).

$$lnY_t = \alpha_0(1-\rho) + (\alpha_1 + \rho \ )lnY_{t-1} - \rho lnY_{t-2} + \varepsilon_t \tag{2.15}$$

So, what's the difference? Recall that it is the logarithm of GNP that possesses those stable time series properties (Blanchard, 1981). This logarithmic specification follows quite naturally from the basic idea of inertia and its likely decay. Orthodox macroeconomics, on the other hand, often employs logarithmic regressions, usually without any justification, or sometimes by assuming, *ad hoc*, a specific type of utility function designed to give the desired relationship (Epstein and Zin, 1989, 1991).

Let us not forget the principal piece to the 'econometric puzzle', i.e., the stylized fact of 'unit roots' in economic data. Is our model of caprice consistent with the great frequency that unit roots are found in economic time series? Again, BIH imbues the appropriate structure. This is readily seen in the most basic representation of inertia and caprice, equation (2.4). When α_1 is one (recall that one or nearly one is its anticipated value), this is the unit root.

In the second order autoregressive representation, AR(2), the first-order autoregression coefficient is $(\alpha_1+\rho)$. Given the frequent positive autocorrelations found in economic data and the socio-economics of trends and fads, it is almost certain that ρ is positive, and, therefore, the first order autoregression coefficient is likely to be at least one, even in the presence of some inertial decay. For AR(2), stationarity depends on the sum of the coefficients, $|\delta_1 + \delta_2| < 1$. Because $\delta_1 + \delta_2 = \alpha_1 + \rho - \rho = \alpha_1$, stationarity requires $\alpha_1 < 1$. Although near unit roots are technically stationary, the associated time series can exhibit great persistence, and statistical tests are likely to accept a unit root because they have low power. Thus, test results consistent with unit roots and nonstationarity are the consequences of the behavioral dynamics of caprice. Even when stationary, BIH implies that economic time series will have near unit roots and considerable persistence.

For US GNP, Rose and others have shown that the evidence is consistent with the existence of a unit root (Stock and Watson, 1986). Using a Dickey–Fuller test on the 1929–1991 logarithmic data leads to the acceptance of a unit root $(t = -.34)$.[10] Unlike traditional theory, we have good reason to expect these 'puzzling' unit roots. Habit and trendy innovations die hard. Together, their effects can be quite persistent and explosive.

Thus, this simple model of behavioral dynamics solves the 'econometric puzzle'. Throughout the remainder of this book, the rich potential of BIH will be illustrated and tested. Returning to Rose's paradoxes, especially intriguing is the resolution of his last two. That GNP is less complicated than its components is not difficult to understand when one realizes that GNP or its growth is the target variable of monetary and fiscal policies. To the extent that these policies are effective, there should be less variability in GNP's time series. Or, even those who do not believe in interventionist policy must admit that the aggregate, GNP, confronts physical, political, social and environmental constraints to its sudden growth or rapid diminution more directly than its components. The major component of GNP, consumption, is also well described by BIH – see Chapter 6.

Rose's most puzzling 'paradox' is that both the annual GNP and the quarterly GNP series can be described by the exact same time series model. Rose (1986) notes that there is no conventional explanation for the peculiar fact that the same model, *with the same coefficients*, represents both the quarterly and the annual GNP series. However, when GNP follows the behavioral inertia hypothesis, one would expect the autoregression coefficients to remain the same. To verify the expected relation between quarterly and annual series, consider a continuous version of the model represented by equation (2.9).

$$E(dY_t/dt) = \alpha_0(1-\rho)+ \rho\, dY_{t-1}/dt \qquad (2.16)$$

If t represents years and q quarters, one could multiply the above equation by dt/dq to derive the quarterly dynamics. By so doing, all variables would be measured by their quarterly rates of change and the slope coefficient would remain the same. However, the constant term, $\alpha_0(1-\rho)$, would be multiplied by $dt/dq = 1/4$. Therefore, the intercept is reduced to one fourth of its annual value to adjust for the expected difference in quarterly dynamics.[11] Changes in the intercept are not considered by Rose, because Blanchard (1981) used detrended data. When applying annual estimates to predict, quarterly, the last consumer recession 1990-1991, reducing the intercept to one fourth its annual estimate improves forecast accuracy, see

Chapter 6. Even the most peculiar properties of GNP's time series are quite easily explained by BIH.

SUMMARY

It would be the final error of reason – the point at which it succumbs to its own *hubris* and passes over into its demoniacal opposite, unreason – to deny that the Furies exist, or to strive to manipulate them out of existence.

– Barrett (1958, p.279)

Given the poor record of empirical economic success, given the surprising ways in which error distributions riddle applied economics, given, indeed, those puzzling economic time series patterns, isn't it time to get serious about caprice? Researchers need not acquire the characteristics of their subjects. Nor do economists need to constrain economic man to be a 'rational' maximizer, even though *homo oeconomicus* may be their alter ego. Being more 'liberal' in our conception of man is not a sign of lax moral constitution. Will people act more 'irrationally' if economics recognizes their inalienable caprice? *The purpose of economic science is not to instruct economic man, but to study him.*

In this chapter, a simple behavioral framework for the study of economic time series is introduced. BIH provides structure for many, but not all, economic time series. Because aggregate flows and prices are analogous to velocity and mass, they may be reasonably expected to harbor inertia. Although variables representing stocks, such as wealth, definitionally contain inertia, their error distributions are better specified through the corresponding flows. Nonetheless, this simple model of inertia and caprice explains a considerable number of well-known empirical puzzles in economic time series. Unlike the orthodox approach, the interaction of inertia and caprice gives a natural explanation to the common types of time series often found in economics, their unit roots and their logarithmic forms. Habit and innovation explicitly imply the autoregression and autocorrelation routinely found in econometric applications.

Equally important is the heuristic value of this framework for explaining economic time series. It explicitly focuses upon those influences that affect the *change* in the dependent economic variables (not their levels) and upon those error terms that generate all the system's statistical properties. These are the factors that dominate econometric results, not equilibrium nor changes in relative prices as orthodoxy would lead us to believe. Contemporary econometrics with its concentration on time series methods is already moving in this direction; BIH merely explains why simple time series models often succeed in describing macroeconomic phenomena.

A likely concern of orthodox economists is whether the simple econometric equations used here are really different from more conventional approaches. Cannot the same type of times series models be found in the empirical literature? Of course, but the lags and time series structures used in the applied econometric literature are generally *ad hoc*, not based on economic theory but appended to a model whenever the data demand. Because orthodox economics does not explicitly acknowledge this dynamic structure, lags and differences are sometimes ignored leading to misspecifications (see Chapters 6, 8 and 9).

Not only does BIH provide a theoretical framework for such econometric models; it is *more general* than orthodox theory. In fact, orthodox empirical economics may be considered a special case of BIH. By specifying βX_t in equation (2.5) (or systems of such influences) through auxiliary behavioral hypotheses (such as budget and other constraints), conventional macroeconomic theories may be embedded in BIH. Even if economic behavior is not entirely composed of inertia and caprice, it may be largely so and, in any case, will be somewhat so. The orthodox approach fails to allow for these dimensions and thereby often discovers the mere artifact of its own methods. Orthodox economics includes inertia and caprice only as *ad hoc* afterthoughts, if at all, and gives them no genuine explanatory power. BIH, on the other hand, begins with a broader conception of human behavior but retains room for conventional explanations to the full extent that they matter. BIH, therefore, is a necessary filter through which economic time series need to be viewed. Because orthodox economists have historically attributed great significance to a theory's generality, the perspective offered here must be seriously considered.

NOTES

*   From the *Journal of Socio-Economics*, **20**, 1991, 37-56.

1   My philosophy of science is quite the opposite of deductivism (Stanley, 1982, 1985, 1991). The purpose of 'playing devil's advocate' is to show that the theory offered here may be defended by the same arguments that are employed to 'justify' fundamental neoclassical propositions. One does not need to accept a Popperian philosophy of science, no matter how rational this may be on its own merit, in order to embrace the following behavioral inertia hypothesis. Mill's method *a priori*, and Friedman's instrumentalism, for examples, give considerable support to the theory of economic dynamics offered here.

2   As every student of economics knows, it is difficult to convince one's friends or spouse of the wisdom of equating at the margin. Those who actually attempt to do so at the supermarket or elsewhere are considered to be quite boorish.

However, everyone has observed repeated behavior in himself and others, often long after the circumstances, which made the habit sensible, have radically changed.

3 Foster (1987) uses the term X_{t-1} rather than Y_{t-1}, but in his context, it has the same meaning.

4 Actually, cointegration requires only that the residuals be integrated at a lower degree. However, most economic applications deal with I(1) and I(0); that is, integration of order one and zero where the latter is stationary.

5 This topic and its relation to BIH are extensively explored in Chapter 7.

6 An alternative methodology of econometrics is developed in Chapter 5.

7 This simple linear model of inertia and caprice can explain many of the properties found in economic time series. It is not, however, meant to be an exhaustive expression of how all stochastic and dynamic elements of economic behavior must be modelled. Rather, this model is but the first, linear approximation, one that is believed to capture the basic dynamic structure of many economic time series.

8 α_1 should nearly always be constrained to be one. In studies of inflation and consumption (Chapter 6 and 7), α_1 is restricted to be one. Here, β is assumed to be zero only for expository purposes and to be consistent with Rose (1986).

9 Given the assumptions of this BIH model, both variables in equation (2.12) are stationary, and conventional testing should be valid.

10 The critical value for the 'no trend case' is –2.908 (MacKinnon, 1991). The augmented Dickey–Fuller test also accepts GNP's unit root ($t = -1.27$).

11 However, quarterly data are often annualized; thus, scaling quarterly variables becomes unnecessary.

3. Economic Inertia as Humean Habit and Stylized Fact

> The extensive examination of the foundations of scientific inference reveals, however, that neither induction by enumeration nor any comparable method has yet been satisfactorily justified. We cannot claim to have a well-established method for ascertaining fundamental probabilities. Hume's problem of the justification of induction remains at the foundation of scientific inference to plague those who are interested in such foundational studies.
>
> – Salmon (1966, p.132)

INTRODUCTION

After decades of distinguished development, what explains the meager record of successful econometric accomplishments? The Lucas critique, specification searches, and data mining have all undermined confidence in econometrics (Lucas, 1976, Leamer, 1983, Leamer and Leonard, 1983). There are few, if any, uncontested empirical economic regularities, and large bodies of empirical evidence refute the most strongly held conventional views; for example, 'rational expectations' or 'efficient markets'. 'Classical econometrics, after all, was designed to seek confirmation of stable equilibrium relationships (Johnston, 1991; Morgan, 1988) whose relevance is now open to question' (Dow, 1997, p.82).

As discussed in the previous chapter, an important symptom of the impotence of conventional econometrics is the poor predictive performance of orthodox econometric models relative to simple, atheoretical time series models. Many economic data sets are nonstationary, autoregressive processes, growing without limit. These nonstationary time series can cause serious problems often leading to 'spurious regressions' that have no genuine explanatory relevance. The clearest lesson that emerges from both the successes and the failures of recent econometric applications is that economic time series harbor great inertia.

'Newton stated his first law in these words: "Every body persists in its state of rest or of uniform motion in a straight line unless it is compelled to change that state by forces impressed on it'" (Resnick and Halliday, 1966, p.82). 'Inertia in physical systems implies that the present velocity of an object is related to its past velocity and the product of its acceleration and time, $v_t = v_0 + at$ (assuming constant acceleration). Or if we observe velocity each period, $v_t = v_{t-1} + a$' (Stanley, 1993b, p.254). In economics, inertia is seen in economic behavior, which follows customs and habits; it is exhibited by persistence in economic time series and reflected by ubiquitous lags and unit roots in econometric applications.

It is now accepted wisdom that most economic time series have unit roots (i.e., $Y_t = \alpha Y_{t-1} + \varepsilon_t$ and $\alpha = 1$) (Nelson and Plosser, 1982). What accounts for this fact? Why is it not explicitly recognized and incorporated into conventional economic theory? The purpose of this chapter is to discuss how inertia is a direct consequence of genuine constraints to human knowledge. Hume's problem of induction and his 'customs and habits' is shown to give a theoretical basis for the behavioral inertia that permeates economic phenomena. It is important to provide a theoretical explanation for inertia because the past half-century of econometric application has discovered no better-corroborated, stylized fact.

This chapter does not attempt to offer a solution to the difficult methodological issues that surround induction and economic empiricism—see Chapter 5. Rather, epistemological limitations are directly employed to explain observed economic behavior thereby jumping over the usual methodological domain.[1] The methodological issues surrounding induction have been widely discussed throughout the philosophical and methodological literature and need not be repeated here.

THE PROBLEM OF INDUCTION: A HUMEAN HABIT

The truly empirical contribution of Hume lay in his revival of the concepts of habit and custom and their importance.   – Dewey (1960, p.83)

Perfect information, or its equivalent, is critical to orthodox economic theory. How can economic agents be expected to make choices that maximize utility or profits if they are not fully aware of the alternatives and all of their consequences? Latsis (1976), for example, considered perfect information an essential part of the theory of the firm, assigning it to the Lakatosian 'hard core' and thereby protecting it from any criticism. Likewise, Friedman (1953) conditioned his 'maximization-of-returns hypothesis' upon the presumption of 'full knowledge'. Nor does the economics of information escape such an onerous epistemological burden. For example, 'rational expectations' requires at least as much 'full knowledge'– perfect information of the central tendency of the relevant distributions and knowledge of the 'correct' theory of corresponding economic processes. But how do economic agents acquire the information they so obviously need? What can any of us know about the world around us, and how do we gain such knowledge? The present task is to discuss how human learning, which is shaped by epistemological constraints, induces a degree of inertia (or habit) into economic choices and behavior.

Can experience, no matter how accurately observed or often repeated, justify our belief in laws? Do past observations warrant predictions of future events about which we cannot have direct experience? David Hume answered: No! A quarter millennium later, his critique of naïve empiricism endures. Hume's skepticism was born from a vain search for a solid foundation upon which to build our empirical knowledge. Hume was an empiricist and believed that we learn about the existence of events, and the causation among them, only through experience. However, his inquiry revealed 'that, in all reasoning from experience, there is a step taken by the mind which is not supported by any argument or process of understanding' (Hume, 1777, p.41).

Long before Milton Friedman's famous essay, 'The Methodology of Positive Economics', and J.N. Keynes (1891) before him, Hume's 'guillotine' employed the same distinctions between 'positive' statements of fact and normative statements about 'what should be'. Like Hume's guillotine, Hume's 'fork' makes a logical distinction that limits the reach of rational inference. 'Hume's Fork forces a choice: between propositions stating, or purporting to state, matters of fact and real existence; and propositions stating, or purporting to state, only the purely logical, not to say tautological, relations between ideas or concepts' (Flew, 1988, p.xi). After making these distinctions, Hume arrived at the insight that only actual experience can teach us about the 'real' world, the future, or the causal interconnections betwixt. Neither normative nor deductive arguments help to explain how the world actually works. Only direct experience contains genuine information, but insufficiently so. With Hume's 'fork', the epistemological problem is centered squarely upon induction (i.e., the added difficulty, nay impossibility, of inferring justifiable general rules or valid patterns from individual instances).

'That even after the observations of the frequent conjunction of objects, we have no reason to draw any inference concerning any object beyond those of which we have had experience' (1739, p.139). Hume's assertion is a challenge that has yet to be met satisfactorily. This challenge has been called the 'problem of induction' – about which controversy still reigns in both the philosophy of science and economics (Boland, 1982, Hausman, 1992, Lawson 1994).[2] The absence of a rational solution to the problem of

induction caused Hume to embrace skepticism. As Bertrand Russell recognized, 'The growth of unreason throughout the nineteenth century and what has passed of the twentieth is a natural sequel to Hume's destruction of empiricism' (Popper, 1972, p.1). Given such fundamental epistemological constraints, any economic theory that supposes otherwise (such as Friedman's 'maximization-of-returns' and 'rational expectations') must be wrong. Nor can economic theories which seek only predictive success succeed on their own instrumentalist terms (Stanley, 1985).

So what is required to justify our beliefs and predictions?[3] Hume identified the necessary missing step as the principle of the uniformity of nature, 'that principle, *that instances, of which we have had no experience, must resemble those, of which we have had experience, and that the course of nature continues the same*' (Hume, 1739, p.89). Having precisely defined the nub of the issue, Hume argued against it. First, there can be no logical, demonstrative argument for the principle of the uniformity of nature because we can always conceive of the possibility of nonuniformity. Next, probable arguments, the only other possible type of demonstration available, will also be found wanting, because all probable reasoning about induction must be circular. '(P)robability is founded on the presumption of a resemblance betwixt those objects, of which we have had experience, and those, of which we have had none; and therefore 'tis impossible this presumption can arise from probability' (Hume, 1739, p.90).

> We have said that all arguments concerning existence are founded on the relation of cause and effect; that our knowledge of that relation is derived entirely from experience; and that our experimental conclusions proceed upon the supposition that the future will be conformable to the past. To endeavour, therefore, the proof of this last supposition by probable arguments, or arguments regarding existence, must be evidently going in a circle, and taking that for granted, which is the very point in question.   – Hume (1777, pp.35-36)

However, all organisms, including economic agents, must genuinely learn from experience, or die! How then do we persist and prosper when there exists no positive solution to the problem of induction; that is, no reliable way to draw inferences about the future from the past? Following Blaug (1992), it may be useful to distinguish the nondemonstrative form of reasoning from experience, 'adduction', from 'induction', both of which are loosely discussed as induction. Adduction is used by science and all of us to learn from experience. Without some form of adduction, science would not be able to progress. Deduction can only repackage old truths (i.e., its premises or assumptions), assumed to be true in the first place. 'Induction', then, is reserved for the principle of logic that allows us to form a general conclusion from knowledge of particular instances. However, no finite number of individual facts, no matter how accurately observed, can ever justify an infallible universal law or a generalization. Justifiable 'induction' does not exist. It is the legendary 'philosopher's stone'. Rather than the mythical, medieval version that turned lead into gold, induction would change data into knowledge, a more valuable transformation in the information age. Adduction is the informal and speculative leap to generalization from limited experience. Unfortunately, it does not carry the weight of logic; its generalizations may, at any moment, be wrong. Nonetheless, we must act on the basis of adductive inferences. Therein lies the practical problem of induction.

It is often overlooked, however, that Hume offered a solution to the 'psychological' implications of the problem of induction, in spite of his skepticism (Popper, 1972). Because practical action requires that people rely on expectations about the future and the consequences of their actions, how do people cope with such a severe limitation to their knowledge? Hume's psychological solution is simple, and basically correct.

> This principle is Custom or Habit. For whenever the repetition of any particular act or operation produces a propensity to renew the same act or operation, without being impelled by any reasoning or process of the understanding, we always say, that this propensity is the effect of *Custom*. By employing that word, we pretend not to give the ultimate reason for such a propensity. We only point out a principle of human nature, which is universally acknowledged, and which is well known by its effects. Perhaps we can push our enquiries no farther, or pretend to give the cause of this cause; but must rest contented with it as the ultimate principle, which we can assign, of all our conclusions from experience.... All inferences from experience, therefore, are effects of custom, not of reasoning. – Hume (1777, p.43)

Hume believed that our ability to draw inferences from experience is a psychological propensity that cannot be further defended or justified.

> There is no internal impression, which has a relation to the present business, but that propensity, which custom produces, to pass from an object to idea of its usual attendant. This therefore is the essence of necessity. . . . Our judgments concerning cause and effect are deriv'd from habit and experience; and when we have been accustom'd to see one object united to another, our imagination passes from the first to the second, by a natural transition, which precedes reflection, and which cannot be prevented by it. . . . (M)en form general rules, and allow them to influence their judgment, even contrary to present observation and experience. – Hume (1739, pp.165, 147)

For Hume, our notions of necessity and causation are born of psychological leaps and predispositions. 'Reason can never shew us the connection of one object with another, tho' aided by experience, and the observation of constant conjunction in all past experience. When the mind, therefore, passes from the idea or impression of one object to the idea or belief of another, it is not determin'd by reason, but by certain principles, which associate together the ideas of these objects, and unite them in the imagination' (Hume, 1739, p. 92).

Such ideas and beliefs lead us to form firm (psychological) rules of conduct on the basis of small (nonrandom) samples of experience. In addition, we have a natural tendency to overextend these general rules. 'For there is a principle of human nature, which we have frequently taken notice of, that men are mightily addicted to *general rules*, and that we often carry our maxims beyond those reasons, which first induc'd us to establish them' (Hume, 1739, p.551).

In order to benefit from experience, we make leaps from observation of conjunctions of events to the presumed cause through custom and habit. Such psychological leaps provide general rules of conduct that become habitual. Although the rules may be in error, we tend to employ them longer than prudent and apply them beyond any justifiable range of application.[4] Thus, we should not be surprised to find inertia in economic actions. Humean rules and habit induce inertia into human conduct. Confronted with inescapable epistemological constraints (i.e., the problem of induction), such behavior represents a 'better-than-optimal' response to limited but *informative* empirical knowledge. Because economic agents have only their experience to guide their decisions, habit or inertia must play a role in economic behavior. Such behavior logically precedes and is therefore more fundamental than any attempt to maximize utility or returns.

Hume's critique of induction is not, of course, the only possible cause of inertia. Although Humean habit provides a sufficient condition for economic inertia, it is not necessary for the existence of inertia. Like all other economic theories, this conjectured explanation of persistence in economic and financial series can never be proved to be the 'true' explanation, but it can be tested and compared with rival hypotheses. 'Nevertheless, the basic fact remains: Hume showed that inductive justifications of induction are fallacious, and no one has since proved him wrong' (Salmon, 1966, p.17). Forthcoming chapters contain many empirical examples of inertia and its importance in economics.

ALTERNATIVE THEORIES OF LEARNING

Over the intervening centuries, psychology has added to our understanding of human and animal learning. Repetition is reinforcing and leads to persistence that does not immediately dissipate as circumstances change. One such mathematical representation of this phenomenon is termed the 'linear learning model' (Estes, 1954, Bush and Mosteller, 1955, Wierenga, 1974, Lilien, 1974, Srinivasan and Kesavan, 1976). In this literature, the probability of purchasing some product next period, P_{t+1}, is linearly related to its current probability, P_t.

$$P_{t+1} = a + b + P_t \qquad \text{(if the product is purchased in period } t\text{)}$$
$$P_{t+1} = a + P_t \qquad \text{(if the product is not purchased in period } t\text{)}$$

Thus, consumer behavior is persistent, and habits are reinforcing. If the above relation is aggregated over the market and if considerations of other effects are included (e.g., prices, income, randomness, etc.), the resulting market demand would become an explicit function of its past value.

Herein lies the point. Because the problem of induction is logically irresolvable, a commonsense guide for practical action is to use habit or inertia forged from past repeated experience. We all must rely on adductive learning, if we are to *rely* on anything.[5] In econometric applications, adductive learning is routinely seen in the inclusion of the lagged values of the dependent variables. Time series models need not be *ad hoc*, as they are often considered from the conventional macroeconomic perspective. Autoregressive structures are the direct consequence of these epistemological limits to human learning.

The most frequent and formal response to the problem of induction by philosophers and social scientists, at least when it relates to practical decision-making, involves Bayesian calculus. 'Bayes' theorem casts considerable light upon the logic of scientific inference. . . . It yields a theory of scientific inference that unifies such apparently irreconcilable views as the standard hypothetico-deductive theory, Popper's deductivism, and Hanson's logic of discovery' (Salmon, 1966, p.120). Because the associated statistical formulas and decision rules are derived through the optimization of seemingly appropriate objective functions (e.g., maximum likelihood), it can be argued that Bayesian decision analysis is the 'rational' way to base our knowledge on experience. As such, it may be considered an application of the 'economic method', broadly interpreted. However, Bayesian inverse probabilities cannot solve Hume's problem; they can only bury it deeper.

Bayesian analysis is based upon an assumed set of prior probabilities. Bayesian inference is justified given the adequacy of the 'priors.' But, how can they, in turn, be justified? At best, such priors could be based upon past experience and previous priors, the latter again having no justification, and so on. No matter where we stop, we will find some unjustifiable proposition, and so the circle endures. Prior probability, or any other probability, cannot be *justified* by past experience alone. At some point, probabilities or probability distributions must be assumed.

Nonetheless, Bayesian inference makes the most efficient use of our scarce informational resources, if we were only to know what we assume. It may, therefore, be revealing to ask what general form Bayesian behavior might take. The updating of prior probability on the basis of the latest experience induces a degree of persistence to information and behavior. Recall the simple Bayes formula: $P(B/E_i) = P(B) \cdot [P(E_i/B)/P(E_i)]$, where $P(B)$ is the prior probability of buying a given product and $P(B/E_i)$ is the revised probability of buying this product given some new experience, E_i. Taking logarithms and simplifying notation yields: $lnP_t = lnP_{t-1} + [lnP(E_t/B) - lnP(E_t)]$. Expressed in this manner, the current propensity to buy, lnP_t, clearly depends on the past propensity, lnP_{t-1}, plus an adjustment for the strength of the buy signal inherent in the latest experience, $[lnP(E_t/B) - lnP(E_t)]$. Thus, a Bayesian economic agent displays persistence in her behavior. Inertia, which may be expressed by a lagged dependent variable, is also a feature of Bayesian behavior. Note also that the last term in the above equation has the general configuration of *dln* (i.e., the change in the logarithm) and is a common pattern found in economic time series.[6]

Bayesian probability calculus does not solve Hume's problem. As Hume correctly anticipated, any reliance upon probability is circular. Bayesian analysis must assume prior probabilities at some level that cannot be inferred from observations alone. However, Bayesian decision analysis can be shown to make optimal use of experience under well-specified conditions, and it leads to behavioral inertia.

Such behavioral inertia may also be derived from utility maximization or from adaptive learning models. When changing routine incurs an additional, quadratic cost, utility maximization implies the same type of dynamic structure. The interested reader should refer to the Appendix for a mathematical derivation.

Other areas of research have linked optimization and inertia. It might be argued that inertia is 'better than optimal'. In an uncertain world, dynamic decisions can give a premium to waiting (Dixit, 1989, 1992, Pindyck, 1991). This premium for waiting can be expressed as upper and lower triggers between which behavior remains the same even though fundamental economic conditions may change. In practical circumstances, this interval of inaction (or inertia) can be substantial. Thus, there will be many particular cases where the status quo gives a higher return than the standard, static neoclassical result. Habit and inertia in economic behavior is also associated with conventional preference theory when there is hierarchical choice (Drakopoulos, 1994). Finally, Akerlof and Yellen (1985) show that inertia in money wages and prices has only small, second order costs as judged from the conventional neoclassical perspective. Thus, an uncertain and dynamic decision environment may well make inertia the rational response.

Although these connections of behavioral inertia to individual utility maximization are likely to give comfort to a neoclassical economist, they do not advance our understanding of inertia. Better reasons for behavioral inertia are Humean habit and the associated constraints to human knowledge. Even though individual utility maximization can be made consistent with almost any behavior,[7] if sufficient adjustments are made, it is not an adequate theory of economic inertia. First, the required *ad hoc* adjustments to utility maximization would be a clear indication of the degenerating nature of the neoclassical research programme. For decades, conventional equilibrium theories and 'rational expectations' were asserted to be incompatible with inertia. It is a poor theory that must be frequently and substantively revised as new facts come to light.

Secondly, any reformulated theory of utility maximization cannot escape fundamental epistemological constraints. According to Hume, individual decision-makers cannot possess the 'full knowledge' of the important data and relevant parameters 'needed to succeed in the attempt' (Friedman, 1953, p. 21). Again, this is the point of Hume's critique of induction, and no one has yet found a solution or a way around it. Individual utility maximization may be made consistent with inertia or any other phenomenon when sufficient auxiliary hypotheses are added, but it remains incompatible with accepted epistemological constraints. Even if we were to embrace some neoclassical theory of inertia, real questions remain about how economic agents learn of the necessary data and parameters. The simple, and more viable, explanation of economic inertia is Humean habit.

Individual utility maximization is empty; it confers only superficial salience not explanatory power to derived hypotheses. Explanatory power is a function of what a theory prohibits; that is, what it forbids to be true (Popper, 1963). Because maximization can appear to 'explain' all possible economic behaviors, it actually explains nothing. Although the neoclassical research programme can appear to expropriate any rival, it does so at a price. By appearing to explain all behaviors, it tells us nothing. The language of optimization makes policy recommendations seem more compelling, and their technical derivation obscures their normative underpinnings. However, behavior that is consistent with maximization (and thereby given the honorific, 'rational') is not as a result more likely to be consistent with observations or to explain actual economic phenomena.

What matters is how people learn about the economy and thereby respond to changes in economic circumstances. Constraints to human learning give form to economic behavior and induce inertia in the responses of economic agents. Like more familiar economic constraints, limitations to human knowledge provide structure to economic activity. Because information is essential to the economics of maximization, constraints to our knowledge are prior to budget or resource constraints. Epistemological constraints cannot be ignored or assumed away without cost. The inability of neoclassical economics to explain the most pervasive stylized fact – inertia and unit roots – is the realization of this cost.

POPPER'S SOLUTION

Another approach to this limitation of empirical knowledge might suppose that economic agents act on the basis of the best scientific information available. That is, they learn in the same general manner that science advances and act accordingly. The philosopher Sir Karl Popper offered such a position as the solution for the problem of induction.

In the 1930s, Popper presented a solution to both the logical and the psychological problems of induction. However, even if we accept his 'solution' as valid, it will not satisfy those who seek justification for their beliefs. Popper, following Hume, clearly admits that the logical problem of induction has no solution. At best, Popper settles a related, but different, question.

> Can the claim that an explanatory universal theory is true or that it is false be justified by 'empirical reasons'; that is, by assuming the truth of certain test statements justify either the claim that a universal theory is true or the claim it is false?   – Popper (1972, p.7)

To this reformulated question, Popper answered in the affirmative. An acceptance of certain observational statements may allow us in some circumstances to falsify a theory. '(W)e might say that Popper has not so much solved the problem of induction, one of his favorite claims, as dissolved it' (Blaug, 1992, p.16). Nonetheless, Popper's reformulation of the problem of induction supplies the best available foundation for our empirical knowledge.

To discuss fully the debate surrounding the adequacy of Popper's solution is beyond the scope of the present essay. The crux of the criticisms of Popper's position concern the Duhem–Quine thesis and whether Popper's 'negative' solution to induction can be used to *justify* the falsity of any theory or statement. The inability to single out, without doubt, specific scientific hypotheses or theories for revision or refutation is a well-accepted tenet in the philosophy of science. Solving the Duhem–Quine thesis and the related pretest/specification dilemma generates an econometric methodology and is the focus of Chapter 5.

The importance of the Duhem–Quine thesis was well known to Popper. In *Logik der Forschung* (1934), he recognized that testing any scientific theory or hypothesis required the conventional acceptance, at least tentatively, of a number of observational statements along with the 'rules' for playing the game. Such a tentative and conventional falsification of scientific theory seems insufficient for those who demand certainty or justification in science.[8]

Although Popper sometimes seems to be saying more, especially when taken out of context, his view of scientific knowledge is entirely nonjustificationistic (i.e., one can never prove or justify the truth or falsity of anything). 'But as Popper has many times emphasized, the man who insists on proof is the man who never learns how wrong he is' (Miller, 1996, p. 200). The central lesson of Popper's solution to the problem of induction remains fully valid and relevant today. That is, there is an asymmetry between empirical support and contradiction, and it is the latter which carries the greater weight. 'It is central to falsificationism or critical rationalism that critical arguments of this kind, though providing no hint of justification, can help to eliminate errors from the hypotheses we propose and (if we make enough decent guesses) enable us to get a little closer to the truth' (Miller, 1996, p. 200).

Returning to the practical issues surrounding the problem of induction, Popper's discussion of the 'psychological' problem is more germane. To address the behavioral implications of the impossibility of induction, Popper proposed a heuristic, the *'principle of transference:* what is true in logic is true in psychology' (Popper, 1972, p.6). Extending this heuristic to economics, we may assume that what is true for science or epistemology will also be true for economic agents. This is essentially Muth's famous proposal for expectations (Muth, 1961). Expectations of economic agents need to be as good as those derived by our best economic theory; otherwise there are profitable opportunities to exploit. This heuristic is the strongest, reasonable assumption that can be made about the information, or the 'rationality', of economic agents. Regardless of one's philosophy of science, there is a great deal of inertia in scientific knowledge. Given this 'principle of transference', such epistemological inertia implies a general inertia in economic behavior as well.

Through Popper's critical rationalism, science advances by the method of trial and error. That is, it grows through critical inquiry, and the best criticism is empirical. Risky conjectures, which explain some phenomenon of interest, are subjected to severe testing to discover their weaknesses. Knowledge grows by seeking truth using bold, permanently tentative conjectures, and by critically and rigorously testing all theories. 'From the amoebae to Einstein, the growth of knowledge is always the same: we try to solve our problems, and to obtain, by a process of elimination, something approaching adequacy in our tentative solutions' (Popper, 1972, p.261). When depicted in such broad empirical brush strokes, philosophers and scientists would generally accept this view.

Although critical rationalism presents a very dynamic view of science (always under threat, constantly being revised), there is also considerable persistence.[9] Theories are needed to interpret observations and tests. Observation is theory-impregnated, and as a consequence, econometric testing is conditional. Theories are not quickly discarded nor rapidly revised, even in the face of abundant disconfirming empirical evidence. Enter inertia. Some would say, *dogma* (Popper, 1963, Hausman, 1992). The full impetus of new empirical experiences will be blunted by the inertia of the scientific enterprise. If economic agents acquire information in a matter analogous to science, inertia will play an important role, and new information will not be entirely reflected in current knowledge or behavior.

Popper's philosophy of science, however, assigns the smallest possible role to dogma in scientific inquiry. In fact, most of his methodological contributions are aimed to minimize the influence of dogmatism in science (Popper, 1959). Popper believed that science changes more rapidly than other philosophers of science.

His critics (for example, Kuhn, Lakatos and Hausman) all give dogma, and thus inertia in scientific knowledge, a greater role. Lakatos conferred virtual permanence to a set of propositions which he called the 'hard core'. These propositions are insulated from all criticism and revision by 'a protective belt of auxiliary hypotheses' (Lakatos, 1970). Only a more 'progressive research programme' can overturn the entire system. The Lakatosian view of science is an explicit compromise between Popper's normative methodology of science and Kuhn's histories.

Kuhn's view of science gives the leading role to inertia (Kuhn, 1962). 'Normal science' extends and refines the accepted theory, but knowledge remains mostly unchanged. Although the 'paradigm' may periodically come into conflict during so called 'revolutions', they cannot be meaningfully compared because they are 'incommensurable'. Because a paradigm is needed to interpret experience and experiment, its adherents will resist major change and dismiss disconfirming empirical evidence as 'anomaly' until a 'crisis' develops and another paradigm eventually supersedes. Both Kuhn's paradigms and Lakatos's research programmes give great weight to stability (hence inertia) in scientific knowledge.

More recently, Hausman (1992) offers an interesting defense of orthodox economics as an inexact science. Although he eschews giving advice (he prefers descriptive over normative philosophy of science), he finds a great deal of dogmatism in economics. Orthodox economists often dismiss findings from other social sciences; for example, the experimental refutation of 'transitivity' by psychologists (Hausman, 1992). There is also a tendency for economists to cordon off economics from all other social sciences. The history of economics shows a great deal of dogmatism; the central propositions of economics have changed little over the last hundred years. Economic knowledge, itself, exhibits much inertia. The open question is not whether economic knowledge resists change, but whether it changes at all in response to empirical evidence.

No matter how progressively practiced and regardless of one's philosophy of science, science will contain some inertia, some persistence, and some resistance to change. At any point, received scientific knowledge goes beyond the most recent scientific experiments or experiences; it must. Therefore, it will also resist the full force of surprise which may be contained in any new empirical information. Inertia is found in the most progressive sciences and human knowledge. Can we demand more from economic agents? If economic agents gain knowledge about the economic world as science learns of the physical and social worlds, there will be a degree of inertia in economic expectations and hence in economic behavior. When economic agents possess the best, humanly obtainable, information and learn about economic reality in the same fashion as the sciences, their behavior will contain substantial inertia.

CONCLUSION

Humean habit readily explains the ubiquitous lags and unit roots found in economic time series data. Inertia is as important and as inescapable for economic phenomena as it is in dynamic physical systems. So why has it not achieved an equivalent status in economic theory and application as it has in physics? If we are to understand the complex dynamics of either physical or social systems, it is imperative to first filter out the obvious patterns of inertia. Otherwise, the causal relations, which adductively emerge, will be thoroughly contaminated with spurious associations.

Humean habit, or behavioral inertia, is as prevalent and as important in economic phenomena as are regularities routinely called 'laws' (e.g., 'law of demand' or Okun's 'law').

Because there exists no logical method of induction, no valid method of generalization from observing individual instances alone, there will be inertia in human knowledge and behavior. Hume believed that custom and habit, based on repeated observation, is the only reasonable basis of action, though logically not justifiable. Custom and habit alone prevent one from falling into the abyss of dysfunctional skepticism. Neither can our most advanced sciences escape the consequences of Hume's problem of induction. Without some persistence there would be no ability to criticize our knowledge and no way to learn from our mistakes. Only by some method of trial and error correction can we learn from experience. Empirical knowledge must contain some dogmatism, or at least persistence; the alternative is chaos.

This limitation of human knowledge is the source of behavioral inertia. Economic behavior can be no better than the information upon which it is based, and our best knowledge exhibits inertia.

Behavioral inertia need not be *ad hoc* nor an afterthought used to make one's statistics look good. It is a basic aspect of economic behavior. Because economic behavior must be based on information held by human agents, limits on human knowledge are the most fundamental constraints. Such informational constraints are prior to 'rational' behavior, to equilibrium theory, and to individual utility maximization. Models of rational choice must presume some set of knowledge possessed by the decision-maker. Any limitation to the agent's knowledge must be explicitly incorporated into the decision model; otherwise, derived behavior will be neither optimal nor 'rational' (recall the theory of 'second best'). Just as the budget constraint outlines the basic shape of consumer theory (that is, the dependence of demand on prices and income), epistemological constraints shape economic behavior. Because there are limits to human knowledge, there is inertia in economic behavior and unit roots in economic time series.

APPENDIX: 'RATIONAL' INERTIA: OXYMORON OR SECOND BEST?

Consider consumption expenditures, and let C_t^* represent the optimal, or 'bliss', level of a consumer's purchases. If the consumer incurs a quadratic penalty, or disutility, for consuming at a nonoptimal level and another quadratic penalty for changing her level of consumption, utility maximization implies a behavioral inertia in economic time series.

Consider the following quadratic utility function:

$$U(C_t) = \Gamma - \gamma_1 (C_t - C_t^*)^2 - \gamma_2 (C_t - C_{t-1})^2 \qquad (3.1)$$

where C_t represents the consumer's actual purchases. The first term, Γ, in this utility function represents the utility at the bliss point, the second term captures the penalty for consuming more or less than C_t^*, while the third term expresses the disutility of change. Change is costly.

Here, the first order conditions become,

$$\gamma_1 (C_t - C_t^*) + \gamma_2 (C_t - C_{t-1}) = 0 \qquad (3.2)$$

or $\qquad C_t = C_{t-1} - (\gamma_1 / \gamma_2) \cdot (C_t - C_t^*)$

Of course, the long run optimal solution will have $C_t = C_{t-1} = C_t^*$. Note that adding the usual budget constraint adds a term involving the Lagrangian multiplier but does not materially affect the subsequent derivations. Also note the inertia; that is, the dependence of current consumption on past consumption, C_{t-1}. Observing that the same structure will hold for t-1 and collecting terms yields

$$dC_t = dC_{t-1} + (\gamma_1 / \gamma_2) \, dC_t^* - (\gamma_1 / \gamma_2) \, dC_t \qquad (3.3)$$

or $\qquad dC_t = \rho \, dC_{t-1} + (1 - \rho) \, dC_t^*$

where $dC_t = C_t - C_{t-1}$ and $\rho = 1/(1 + \gamma_1 / \gamma_2)$. The remaining step is to postulate what the change in the bliss level may depend on, $X_t \lambda + e_t$. Substituting this into equation (3.3) above, we find:

$$dC_t = \rho \, dC_{t-1} + X_t \beta + \varepsilon_t \qquad (3.4)$$

for β as $(1 - \rho) \lambda$ and $\varepsilon_t = (1 - \rho) e_t$. This relation is the behavioral inertia hypothesis – see equations (2.11) and (6.4). Thus, behavioral inertia can be made consistent with maximization.

Nonetheless, this exercise in differential calculus serves little purpose. First, the existence of a bliss point may itself cause technical problems for the individual-utility-maximization research programme. Bliss points can invalidate Arrow–Debreu competitive equilibrium and make prices nonpositive (Takayama, 1985). Secondly, when C_t^* is more broadly interpreted as some optimal consumption level, this derivation begs the question of whether and how utility might be maximized. Lastly and most importantly, the individual decision-maker must still be assumed to possess 'full knowledge' of all the relevant data and parameters. Thus, reenters Hume's problem of induction.

NOTES

1   To clarify this potentially difficult intellectual landscape, one may identify a hierarchical structure for economic knowledge (Stanley, 1986b). 'Epistemology' entails philosophical theses about knowledge and truth. 'Methodology consists of rules, procedures, and methods for the production of knowledge. . . . It is at the methodological level that we seek practical methods to achieve our goals' (Stanley, 1986b, p. 88). 'Theory', in contrast, involves statements and explanations about the interrelationships among the 'facts'. And, the facts are descriptions of observed events. Inertia in economic time series is a fact which conventional optimization and equilibrium theories fail to explain. Yet, Hume's practical solution to the problem of induction may serve as an economic theory more fundamental than utility maximization. Epistemology begets economic theory, regardless of the viability of inductivism for economic method.

2   Lawson (1994) criticizes conventional econometrics and orthodox economics as being inductivist, that is, crucially dependent on the constant conjunction of events, and he offers an interesting alternative, 'critical realism'. Without question, economists have employed a great deal of inductivist rhetoric, when fashionable. My criticism of orthodoxy, however, is in no way dependent on an inductivist interpretation of economic method. In fact, economics is quite eclectic containing important elements of conventionalism, instrumentalism, apriorism, and Cartesian intuitionism (Stanley, 1982, 1985, 1986b). For the present discussion, I only wish to claim that economic phenomena, and our knowledge of them, exhibit considerable persistence, regardless of which of these 'isms' one ascribes to economic methodology.

3   The interpretation below of Hume's skepticism and his critique of induction parallels Fogelin (1985) and Flew (1988).

4   The neoclassical reliance on individual utility maximization is an excellent illustration of such a Humean habit.

5   Relying on any information is risky, no matter how good one's knowledge may seem (Popper, 1972).

6   Throughout this book, it is shown that: $dY_t = \alpha_0 + \alpha_1 \, dY_{t-1} + \beta X_t + \varepsilon_t$, with or without logarithms, is a common explanatory structure for economic time series (see Chapters 2, 6 and 7).

7   A notable exception concerns intransitivity, or framing effects, found in many situations by economists and psychologists. Because transitivity is at the very core of 'rational utility maximization', trying to accommodate this empirical anomaly is especially problematic for the neoclassical research programme.

8   Of course, empirical falsification is more complex than sketched here – see Chapter 5.

9   Lakatos and Musgrave (1970) present an extended discussion of the relative
    importance of change and stability in science. Supporters and critics of both
    Kuhn and Popper agree that each plays a role in the development of science; the
    debate is over their proper balance.

4. Caprice: Dostoevsky's Uncertainty Principle*

Though custom and habit may be strong arbitrators of human action, they are not alone. Because human nature contains an irreducibly random potential, economic theory must also explicitly embody stochastic elements. Economic agents may at any moment take random, or even perverse, actions. Yet, orthodox economic theory depends fundamentally on the notion that economic behavior is rational or optimal and, in any case, deterministic. The failure of conventional economic theory to incorporate genuine uncertainty into its core denies that human economic agents are intelligent or have free will. This failure to account properly for capricious economic behavior and to filter out inertia is largely responsible for the weak record of empirical success.

DOSTOEVSKY'S UNCERTAINTY PRINCIPLE

Dostoevsky observed the irreducibly stochastic aspect of economic behavior more than one hundred years ago. His '*Notes from Underground*' contains a prophetic statement of the fundamental limits to economic knowledge.

> (N)ew economic relations will be established, all ready-made and worked out to mathematical exactitude, so that every possible question will vanish in the twinkle of an eye, simply because every possible answer to it will be provided. ... Of course there is no guaranteeing (this is my comment) that it will not be, for instance, frightfully dull then (for what will one have to do when everything will be calculated and tabulated), but on the other hand everything will be extraordinarily rational. ... I, for instance, would not be in the least surprised if all of a sudden, *à propos* of nothing, in the midst of general prosperity a gentleman with an ignoble, or rather with a reactionary and ironical, countenance were to arise and, putting his arms akimbo, say to us all: 'I say, gentleman, hadn't we better kick over the whole show and scatter rationalism to the winds, simply to send these logarithms to the devil, and to enable us to live at our own sweet foolish will!' That again would not matter, but what is annoying is that he

would be sure to find followers – such is the nature of man. And all of that for the most foolish of reasons, which, one would think, was hardly worth mentioning: that is, that man everywhere at all times, whoever he may be, has preferred to act as he chose and not in the least as his reason and advantage dictated. And one may choose what is contrary to one's own interest, and sometimes one *positively ought* (that is my idea). One's own free unfettered choice, *one's own caprice* . . . is that very 'most advantageous advantage' which we have overlooked, which comes under no classification and against which all systems and theories are continually being shattered to atoms.

– Dostoevsky (1864; 1956, pp. 70-71) (last emphasis added)

'This book published in 1864 is one of the most revolutionary and original works in the world of literature' (Kaufmann, 1956, p.13). Dostoevsky presaged our present age of uncertainty – before marginalism and before Marx's *Capital*! More profound portrayals of human behavior have rarely been made. He anticipated and rejected marginalism and neoclassical economics. Dostoevsky's perceptions represent an economic analogue to Heisenberg's uncertainty principle. Recall that Heisenberg's uncertainty principle asserts that we cannot know both the position and the momentum of an electron beyond a certain level of accuracy, a level that corresponds to Planck's constant.

Heisenberg's uncertainty principle addresses the fundamental stochastic nature of even our 'hardest' science, physics. However, it does not imply that reality or science must be subjective or the many other things that have been ascribed to it. As Mirowski (1989a) observes, 'Heisenberg's 'uncertainty principle' was thought to support all sorts of outlandish philosophical positions, from solipsism to the necessity of the existence of free will' (p.219). Because there is no obvious reason to suppose that economic agents should behave as if they were 'electrons', Heisenberg's uncertainty principle does not directly apply to economics. However, an analogous relationship is at work in complex economic systems. Although stated by Dostoevsky long before its physics counterpart, this economic 'uncertainty principle' has been overlooked.

Like Heisenberg's uncertainty principle, Dostoevsky reveals the fundamental limits of scientific knowledge, at least as it concerns the human sciences. If someone were to discover some set of deterministic laws that govern economic affairs, that knowledge would itself create uncertainty because its possessor may consciously *choose* not to obey these laws. Whoever knows the precise economic equations might exploit this special knowledge for profit thereby changing the underlying circumstances upon which the equations were based. Or perhaps, the human quest for liberty, for freedom of action, may be stronger than purely economic motives.

Dostoevsky's uncertainty principle describes a human nature that can cause at least one person to do the unpredicted – for the pure joy of truly independent choice.

> And how do these wiseacres know that man wants a normal, a virtuous choice? What has made them conceive that man must want a rationally advantageous choice? What man wants is simply *independent* choice, whatever independence may cost and wherever it may lead. And choice, of course, the devil only knows what choice.
>
> – Dostoevsky (1864, pp. 71-72)

Orthodox economics is predicated upon a belief in the sovereignty of independent choice for economic agents. In fact, this is the basis for the methodological individualism, which is so central to neoclassical economics. Ironically, however, there is an epistemological tension between the preference for freedom of choice and a requirement of stable and well-behaved individual preferences.

To make this argument a bit clearer, let us more formally state our terms and reasoning. A free economy may be defined as one in which everyone is at complete liberty to interact in the economy as they wish. That is, in a free economy economic agents can choose any feasible alternative they wish within, of course, the usual economic limits defined by income, technology, resource availability, etc. Now, we are ready to state our central conclusion.

Dostoevsky's Uncertainty Theorem: A free economy contains an irreducible amount of uncertainty that is at least as great as the economic power of one economic agent, ε.

Proof: Suppose not. That is, suppose that the economy is knowable to a degree greater than that which can be influenced by one individual. Or, let κ represent our ignorance in fully knowing the economy, and suppose $\kappa < \varepsilon$. If this were true, then someone (perhaps even an economist!) would know the conditions of the economy to a greater degree than he/she could affect. But since the knower is also an economic agent who is completely free to choose in a free economy, this very knowledge might *possibly* cause the knower to change the economy . . . or not. Such knowledge creates its own uncertainty – an uncertainty at least as great as ε. Therefore, the only way to maintain a knowable economy is to prohibit 'perverse' actions by the knowers, and that would mark the end of the *free economy*.

This interaction of economic agents' knowledge of the economy and their subsequent behavior is not merely the subject of idle philosophical speculation; it is the stuff of daily Wall Street machinations. In an era of corporate raiders and merger mania, the mere rumor of a potential takeover is sufficient to make a stock's price soar or fall. '(B)ut what is annoying is that he would be sure to find followers – such is the nature of man' Dostoevsky (1864; 1956, pp. 70-71). Such price changes are often self-fulfilling. Regardless of the accuracy of the initial rumor, a drastic price increase will tend to rationalize itself. Should the information prove to be incorrect, prices need not be immediately 'corrected', as conventional theory demands. Such 'irrational' price swings often exhibit an inertia of their own (Chapter 10). Orthodoxy, of course, does not deny that 'random' factors can affect prices, but it does require the effect of 'nonfundamentals' to be purely random.[1] The existence of predictable statistical properties for 'random price movements' may serve as a test of orthodox theory. In fact, considerable empirical evidence has accumulated through the study of rational expectations, efficient markets, and economic time series that makes the conventional characterization of price movements quite suspect (LeRoy, 1989, Camerer, 1989, Shiller, 1984).

Bacharach (1989) has termed a similar phenomenon the 'Orpheus effect' because, 'no sooner do agents' eyes fall upon the basic model than it turns to stone' (p. 340). In Bacharach's model there are two equations – one represents the usual choice-situation in which our decisions depend upon some 'parameter' (for example, price), and the other models how this 'parameter' is determined by the actions of all agents together. Should some agents come to know these equations, they will cease to be true. Because agents act as *price-takers* in the first equation but learn that they are *price-makers* from the second, it would be 'irrational' for agents not to change their behavior and hence the equations that define the economy. Bacharach goes on to show that this effect applies to the competitive model and concludes that competition is not 'rational'.

Binmore makes an analogous criticism of orthodox game theory.

> (T)raditional game theory is unsatisfactory insofar as the behavior of ideal 'perfectly rational' players is treated axiomatically à la Bourbaki. In the first place, it does not 'deliver the goods'. For games of any complexity, confusion reigns supreme about what the 'correct' analysis ought to be. . . . In the second place, doubts are appropriate about the logical foundations of the traditional approach. It is, by now, a cliché that completeness is incompatible with consistency for formal deductive systems.
>
> – Binmore(1987, pp. 9-10)

By applying Gödel's undecidability theorem to equivalent issues such as those addressed by Dostoevsky's uncertainty principle, Binmore argues that a 'perfectly rational' Turing machine cannot both fully know the game and, at the same time, be a player. 'It is in this sense that the claim that perfect rationality is an unattainable ideal is to be understood' (Binmore, 1987, p.206). Clearly, something analogous to Dostoevsky's uncertainty principle reigns even in the heart of orthodox economic game theory. 'The result is the construction of magnificent mathematical edifices of which a medieval scholastic might justly be proud, but little in the way of genuine progress' (Binmore, 1988, p.10).

But what about 'rational expectations' the neoclassical economist may wonder. First, this orthodox defense of the Newtonian paradigm from the onslaught of 'irrational' stochasticism is itself stochastic. Recall that rational expectations theories postulate that economic agents correctly know the average values of future decision parameters. Because this knowledge is incomplete (concerning averages not precise realizations), it does not directly violate Dostoevsky's uncertainty principle. However, Dostoevsky's uncertainty principle does prohibit agents with 'rational expectations' from knowing precisely how the economy works. Rational expectations theorists often argue that it is possible for all agents to possess the same 'rational expectations' and, at the same time, a knowledge of the true economic relationships. Otherwise, their position lacks a certain consistency, and the possession of such knowledge is often used as the justification of these 'rational expectations' in the first place. Bacharach (1989), however, contends that the Orpheus effect applies to these agents as well. As before, when agents learn how the economy operates, their decision problem changes and so does the manner in which the economy operates. With such knowledge, rational agents are forced into a game theory environment, and no telling where that leads. '(T)he rational expectations hypothesis, correctly applied, therefore leaves us as far from determinacy as ever' (Bacharach, 1989, p.341).

Caprice is a manifestation of intelligence, and intelligence involves hierarchy and recursion (Hofstadter, 1979). Intelligent agents have the ability to question, evaluate, and revise their own choices, generating 'meta-preferences' – preferences among preference relations (Sen, 1979). One ingredient in the intelligent individual's meta-preference relation may be the degree to which choices are really free and agents are truly autonomous. Thus, simple choices for intelligent agents will remain uncertain, for they will always have the option of not obeying their own simple-minded preference relation, or in other words, of changing their minds. Genuine 'freedom to choose' undermines the usual notion of determinism, creating uncertainty and 'caprice' in all aspects of economic behavior.

Dostoevsky's uncertainty principle implies that there will be some randomness or unpredictability in human economic behavior and choice. If economic agents are permitted to have intelligent free will, economic theory will contain a degree of uncertainty. The strictly deterministic theories of orthodox economics are misplaced and ultimately counterproductive. Nor does it suffice to graft a random error term upon the applied econometric model derived from deterministic theory. As discussed in the next chapter, this practice jeopardizes the empirical nature of econometrics and creates a dilemma – the pretest/specification dilemma. Aside from its descriptive accuracy, there are sound practical and methodological reasons to embed stochastic elements explicitly into economic theory.

THE NATURAL INHERITANCE OF CAPRICE

Caprice has evolutionary value. It provides a mechanism of behavioral variation for our higher-order social evolution. Evolution teaches us that biological characteristics are inherited from one generation to the next with 'blind' variations that lead, once in a great while, to improvements that are retained (Campbell, 1987). Caprice, therefore, may be a necessary catalyst for long run economic growth and for advancing human societies.

The evolutionary approach has had a long and variegated history in economics – from Malthusian population dynamics to Marshall's biological analogies and Veblen's evolutionary science, and from American institutionalism and Schumpeter's 'Theory of Economic Development' to Nelson and Winter's evolutionary theory and the orthodox defense of maximization by Alchian and Friedman. The evolutionary paradigm does have something to offer economics, if not applied defensively.[2] For instance, it can liberate economic theory from its sterile, static and deterministic chains – that is, from the *Zeitgeist* of its outmoded and misunderstood physics (Mirowski, 1988).

Evolution has also been advanced as the model of scientific discovery and the growth of knowledge and learning, in general (Popper (1972, Campbell, 1974, Radnitzky and Bartley, 1987). Virtually no contemporary philosopher of science believes that science grows in a continuous linear fashion. Coming the closest to this ideal is Kuhn's view of 'normal science'. But for Kuhn (1962), the slow exploration of a received paradigm is punctuated by revolutions that cause a radical rewriting of the history of science. Is this not evolutionary, as well as revolutionary?

Science does not grow by the slow accumulation of facts, as is commonly believed – recall the problem of induction. It is rather those exceptions to the rule of facts that prove the most progressive. Popper, Campbell and other evolutionary epistemologists remind us that all forms of learning involve trial and error. Many alternatives are offered (sometimes unconsciously). Those which do not withstand empirical tests will be eliminated. The schema often used by Popper is:

$$P_1 \longrightarrow TT \longrightarrow EE \longrightarrow P_2$$

(Popper, 1972), where P_1 is the problem, or issue, with which we begin. *TT* is a tentative solution or theory for the issue in question. It remains quite tentative, never 'proven', no matter how compelling the evidence may seem. *EE*, error elimination, is the most important step in the process. In science, *EE* is primarily empirical. The advance of our knowledge depends crucially on how well or poorly we carry out this step. Finally, there is P_2, the new problem-situation which results from the unanticipated surprises and remaining puzzles that always follow the preceding two steps. This is an evolutionary process where perfection is not accessible to mortal man. The wondrous varieties of life and our scientific knowledge simply evolve through random variation and selective retention. In science, at least, we have some control over the selection mechanism.

The behavioral inertia hypothesis reflects the inherently evolutionary nature of economic behavior. Clearly, the current generation as well as current behavior is related to past generations; thus, there will be inertia in observed traits and behaviors. Next, random variation and selective retention will provide the stochastic dimension. However, even this stochastic behavior will involve some pattern. The types of variations that were successful in the most recent past will tend to remain successful in the near future, implying positive autocorrelation among the innovations (i.e., $\rho > 0$). My basic model of inertia and caprice allows for both autocorrelation and any other explanation of the selection mechanism– recall equation (2.7).

The behavioral inertia hypothesis can, indeed, capture the dynamics of evolution, but can it decipher the caprice of man? Admittedly, this approach represents a tentative first step towards an evolutionary theory of economic behavior. Nonetheless, it is capable of explaining a considerable number of observed features in economic time series. BIH is simply a framework in which to study the dynamic behavior of economic time series, to sort out the signal from the many spurious patterns. Its advantage lies in its focus on the fundamental forces of inertia and innovation and its ability to explain many of the puzzling features found in economic data.

SUMMARY

Economic theory requires an element of genuine uncertainty. Such stochasticism must be made an explicit part of economic theory if theory is to be consistent with intelligent decision making and if theory is to improve through empirical experience. Because such stochasticism is adverse to the classical physics metaphor which still haunts the ruling orthodox economic paradigm (Mirowski, 1989b), this proposal is unlikely to be readily accepted. However, the history of twentieth century physics clearly demonstrates that progress can be made when fundamental randomness is incorporated into the nucleus of theory. Contrary to the beliefs of some of the most respected physicists, notably Einstein, the inclusion of genuine uncertainty into the description of the physical world led to the most empirically successful theory of physics, quantum mechanics. In the following chapter, it is argued that genuine empiricism in economics requires the explicit incorporation of stochastic behavior into economic theory. Otherwise, economic theory cannot be brought into contact with observation. Without such contact, economic theory can neither be corroborated, nor falsified. Without empirical tempering, economic theory corrodes.

Against the conventional economic view, I believe that people are intelligent, capable of genuine learning and innovation. Contrary to the orthodox view, the behavior of economic agents is dominated by inertia and caprice. Much of the remainder of this book is devoted to demonstrating the power of inertia and caprice in explaining economic phenomena. Economists need not constrain man to maximize. Nor, is it efficient to do so. If our purpose is to study economic man, we have no genuine choice but to incorporate the stochastic manifestations of economic behavior into our most fundamental economic theories.

NOTES

* From the *Journal of Socio-Economics*, **20**, 1991, 37-56.

1 Search theory and the economics of information also deal explicitly with randomness, but not the profound uncertainty discussed in this chapter. However, if search theory were used to derive explicit equations of economic behavior, including the type of error distribution, then it could become the type of economic theory that I am advocating.

2 With regard to the use of evolution to defend the orthodox theory of the firm, a few words of clarification are needed. To suppose that firms behave as if they are maximizing because if they were not maximizing then they would not survive is, *at best*, circular reasoning. As succinctly summarized by Blaug (1980): '(T)he problem with the Alchian thesis is the same as the problem of reading meaning into 'the survival of the fittest' in Darwinian theory: to survive, it is only necessary to be better adapted to the environment than one's rivals, and we can no

more establish from natural selection that surviving species are perfect than we can establish from economic selection that surviving firms are profit maximizers' (p.119). Behavioral theories of the firm – for example, satisficing, bounded rationality, or X-efficiency – permit firms to survive and prosper without maximizing. Etzioni (1987) also questions the logical and empirical basis of recent 'strenuous efforts to shore up the beleaguered neoclassical paradigm', by using the evolution of 'rules of thumb' (p.496).

5. Empirical Economics?
An Econometric Dilemma with only a Methodological Solution*

> For myself, I am interested in science and in philosophy only because I want to learn something about the riddle of the world in which we live, and the riddle of man's knowledge of that world. And I believe that only a revival of interest in these riddles can save the sciences and philosophy from narrow specialization and from an obscurantist faith in the expert's special skill and in his personal knowledge and authority.
>
> – Sir Karl Popper, *Logic of Scientific Discovery*, 1959, p.23 .

Conventional econometric practice begins with a general model or family of models. Various model specifications are explored, and the one that best fits the data is chosen. If, however, researchers regard the chosen model as merely a convenient summary of the data, what can be learned about economic theory or our explanation of economic phenomena? Nothing, unless theory is held in genuine risk of rejection or revision by observation.

Rarely does applied econometrics begin with a theory (and when it does, it is utility theory). More rare still are those studies where a specific utility function is used to derive the researcher's econometric model. Because econometric models are not regarded as the theory under examination, researchers usually do not bother to accumulate evidence, for or against, a specific econometric representation. Rather, the development and application of new statistical techniques propels model evaluation and development.

Econometric inference is only as trustworthy as the underlying statistical assumptions. The necessary assumptions concern specific distributional properties of the errors in the associated econometric model.[1] Such errors receive little attention from economic theorists and are added grudgingly at the end of econometric models. Nonetheless, it is the proper specification of these error distributions, along with the exact structure of the interdependence, that sanctions our empirical economic inferences. The necessity of correctly specifying the underlying statistical model is always

55

at issue in actual econometric applications. Questions of proper specification affect the interpretation of any empirical economic evidence. Unfortunately, we can never know whether our economic models are correctly specified.

The purpose of this chapter is to reveal the epistemological constraint, the 'Duhem–Quine thesis', that lies at the heart of econometrics and to offer a methodological solution.[2] The fundamental nature of this epistemological limitation prohibits technical solution. Rather, a sound empirical economics requires an explicit methodological solution to the pretest/specification dilemma. The acceptance of this methodological proposal would change what economists deem as 'theory' and the way in which conventional 'economic theory' is regarded.

THE PRETEST/SPECIFICATION DILEMMA

> Blind mechanical application of one particular criterion, or many criteria, is not a satisfactory strategy. All of the criteria suffer from the defects of preliminary-test estimation.   – (Griffiths, Hill, and Judge, 1993, p. 342)

Making errors is an inevitable consequence of statistical analysis. In fact, mastering error distributions is the basis of statistical models and reasoning. Both statistics and econometrics make fallibility their foundation and their strength. Although statistical methods adequately confront probability and error when the generating distributions of the relevant processes are known, *these distributions are not generally known.* Economists have been especially reluctant to regard probability and error distributions as part of the phenomenon about which they need to theorize.

Econometric techniques are only as good as the accuracy of the assumptions upon which they are based. A specific statistical test or econometric model will give valid implications, albeit probabilistic ones, to the extent that the underlying statistical and causal structures have been correctly identified and modelled, i.e., the problem of specification. Unlike Friedman's 'positive economics' which asserts that the assumptions of economic theory are irrelevant (Friedman, 1953, Blaug, 1980), econometricians fully acknowledge the dependence of empirical inference on statistical assumptions. The importance of the specification problem for applied econometrics is well accepted. Because proper specification directly affects the quality of our econometric methods, its importance is fundamental. There is no escape from the acceptance of some statistical assumptions when making econometric inferences, and these assumptions cannot be unambiguously examined by further econometric testing (not even within usual levels of statistical risk).[3]

'Most techniques for hypothesis testing in econometrics, however, simply, allow one to test restrictions on a model more general than the one being tested, conditional on the more general model being valid' (Davidson and MacKinnon, 1981, p.781). Thus, specification testing leads to an infinite regress. At any point, the statistical interpretation of previous steps can be completely revised if the more general model is found wanting. The real problem is not knowing whether a particular misspecification is present. Any empirical inference or judgment of a model may later be revised on the basis of the *same empirical information*. After one identified problem is remedied, there is no guarantee that other specification problems will not also be present, or worse, that these other problems caused a misidentification of misspecification and therefore an application of an inappropriate remedy.

It may be instructive to recall the recent history of accepted econometric practice, circa 1950-1980. The 'illusion of technique' beguiled more than one generation of econometricians into the false belief that each problem (e.g., autocorrelation) had its own technical remedies (e.g., Hildreth–Lu, Cochrane–Orcutt, etc.) (Barrett, 1958). Standard econometric textbooks and conventional practice made it obligatory to check for autocorrelation and, when found, to apply an accepted technical remedy. However, we now know that thousands of such conventional econometric applications were based on misspecified and misleading fitted relations that produced poor predictions and invalid inferences. Conventionally accepted, technical remedies only exacerbate the problem. The source of this problem is that many standard economic variables are nonstationary (at least, when observed as a time series). Because traditional tests of autocorrelation (e.g., the Durbin–Watson statistic) implicitly assumed stationarity, the routine and mechanical application of this specification test is misleading and often counterproductive. It is now generally accepted that nonstationary regressor can give an erroneous appearance of a good statistical relationship where none actually exists, 'spurious regressions', and an accompanying, poor Durbin–Watson statistic (Granger and Newbold, 1975).[4] Recent developments in econometrics (in particular, times series analysis and especially the consequences of nonstationarity and cointegration) have forced drastic revisions to the interpretation of decades of empirical economic inquiry.

At this moment, the set of specification error tests is a ragbag of miscellaneous procedures. The chief difficulty occurs with the presence of more than one error and with the resulting problem of how to isolate and identify the separate effects.   – (Ramsey and Kmenta, 1980, p. 11)

At any point, our empirical inferences may be in error. Econometric analysis is fallible not merely because statistical reasoning is probabilistic and thus always risky, but because the statements of probability and significance levels used to assess econometric reasoning may themselves be wrong. Attempting to detect and correct potential misspecification leads to a dilemma. The very act of testing for the misspecification invalidates classical econometric inferences, at least as conventionally uttered. A considerable literature has grown around this issue under the label 'preliminary-test or pretest estimation' (Judge and Bock, 1978, Judge *et al.*, 1985). When an econometric model has been 'pretested' by a specification or model selection test, the second step of applying some conventional estimation procedure (e.g., least squares) no longer gives the statistical results conventionally assumed. The prescreening of an econometric model changes the distributional properties of subsequent statistical analyses, yielding statistics that have 'virtually unknown sampling properties' (Griffiths *et al.*, 1993, p.344). When our econometric models are subjected to an initial round of specification testing, the resulting statistical inferences no longer have the properties that they profess to possess. Pretesting may cause the results to be biased, and they will typically overstate their reliability. The insolubility of pretest bias has led to a call for a more modest econometric methodology. '(P)rogress can only be made by tempering of one's conclusions: confident conclusions . . . are wholly inappropriate and must be replaced by less confident statements which implicitly recognize the pre-test nature of the process' (Darnell and Evans, 1990, p. 147).[5]

Our dilemma then is this: if we do not test for the proper statistical specification of an econometric model, conventional inference is suspect because the necessary assumptions of these models are routinely violated in practice. If, on the other horn, we do test our model's specification, we introduce unknown distortions into conventional estimates and inferences. Little is known about the properties of econometric estimators in a multi-stage pretesting environment (Giles and Giles, 1993).[6] Yet, this is precisely the typical environment of applied econometrics and empirical economic investigations. Given the current state of econometric knowledge, neither the properties nor the validity of reported estimates in applied econometrics are known. It is acknowledged that there is no econometric solution to this dilemma (Darnell and Evans, 1990, pp. 70-73) nor, would I argue, can there be. This econometric dilemma is a reflection of deeper philosophical limitations and will not yield to a technical solution no matter how elaborate or adroitly executed. The pretest/specification dilemma may be managed only by methodological decision.

The current state of econometric practice is rather like the practice of medicine where a test used to identify cancer may also be positive when the patient has emphysema or the common cold. Needless to say, the treatment for the former may not be beneficial to the patient who actually has one of the latter. Unlike medicine, however, econometric practice may not be able to learn even by trial and error because the econometrician can never conduct a postmortem examination of his patient to discover the 'true' cause of his model's statistical symptoms or inaccurate predictions.

METHODOLOGICAL SPECIFICATIONS

Obviously, the omnipresent possibility of misspecification is a critical issue for empirical economics. To understand fully the potential consequences of this problem on the quality of economic knowledge, let us distinguish more clearly among several levels of the issues.

1. *Problem-Situation (PS):* When *unknown*, and *unknowable*, specification errors are present (a genuine possibility in any econometric application), statistical inference loses its claim to validity. The distributional properties and biases of statistical tests are likewise unknown, making econometric results suspect.

Depending on the way we conceptualize this enigma, different questions and approaches are suggested. Conventional econometric practice considers the specification problem in more technical terms concerning the following questions.

2. *Econometric Specification Problem (ESP):* Are the disturbances normally, independently, and identically distributed? Are the independent variables correlated with the error terms, and are they stationary? How can specification errors be detected? When found, how can the effects of misspecification be estimated and corrected?

The econometric literature on specification is long and the offered solutions many.[7] Implicit in the econometric formulation is that misspecification can be identified, and once identified it can be remedied. Although this may be true in specific cases where the rest of the economic and statistical background knowledge can be considered unproblematic, there exists no unambiguous general test for misspecification.[8]

At a more general level, the specification problem becomes a fundamental methodological issue for empirical economic science.

3. *Methodological Specification Problem (MSP):* How can the results of statistical/empirical investigations be understood or justified? How can economic theory benefit from empirical experience? What methodological procedures or processes can insure that statistical analysis will generally lead to advancements of knowledge?

Although econometricians and statisticians are quite aware that their techniques are related to methodological issues of theory choice, few willingly venture into philosophical seas. The Duhem–Quine thesis, however, mingles the seemingly safe harbor of technical mathematical statistics with more salty philosophical seas. According to Duhem (1906), any empirical test is a test of the entire body of scientific knowledge, and no part can be singled out for special blame or credit. As Quine (1953, p. 43) states,

> Any statement can be held true come what may, if we make drastic enough adjustments elsewhere in the system. Even a statement very close to the periphery can be held true in the face of recalcitrant experience by pleading hallucination or by amending certain statements of the kind called logical laws (e.g., the law of the excluded middle). . . . If this view is right, it is misleading to speak of the empirical content of an individual statement. . .

Yet econometric practice alleges just the opposite – that economic data can test the value of single parameters and particular hypotheses. The problem, as everyone fully realizes, is that each hypothesis test is conditional on a host of structural and distributional assumptions. Nonetheless, it is a mistake of econometric method to treat these assumptions as a proven part of our 'background knowledge' when there is little, if any, empirical information to support them. Often, in fact, there is a great deal of evidence suggesting that the conventional assumptions are wrong.

The inability to single out, without doubt, specific scientific hypotheses or theories for revision or refutation is an well-accepted tenet in the philosophy of science. Scientific theories are under-determined by empirical evidence. Many theories and interpretations of given empirical tests will be consistent with the current state of our empirical knowledge. Theories are more general than empirical information. A theory's implications or meanings are not exhausted by any set of empirical information available to science. No one denies the logical implication of the Duhem–Quine thesis, but its implications for scientific knowledge remain somewhat in contention.

Cross (1982) applies the Duhem–Quine thesis to economics and demonstrates the impossibility of independent empirical testing. To illustrate the impact of the Duhem–Quine thesis, Cross discusses how testing the deceptively simple economic hypothesis that the demand for money is stable, H_0, requires an unreasonable proliferation of additional hypotheses:

H_1	the hypotheses used to define a relevant set of explanatory variables, $M^D = M^D(...)$;
H_2	the functional from of M^D ...,
$H_3, H_4, ..., H_\infty$	auxiliary hypotheses about the rest of economic theory;
$O_1, O_2, ..., O_M$	the hypotheses adopted regarding the measurement of the variables involved in the theory;
$T_1, T_2, ..., T_M$	hypotheses regarding the appropriate time lag structures involved in the H_2 relationship;
$I_1, I_2, ..., I_N$	the hypotheses sufficient for the identification of H_2 from the observations;
$C_1, C_2, ..., C_P$	the hypotheses underlying the *ceteris paribus* clause;
$E_1, E_2, ..., E_Q$	hypotheses regarding the generation of the error terms in H_2;
S	the statistical inference rule adopted;
D	boundary conditions which delineate the range of empirical observations commensurate with the H_0 hypothesis

– Cross (1982, p. 324)

A weakness in any one of the above hypotheses may, of course, be the reason for an apparent refutation or disconfirmation of H_0. Thus, the simplest economic hypotheses are not independently testable.

Returning to the specification problem (ESP), it is clear that the acceptance of the Duhem–Quine thesis provides an answer, albeit a negative one. Acceptance of the Duhem–Quine thesis implies that there exists no set of specification tests that can guarantee the validity of any particular empirical test of an economic hypothesis. Falsifying or supportive evidence can always be attributed to one or more of the many auxiliary statistical hypotheses. We can never be certain of the meaning, or even the probability, of a given econometric test. Nor can we be sure which of a potentially infinite number of auxiliary hypotheses is responsible for the test results. There is no strictly *logical* way to legislate a given hypothesis 'out-of-bounds' of empirical testing. As discussed above, the pretest-specification dilemma keeps the validity of econometric inference in serious doubt. The conventional econometric approach of developing new and/or more general specification tests and estimators cannot be genuinely successful. That is, there exists no technical solution to the pretest/specification dilemma.

The route around this econometric dilemma is methodological (MSP). Only by explicitly adopting methodological principles for an empirical economics can we harbor any hope of testing economic hypotheses of interest. By convention, we need to accept rules of statistical inference (i.e., Neyman–Pearson hypothesis testing) and a collection of statistical estimation techniques and specification tests that represent the best econometric practice. By accepting a set of such methodological restrictions we can 'rationally' interpret empirical economic results. This suggestion is not radically different, in principle, from current econometric practice.[9] If econometrics has found a coherent interpretation of some empirical analysis, it is because we have accepted, perhaps tacitly, a variety of conventional methods and standard statistical techniques. To the extent that econometrics 'works', it is due to the methodological acceptance of a variety of statistical techniques, rules of aggregation, and rules of correspondence between observed economic data and theoretical concepts.

The principal problem with the current econometric methodology is that no one believes in it, least of all econometricians. Econometricians do not, as a rule, believe that all the necessary statistical conditions required for correct specification hold in any given application. This is why specification searching and testing are so important and so often employed in applied econometrics. The loss of faith in current econometric practice is clearly expressed by Leamer and Leonard:

> Empirical results reported in economic journals are selected from a large set of estimated models. Journals, through their editorial policies, engage in some selection, which in turn stimulates extensive model searching and prescreening by prospective authors. Since this process is well known to professional readers, the reported results are widely regarded to overstate the precision of the estimates, and probably to distort them as well. As a consequence, statistical analyses are either discounted or completely ignored. (1983, p. 306)

Econometricians continue to avoid 'biting the methodological bullet' of accepting some explicit set of reasonable procedures for hypothesis and specification testing.

Nonetheless, econometric techniques force us to accept some specification as given if we wish to test empirically any economic proposition. When there is reason to believe that our model is correctly specified (because it has passed certain specification tests or perhaps from past empirical investigations), then we might interpret the results of our statistical analyses as a test of some particular economic hypothesis. The logic of current practice treats proper econometric specification at some level as if it were accepted background knowledge. That the regression error, ε, is distributed independently and identically, independent of X, is regarded, most often, as if it were a widely accepted fact. If these statistical properties are not assumed at one level of generality, they, or the equivalent, must be presumed at a more general level. Econometricians fully recognize that these demanding properties are not such obvious facts and need to be empirically verified. However, empirical testing requires that the background knowledge be *relatively hard*. One might imagine econometric results as a hammer, the requisite background knowledge as the anvil, and the theory under test as the nut we wish to crack.[10] The background knowledge (in this case, the correct econometric specification) must be at least as well known as the hypothesis under test if our efforts are to be rewarded.

> 4. *Methodological Proposal (MP):* Economic theory should include stochastic hypotheses about economic behavior and error. Such information should be sufficient to identify the econometric model and to test relevant hypotheses. That is, economic theory should be fully articulated.

Acceptance of this principle can permit us to escape the dilemma of econometric specification. Because it is not likely that the necessary distributional assumptions will gain the status of 'fact' or common knowledge, they need to be incorporated explicitly into economic theory. Empirical testing would then jointly apply to a full theoretical system including the more traditional types of economic theory as well as hypotheses about stochastic economic behavior and error. A similar understanding of the role of economic theory and empirical testing is beginning to sprout from experimental economics. 'Ultimately, the procedures under which a theory is tested should be part of the theory. But this step requires theorists' models to reflect a close understanding of the circumstances that produced the observations' (Smith, 1994, p.129).

Some econometricians may regard this solution as merely rhetorical. What is called 'theory' is simply altered. Although this methodological proposal (MP) is, on the surface, largely definitional (or 'rhetorical' if you wish), it has profound implications for practice when seriously followed. Its purpose is to revise what economists regard as 'theory' and how economists respond to unsupportive empirical evidence. Others may fear that economic theory would become little more than a collection of commonsense, simple hypotheses concerning supply and demand, and behavioral patterns such as habit or inertia. However, empirically sharpened common sense would represent an important scientific advance over untestable, often tautological, conventional economic dogma such as individual utility maximization. The importance of what is now misnamed as 'theory' (i.e., individual utility maximization or optimization) would be greatly lessened (Stanley, 1986b).

Most practicing econometricians recognize that 'maximization' provides little actual guidance to the construction of econometric models. Models derived from optimization theory are rarely estimable, providing mostly hints rather than exact specification (Spanos, 1990). Particular models are chosen more for their tractability or convenience in a given application.

> Maximization theory does not *explain* how economic agents behave; it tells *economists* how to restrict their models, how to infer predictions, and how to make policy recommendations. In other words, this economic theory has adopted the role of methodology. *Maximization* is economic *methodology* as practiced. It is not itself a theory. Instead, it represents a mechanism by which specific theories about market processes are derived and justified.
>
> – Stanley (1986b, p. 92)

PROPOSED VS. CONVENTIONAL ECONOMETRIC METHODOLOGY

The problem with current practice is that it is almost impossible to learn from empirical experience. Conventional optimization is so general and so vague that it is always possible to blame auxiliary hypotheses or a particular specification of maximization as the source of any empirical shortcoming. Even when a large body of *experimental* evidence accumulates against the core of neoclassical economics (e.g., the transitivity axiom vs. repeatedly observed preference reversals), contemporary practice allows economists to deflect such criticism almost indefinitely. Current economic practice is so dogmatic that the apriorist philosopher, Daniel Hausman, finds it indefensible (Hausman, 1992). Because econometrics involves nonexperimental data that cannot easily be independently replicated, supporters of a given theory can be quite intransigent in how they interpret disconfirming evidence. Particular specifications of individual utility maximization are not considered to be of great importance and are changed for the least of reasons; thus, empirical evidence, for or against, is not actually brought to bear on what is generally regarded as 'economic theory'. It might be argued that no economic theory has been discarded on the basis of its empirical record (Grunberg, 1966, Spanos, 1986). Or, one might question whether econometrics is genuinely empirical at all (Mirowski, 1989b).

In a laudable, but failed, attempt to 'recast the "traditional" approach into a methodologically acceptable strategy. . .', Darnell and Evans (1990, p.148) sketch the conventional empirical economics as:

1. *Theory:* Through deduction, the main hypothesis renders potentially observable implications (termed 'predictions').
2. *Econometric Model:* With the assistance of auxiliary hypotheses, theoretical implications are expressed in the form of a regression model.
3. *Specification Testing:* The model's error distribution is either accepted by the data or not.
4. *Empirical Test of the Main Hypothesis:* The theory is either rejected by the data or not.

Alternatively, the traditional approach may be represented by a schema (see Figure 5.1).[11]

Figure 5.1 clearly draws out two key attributes of the conventional methodology. First, theoretical activity (e.g., Main Hypothesis + Auxiliary Hypotheses + Deduction = Prediction) is held apart from any intimate empirical contact. Although 'prediction' may sound an empirical note, it merely represents potentially observable theoretical consequences such as: 'the economic variable Y is expected to be related to the economic variables listed in set X. . .' (Darnell and Evans, 1990, p. 65). Before these 'predictions' are actually brought into empirical risk, many additional auxiliary hypotheses are required. Thus, conventional methodology insulates theory from the cold draft of empirical testing.

Second, the traditional approach will maintain the main hypothesis come what may. If empirical evidence shows that the testable regression model is misspecified, the *auxiliary hypotheses* must then be modified. Or, if the regression model survives the pretesting stage and the main hypothesis is found to be inconsistent with known facts, the conventional approach again calls for a modification of the *auxiliary hypotheses* rather than the main hypothesis. Theory is permitted to be empirically modified only after all possible alterations of the auxiliary hypotheses are found to be empirically untenable. '(A) final rejection of H results after the possible modifications to the auxiliary hypotheses *all* lead to either a rejection of the main hypothesis as the result of regression analysis, or an inability to test that hypothesis directly within the regression equation' (Darnell and Evans, 1990, p. 66; emphasis added). However, the day of empirical reckoning may be postponed indefinitely, because the number of *possible* modifications (many of which have no readily observable consequences) to the auxiliary hypotheses has no limit. It is difficult to improve our explanations of actual economic phenomena, to discover new ones, or to learn from experience when empirical method sanctions incessant deflections of unfavorable empirical findings. Rather than mitigate the effects of the Duhem–Quine thesis, conventional econometrics wallows in its ambiguity, thereby postponing empirical learning and progress indefinitely.

Figure 5.1: Traditional Econometric Methodology

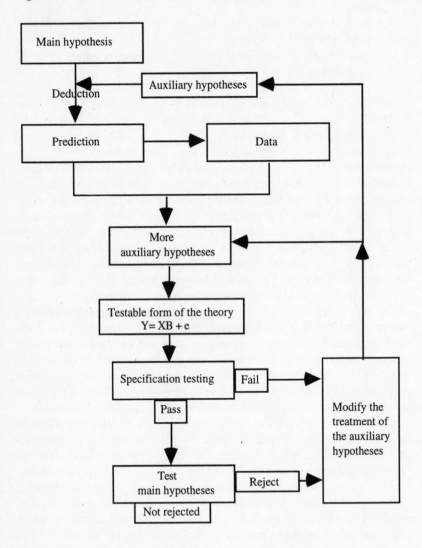

Source: *Darnell and Evans (1990, p.66)*

To correct identified problems in the traditional methodology, Darnell and Evans (1990) suggest some changes. First, because there is no solution to the pretest/specification dilemma, 'we must adopt the methodological norm that no Type II errors have been committed at the pre-test stages' (Darnell and Evans, 1990, p. 73). Such a strategy is especially pernicious when it is well known that many specification tests have low power (i.e., are unlikely to find existing problems). Although methodology must contain an element of convention, assuming away the specification problem does not lessen the damage it may cause to our empirical inferences. This 'methodological solution' might be commendable if, as the authors desire (1990, p. 148), it would lead to a more aggressively empirical, or more 'falsificationistic' economics. However it is much more likely that economists will ignore this methodological norm when it suits them, i.e., the 'teflon factor' (Poirier, 1988). That is, the first economist whose well-respected hypothesis is rejected because of this 'methodological norm of confirmation' will likely cry foul and blame the pretests or unknown specification errors for the apparent empirical refutation. Even if an empirical rejection of the main hypothesis is methodologically accepted, the conventionally endorsed response (recall Figure 5.1) is to make some distant modification of auxiliary hypotheses, which is, in any case, the same response as that recommended for failure at the pretesting stage.

So where do these modifications leave us; what has empirical economics gained? '(C)onfident conclusions based upon the assertion that no Type II errors have been committed are wholly inappropriate and must be replaced by less confident statements which implicitly recognize the pretest nature of the process' (Darnell and Evans, 1990, p. 147). In other words, the adoption of their 'methodological norm of confirmation' provides no genuine solution to the pretest/specification dilemma.

To what then do empirical researchers have to cling? Their own subjective degrees of belief, for this is the interpretation of probability, hence knowledge, advanced by Darnell and Evans (1990). Darnell and Evans (1990) correctly identify the central problem with the conventional frequency interpretation of probability for econometric modelling. To avoid these real problems, they adopt a subjective view of probability but incredulously eschew Bayesian statistical inference. Thus, they have chosen the worst of both worlds – a belief interpretation of probability and knowledge without the powerful inferential mechanism of Bayesian analysis or, from the opposite perspective, the rigid limitations of classical statistical inference that yields only stronger or weaker subjective beliefs. Ironically, although Darnell and Evans (1990) claim a Popperian perspective, they fail to adopt the solution to this problem of probability interpretation advanced long ago by Popper. Popper's propensity interpretation entirely circumvents the demand of classical statistics for repeated experiments or the Bayesian dependence on subjective degrees of belief.

There is a simpler, more direct approach to empirical testing that genuinely answers the pretest/specification dilemma (see Figure 5.2). First, an explanatory theory is proposed as a tentative solution to specific economic issues or problems. This notion of theory includes all the stochastic assumptions required to specify the econometric model fully. To the extent possible, theory should be equivalent to the testable form of the theory that is brought into direct contact with empirical observations. That is, steps 1 and 2 in Figure 5.2 are to be made as close as possible.[12]

Next lies the principal activity, empirical testing. Unlike the conventional view, problems found either during specification testing or when testing the 'main hypothesis' are equally regarded as evidence against the *theory* under examination. Whether the error distribution is found to be misspecified or some important coefficient has the wrong sign, the researcher is obligated to find an explanation for the observed empirical deficiency. However, before a theory is empirically refuted, an alternative explanation for the theory's past successes and failures (i.e., 'falsifying hypothesis'), which is itself a theory, must be proposed, tested and corroborated (Popper, 1959).[13] Success at this stage will lead to a new or revised theory that incorporates the falsifying hypothesis, and the entire process is repeated. Whenever a given theory has yet to be rejected by the data, it may be tentatively accepted for practical application but not without risk. Empirical testing never ceases. The best theories survive demanding empirical testing and thereby earn our reliance for application.

It is important to realize that the proposed methodology is not subject to the pretest/specification dilemma. Because it does not rely on any hierarchy of statistical testing or upon an inductive search for suitable econometric models, there is no pretest bias. Although there is always the possibility of specification error, specification tests are elevated to genuine tests of the theory under review. Several implications may be derived from the theory and separately tested. If the rejection of one statistical test is actually due to the failure of some other implication, no problem results from the perspective of the proposed approach. The failure of any implication represents an empirical rejection of and a poor reflection on theory. When a theory is completely specified, any empirical weakness represents a *theoretical* flaw.[14]

Unlike the traditional econometric approach, the proposed methodology does not attempt to isolate or insulate selected parts of the theoretical edifice nor does it rely on specification searches to identify the appropriate econometric model. Proper specification is an essential constituent of the

Figure 5.2: Proposed Econometric Methodology

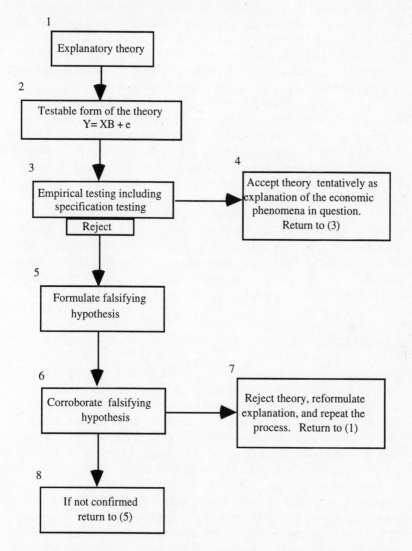

theory; it need not be discovered in the data. This approach integrates specification testing with traditional hypothesis testing and thereby strengthens the power of empirical analysis. See Chapter 6 for an application of this econometric methodology to theories of consumption and alternative explanations of the 'consumption puzzle'.

This methodological proposal is offered as a way to take empirical evidence seriously. By transforming what is regarded as theory, the specification problem can be solved, and the Gordian knot of indefinite specification error testing and model estimation can be cut. Exact statistical specification can be assumed to be known as part of H_0, the composite hypothesis under examination. If empirical evidence is found against the theory or its specification, it is a disconfirming instance of the *theory* under test. Problems of model specification could not then be used as a scapegoat for unwanted findings. In fact, tests for specification errors would clearly become tests of the theory in question. If the main hypothesis is rejected or if a specification test uncovers a problem, the *theory* would be implicated and an alternative formulation or a radically new theory would be sought that might be consistent with the evidence. Such a methodology would also have the desirable side effect of forcing economists to take empirical evidence seriously and to discuss explicitly the stochastic nature of economic behavior.   This proposal seeks a reversal of the narrow specialization of economic theorists and econometricians by more fully integrating these fields through empirical testing.   Unless some methodological decision is taken, empirical economics will continue to be largely a deception.[15] Worse yet, we will fail to learn from our mistakes.

ILLUSTRATION

Conventional econometric practice, when it is applied, begins with a general model or family of models, often involving prices, income, wealth, taxes, etc. Various model specifications are explored and the one which best fits the data is chosen. If, however, researchers regard the chosen model as merely a convenient summary of the data, what can be learned about economic theory or our explanation of economic phenomena? Nothing, unless the researcher's theory is held in genuine risk of rejection or revision by observation.

Rarely do empirical researchers begin with a theory (usually then, utility theory). More rare still are those studies where a specific utility function is used to derive the researcher's econometric model.[16] When econometric models are not regarded as the theory under examination, researchers have little reason to accumulate evidence, for or against, a specific econometric representation. Rather, it is the lure of technique that propels model evaluation and evolution.

On the other hand, there is no scarcity of econometric models purporting to explain a given economic phenomenon. The excess supply of these models underscores how little the field values them. Consider, for example, the consumption function and the associated 'consumption puzzle' which has attracted more econometric attention than any other single economic phenomenon. Chapter 6 furnishes a detailed econometric analysis of this topic. Despite more than a half-century of econometric modelling, there is no coherent professional consensus regarding the proper empirical representation of the consumption function.

To further contrast my approach with conventional reasoning, take the rare case where a researcher assumes a specific utility function to investigate, for example, charitable contributions. Individuals (or families) choose consumption, c_j, and charitable contribution, g_j:

$$
\begin{array}{ll}
\underset{c \& g}{\text{Max}} & c_j + \alpha_j \ln(1+g_j) \\
\text{S.T.} & c_j + p_j g_j \leq I_j \\
& c_j \& g_j \geq 0
\end{array}
\tag{5.1}
$$

where I_j is individual j's income, p_j is the price of one dollar of charity, and α_j is a preference parameter that permits individual differences. Furthermore, if $\alpha_j = \exp(X_j \beta + \varepsilon_j)$ for $\varepsilon_j \sim N(0,\sigma^2)$ and independent of $\varepsilon_{j,}$, p_j, X_j and $I_{j,}$, hen $\ln(1+g_j)$ has a standard Tobit representation:

$$
\ln(1+g_j) = X_j \beta - \ln p_j + \varepsilon_j
\tag{5.2}
$$

Because all necessary variables, functional forms, and stochastic processes are explicitly stated in the utility theory, this theory of charitable contributions is empirically testable by observations on g_j, X_j and p_j. Better still, this theory has specific testable implications: charitable contributions do not depend on an individual's income and the coefficient of $\ln p_j$ must be equal to minus one. These restrictions on observable behavior greatly enhance the theory's empirical and policy importance. However, it is unlikely that an applied researcher will take these restrictions seriously and not loosen them as the occasion demands. And, it is less likely that one would reject this theory of charitable contributions in the almost certain case that income is found to be empirically important. Conventional econometric practice would embed this theory's empirical representation in a more general econometric model (most likely including income). However, rather than testing the theory's restrictions for possible rejection of the above utility theory, various effects would be estimated and reported. At the applied level, more flexible approaches will be offered, the results will be claimed to be consistent with some unspecified utility function, and nothing will be learned.

Against this view, my approach would take the theory's restriction quite seriously. For example, when evidence is found for the importance of income, a falsifying hypothesis need be offered and confirmed if this specific theory of charitable contributions is to be empirically refuted. The most obvious explanation for the importance of income and the one which demands the least drastic revision of the previous theory is that the preference parameter, α_j, is itself a function of income. This new utility theory and associated econometric model could be tested; if confirmed the old version would be empirically rejected. When some other empirical implication is statistically rejected (for example, if equation (5.2) does not have a unitary price coefficient), yet another hypothesis that explains this empirical weakness and past successes would need to be proposed and corroborated before the amended utility theory is revised. At each step, the statistical rejection of theoretical implications is used to stimulate further theoretical development and refinement, resulting in theories that explain increasingly wider empirical phenomena. Thus, economic knowledge grows.

CONCLUSION

The purpose of econometrics is to apply and test economic theory with actual economic data and thereby to learn from the experience. Econometrics is meant to be empirical. Unfortunately, the purely technical approach to the specification problem provides no 'rational' means of interpreting econometric results. The plethora of specification error tests that one can find in the econometric literature often provides ambiguous or mutually inconsistent results for any given empirical application. Furthermore, this ambiguity is inescapable when one considers both horns of the pretest/specification dilemma. Under the current practice, an economist who is unhappy with the empirical record of his favorite theory can conduct exhaustive specification tests and searches until by luck or error a more fitting model is found or an insignificant auxiliary hypothesis can be blamed. Such is our current econometric custom.

If economic theory is not genuinely vulnerable to empirical testing or revision, can we learn from experience? It is no surprise that economic story-telling perennially lags behind our last economic crisis.[17] The problem is not that economists make mistakes or that economic theory is sometimes wrong due to the complex nature of human behavior. All sciences share such sins. The unforgivable sin is that economists refuse to learn from their mistakes. If economics cannot profit from experience, it is not an empirical science.

The inability of econometrics to effectively refute economic theory is a serious criticism of its scientific merit. It might be argued that no economic theory has been discarded on the basis of its empirical record (Grunberg, 1966). Or, one might question whether econometrics is genuinely empirical at all (Mirowski, 1989c). Some, in fact, regard falsifiability as the criterion of science (Popper, 1959, 1963, Blaug, 1980).[18] The Duhem–Quine thesis or its econometric shadow, the pretest/specification dilemma, explains much of the historic difficulty in empirically refuting economic theory. However, these methodological limitations need not render econometrics empirically impotent. Witness the natural sciences. Although they too suffer from the methodological problems associated with the Duhem–Quine thesis, the critical attitude of the natural sciences has sometimes permitted effective empirical criticism. The recognition of these limitations can, in fact, form the basis of a reasonable empirical methodology.

NOTES

* From the *Journal of Economic Issues*, **32**, 1998, 191-218.

1 Although robust and semiparametric procedures (Wooldridge, 1991, J.L. Powell, 1984, 1986, Robinson, 1988, Peters and Smith, 1991) are less dependent on specific distributional assumptions, their validity, nonetheless, remains conditional on restrictive assumptions.

2 Sawyer *et al.* (1997) provide a primer on the Duhem–Quine thesis and its relevance to economics.

3 Although there are more robust strategies for specification testing which some may believe can circumvent the complex interdependence of econometric inference and specification, none are free of restrictive assumptions. 'Robustification' comes at the price of lower power and questionable small sample properties. Though dependent on fewer assumptions, robust tests are, nonetheless, dependent. Even the most robust specification test 'implicitly or explicitly imposes correct dynamic specification under the null hypothesis' (Wooldridge, 1991, p. 37).

This argument applies equally well to less traditional testing strategies – e.g., non-nested and nonspecific testing: J.A. Hausman (1978), Hillier (1991), Morey (1984), Nakamura and Nakamura (1981), Pesaran and Deaton (1978), Pesaran (1982), Peters and Smith (1991), Powell (1984, 1986), Ramsey (1969 & 1974), Robinson (1988), Thursby (1979, 1981), Thursby and Schmidt (1977), White (1982, 1989), and Wooldridge (1991).

4 Ironically, the Durbin–Watson statistic is better suited to detect spurious regressions than genuine autocorrelation in typical time series applications (Hendry, 1986, Engle and Granger, 1987).

5   Neither robust regression diagnostics nor specification testing avoids this problem. Although one robust test may be employed in the place of several parametric tests, the use of robust regression diagnostics is a form of preliminary-testing. Wooldridge (1991), for example, recommends employing t-statistics, robust to heteroskedasticity and serial correlation, to test the regression coefficients in conjunction with his robust regression diagnostics. The properties of these t-tests conditional on passing the RB-LM test remain unknown. Such prescreening will again affect the properties of subsequent hypothesis tests of particular parameters in unknown ways – whether these tests are robust or more conventional. Because tests of specific parameters are often the main objectives of empirical economic inquiry, the validity of econometric inference remains in doubt.

Stein-rule or instrumental variables estimators, for example, are sometimes employed as an alternative to specification or model selection testing (Judge and Bock, 1978). However, such a strategy leads us back to the problem with which we began – the specification problem. Can we know whether the assumptions upon which these methods are based (whether regarded as more 'robust' or not) are valid? Do our inferences mean what they claim? Like more conventional estimators, Stein-rule or instrumental variable methods depend upon restrictive statistical assumptions and presuppositions about the nature of the investigated relationship and the variables used to represent it. Thus, no estimator – 'robust', unconventional, or otherwise – avoids the very real question of proper specification. Although econometricians possess a large and diverse 'ragbag of miscellaneous procedures' for estimation and specification testing, none are free from making restrictive assumptions.

6   Robustification of regression diagnostics can make the dilemma more pronounced and less tractable when, as Wooldridge(1991) suggests, they are used in conjunction with more conventional statistics.

7   For representative examples, see Davidson and MacKinnon (1990), J.A. Hausman (1978), Hillier (1991), Morey (1984), Nakamura and Nakamura (1981), Pesaran and Deaton (1978), Pesaran (1982), Peters and Smith (1991), Powell (1984, 1986), Ramsey (1969 & 1974), Robinson (1988), Thursby (1979, 1981), Thursby and Schmidt (1977), White (1982, 1989), and Wooldridge (1991). Any standard econometric textbook will present an introduction to the mathematics and statistics of specification error and offer several statistical tests.

8   To anticipate a potential misunderstanding, the type of ambiguity of specification testing discussed here goes well beyond the conventional risk associated with the type I and type II errors, i.e., α and β. With misspecification we run an additional, *unknown* risk that our whole test procedure may be inappropriate, thereby losing control over the conventional significance level, α.

9 Recognizing the importance of convention in econometric inference plays an essential role in the recent methodological defense of conventional econometrics (Darnell and Evans, 1990).

10 This metaphor comes from Lakatos (1970, p. 186). Although he uses it to discuss 'naive falsificationism', no such limited interpretation is implied here. In Lakatosian terms, the approach to empirical testing taken here is a variant of 'sophisticated falsificationism'.

11 Darnell's and Evans'(1990) views of conventional econometric methodology are presented because they provide the most explicit and most favorable treatment of conventional econometrics.

12 A potential wedge between theory and its testable form concerns how best to relate various theoretical concepts to observable magnitudes. For example, the notion of price is inherently a specific, disaggregate phenomenon. Yet, empirical economics is forced to aggregate across space and/or time. Thus, some ambiguity will always remain concerning which aggregate or index best reflects theory. My solution is to adopt a rule of correspondence as part of the theory. However, due to the history of the aggregation and related problems in economics, it is unlikely that any such methodological convention will be universally adopted. Thus, the conceptual difference between a theory and its testable form is reluctantly acknowledged in Figure 5.2.

13 For example, the behavioral inertia hypothesis serves as a falsifying hypothesis for the 'expectations-augmented' Phillips curve – Chapter 7.

14 The only problem created by this approach is the expansion of α, the probability of falsely rejecting a true null hypothesis (a.k.a., type I error). Because this recommendation implies multiple testing, for specification and coefficient magnitudes, some adjustment for α, such as Bonferroni, will become necessary. A reasonable suggestion is to test all hypotheses at the .01 level to accommodate the compounding of α.

15 Extensive illustrations of the econometric methodology proposed in the previous section are offered in Chapters 6 and 7; here only a quick caricature is drawn.

16 Even in these cases, typical practice is to search exhaustively over the data for a suitable model specification and then to tack on a theoretical derivation of this specific model, *ex post*.

17 Or good fortune. The low rates of recent inflation and unemployment in the US cast doubt on conventionally accepted views.

18 The notion of using falsifiability as the 'demarcation of science' is a bit outdated and certainly out of fashion. It was originally proposed in the 1930s as part of Popper's criticism of logical positivism. Popper and his followers have since broadened their view to focus on whether a position can be *criticized* (Popper, 1982, Radnitzky and Bartley, 1987). Nonetheless, from this broadened perspective, empirical disconfirmation remains a very powerful form of rational criticism.

Recently, Redman (1994) tells an interesting and important story of the failure of Popperian falsificationism in the early econometric efforts of the Cowles Commission. However, any failure of econometric practice cannot be fairly attributed to falsificationism because it has never been fully implemented in economics. To discuss and defend Popperian falsificationism for econometrics would require a separate essay. However, to make one indicative point, no econometrician has recognized the need for constructing and testing a new theory (i.e., a 'falsifying hypothesis') before the original theory under empirical examination may be regarded as 'falsified' (recall Figure 5.2).

6. Ain't Misbehavin' – Capricious Consumption or Permanent Income?[*]

> The empirical consumption function, referring to the relationship between consumers' expenditure and income, is undoubtedly one of the first and most intensively researched topics in macro-econometrics.   – Spanos (1989, p.150)

> Few subjects in macroeconomics have received as much attention as the relationship between aggregate consumption and aggregate income.
> – Christiano et al. (1991, p.397)

Because the development of Keynesian economics was contemporaneous with the inception of econometric analysis and because the consumption function is fundamental to Keynesian economics, the empirical estimation of the consumption function has received greater attention than other econometric application. Given such scrutiny, is there anything new to be learned?

Yet several reviews question the very core of the 'stylized history' of consumption research (Bunting, 1989, Spanos, 1989, Thomas, 1989). A careful study of the history of early econometrics rejects the existence of the empirical consumption puzzle and the conventional story told by the textbooks.

Recall that the consumption puzzle is the observed difference between estimated long and short run marginal propensities to consume (MPC) or between average propensity to consume and the MPC. It was the impetus for the development of the permanent income hypothesis and the life-cycle theories of consumption. Other studies, (Deaton, 1987, Stock, 1988, Campbell and Deaton, 1989, Campbell and Mankiw, 1990, Christiano et al. 1991, Fuhrer, 1992), force us to reconsider the conventionally accepted theories of consumption. What then are we to make of the long, yet mixed record of empirical economic research on consumption? How can observed consumption expenditures be explained? If the orthodox interpretation of the best-studied empirical economic phenomenon is questionable, what does this imply about the empirical content of conventional economics, generally?

77

The purpose of this chapter is to show how a simple model of behavioral dynamics can explain observed consumption, previous research findings, and the puzzling empirical results found in many of the earlier consumption studies. The behavioral inertia hypothesis (BIH) introduced in Chapter 2 is employed to explain and forecast aggregate consumption expenditures. The basic behavioral forces of inertia and caprice go further towards explaining consumption expenditures than more accepted theories such as the permanent income hypothesis or recent advances in econometric analysis such as cointegrated variables and time series models. Although others have referred to habit or inertia when faced with disconfirming evidence, none have shown how a cohesive, well-integrated model of inertia can explain many of the puzzles found in economic time series. Parsimony and predictive success are often cited as desirable properties of economic models (Friedman, 1953, Caldwell, 1982). This simple framework of behavioral dynamics, BIH, provides both.

MISBEHAVIN': PERMANENT INCOME AND THE CONSUMPTION PUZZLE

Economic legend relates that early attempts to estimate the consumption function ran into difficulties in the 1940s, difficulties which eventually led to a number of renowned economic theories: Duesenberry's (1949) relative income hypothesis, Modigliani's (1949) life-cycle hypothesis, and Friedman's (1957) permanent income hypothesis. These theories are advanced in textbooks and continue to drive research. Briefly, the 'stylized facts' about this early episode of econometric history are (Spanos, 1989, Thomas, 1989):

(1) Using short run time series data, the consumption function was estimated as, $C = b_0 + b_1 Y$. Where C is real consumption expenditures, Y is real disposable income, $b_0 > 0$, and $b_1 < 1$.

(2) Initial estimates of the consumption function greatly underpredicted the period just after the Second World War.

(3) Kuznets found that the APC was constant, contradicting the consumption function stated in (1), above.

(4) The analysis of cross sectional data revealed lower MPCs (*i.e.*, b_1) and shifting intercepts (*i.e.*, the 'ratchet effect').

These historical 'facts' constitute the 'consumption puzzle' with which the economic profession continues to struggle.

This 'consumption puzzle' may be illustrated graphically – Figure 6.1. Line AB represents the 'true' relationship between consumption and income, their long run relationship, or the relationship between 'permanent income' and 'permanent consumption' depending upon your choice of explanations. In contrast, the less steeply sloped lines (CD, EF, GH) are those estimated by ordinary least squares (OLS) using observed income and consumption for different short run time periods or different cross sections. Now the above 'stylized facts' can be concisely illustrated. Lines CD, EF, GH each conform to point (1) and their differences reflect the 'ratchet effect' described in (4). The constancy of the APC, point (3), is exhibited by the fact that the 'true' relationship AB goes through the origin. Finally, the underprediction of consumption can occur if any of the estimated relations CD, EF, or GH is used to make predictions for values of income larger than their sample means. The gap, BH in Figure 6.1, represents such an expected prediction error when our planning value is Y_{t+1} and the fitted relation GH is used (Stanley, 1988). The most important feature illustrated by this graph is the striking difference in the estimated MPCs found among these distinct types of consumption relations. The differences among estimated MPCs define the 'consumption puzzle' and require explanation.

Figure 6.1: The Consumption Puzzle

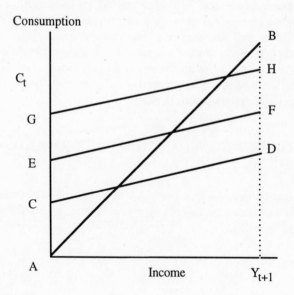

To resolve the seemingly contradictory empirical findings, the next generation of consumption theories added new or different explanatory variables to the consumption function. Duesenberry's relative income hypothesis employs past peak income levels, Modigliani's life-cycle hypothesis adds wealth to the consumption function, and Friedman's permanent income hypothesis relies on the concept of 'permanent income'. It is commonly believed that these theories, in their own fashion, successfully account for the stylized history of early econometric estimation of consumption. However, there are considerable problems with such an interpretation.

Several reviews (Spanos,1989, Thomas 1989, Bunting 1989) cast doubt on the received view of this episode of econometric history. A more careful analysis of the stylized facts dismisses them altogether, without recourse to the second-generation consumption theories (Spanos, 1989, Thomas, 1989). Specifically, Thomas (1989) questions the dominance of the simple linear form of the consumption in early econometric work – recall (1) above. Spanos (1989), on the other hand, shows that this simple linear consumption function and the model used by Kuznets, recall (3), are statistically invalid. Econometric misspecification also clarifies the remaining stylized facts, (2) and (4). Omitted variables, errors-in-variables, as well as other types of misspecification biases can easily generate the observed patterns of estimated consumption. Hence, the 'stylized facts' uncovered in the early econometric work and widely accepted are misleading. From this perspective, the second generation of consumption theories of Friedman, Modigliani, and Duesenberry are simply unnecessary because no 'consumption puzzle' needs to be solved.[1] The answer to the puzzle then is to find a statistically adequate model of consumption in the first place. Progress will be made if a tentative solution can also clarify previous successes and explain past difficulties.

CAPRICIOUS CONSUMPTION: THEORY AND EMPIRICAL RESULTS

Consumption expenditures and many other economic phenomena may be usefully separated into two constituent components, 'inertia' and 'caprice' (recall Chapter 2).

$$C_t = \alpha_0 + \alpha_1 C_{t-1} + \eta_t \qquad (6.1)$$

where:

C_t is consumption at time t

C_{t-1} is the previous value of consumption

η_t is everything that might cause consumption to change, the caprice.[2]

In the absence of any 'outside forces', consumers will attempt to maintain their standard of living. Thus, we would expect α_1 to be equal to one, or perhaps somewhat less with inertial decay.

The challenge is to model the caprice, η_t, correctly. A general expression for caprice is:

$$\eta_t = X_t\beta + \rho\eta_{t-1} + \varepsilon_t \qquad (6.2)$$

where:

X_t is a 1 x k vector of explanatory variables

β is a k x 1 vector of regression coefficients

ε_t is the irreducibly random part of caprice

ρ is the autoregression coefficient for caprice.

The first term in the above expression, $X_t\beta$, identifies the deterministic aspects of the phenomenon in question. The second term, $\rho\eta_{t-1}$, in equation (6.2) captures 'fads' or 'trends' in consumer's caprice and the speed with which consumers adopt to change. Together, equations (6.1) and (6.2) incorporate inertia in consumers' standard of living and in its change, and they embody what I call the 'behavior inertia hypothesis'.

Considerations that may help determine the explanatory variables, X_t, include supply and demand. However, for the purposes of finding an adequate statistical model, we do not demand that it be derived explicitly from maximization. In fact, inertia and caprice can supplant individual utility maximization altogether; they are entirely sufficient to derive the usual empirical generalizations of consumer theory. This insight was recognized by Becker (1962) who used inertia and 'impulsiveness', defined by completely random choices in the consumption opportunity set, as a basis for the law of demand. 'For example, impulsive households tend to have negatively inclined demand curves because a rise in the price of one commodity would shift opportunities towards others, leaving less chance to purchase this one even impulsively' (Becker, 1962, pp. 12-13). These changes in the budget constraint give rise to an inverse relation of price and quantity whether consumers act out of caprice, inertia or both. Similarly, the pull of an increase in real income would induce an increase in total consumption expenditures for the average of random, yet feasible consumption choices. Thus, inertia and caprice alone are sufficient to justify the dependence of consumption expenditures on real disposable income as well as the interest rate (because the interest rate reflects the price of current consumption). Maximization is simply unnecessary, a complication that adds no explanatory power. Parsimony demands the rejection of individual utility maximization as a theory of consumption expenditures.[3]

Although BIH can be derived from utility maximization (recall the Appendix of Chapter 3), little is gained by this exercise. Models derived from optimization theory are rarely estimable, providing mostly hints rather than exact specification (Spanos, 1990). Why must *economists constrain man to maximize?* At best, maximization represents but one possible theoretical approach. Elsewhere, I have argued that individual utility maximization is not theory, but rather methodology (Stanley, 1982, 1986b, 1991b). It is unlikely that these results, or any other, will convince orthodox economists who are committed to the ruling paradigm to consider alternatives to maximization. To them, optimization is the very definition of economic theory. Any other explanation, therefore, has no theoretical foundation and is often maligned as '*ad hoc*'. Such dogmatism is the source of the 'measurement without theory' debate of the 1940s (Mirowski, 1989) and the 'assumptions debate'. Yet even defenders of neoclassical economics cannot defend its dogmatism, e.g., Hausman (1992). Although BIH may also be used in conjunction with more conventional economic theory, it quite intentionally avoids utility maximization.

Returning to previous equations, a little algebraic manipulation implies a second order autoregressive structure.

$$C_t = \alpha_0(1-\rho) + (\alpha_1 + \rho)C_{t-1} - \rho\,\alpha_1 C_{t-2} + X_t\beta + \varepsilon_t \qquad (6.3)$$

When $\alpha_1 = 1$, this relation may be equivalently expressed in differences as:

$$dC_t = \alpha_0(1-\rho) + \rho dC_{t-1} + X_t\beta + \varepsilon_t \qquad (6.4)$$

where:

$$dC_t = C_t - C_{t-1}$$
$$dC_{t-1} = C_{t-1} - C_{t-2}$$

X_t should not be highly correlated with past consumption, C_{t-1}, because X_t is a predictor of the *change* in consumption, neither its present nor past levels.

Before estimating equation (6.3) or (6.4), we must specify the X_t variables. Following Keynes, disposable real income is an obvious choice, but there are other reasonable candidates including: interest rates, consumer sentiments, and prices. Recall, however, that $X_t\beta$ is meant to explain the *change* in consumption. Hence, the change of disposable income, dY_t, will be used for X_t.[4]

When change in disposable income, dY_t, is chosen as the explanatory variable equations (6.3) and (6.4) yield:

$$C_t = \alpha_0 (1-\rho) + (\alpha_1 + \rho) C_{t-1} - \rho \alpha_1 C_{t-2} + \beta_1 Y_t - \beta_1 Y_{t-1} + \varepsilon_t \quad (6.5)$$

or

$$dC_t = \alpha_0 (1-\rho) + \rho \, dC_{t-1} + \beta_1 \, dY_t + \varepsilon_t \quad (6.6)$$

where $0 < \alpha_1 \le 1$, $0 \le \rho \le 1$, and $0 < \beta_1 \le 1$. Estimating the above relation without any parameter restrictions, using the natural logarithm of real US expenditures and income, 1929-1991 (1982 base year), and excluding WWII,[5] we find

$$\ln\hat{C}_t = .022 + .968 \ln C_{t-1} - .118 \ln C_{t-2} + .621 \ln Y_t - .474 \ln Y_{t-1} \quad (6.7)$$
$$\phantom{\ln\hat{C}_t =} (9.55) \quad (-2.28) \quad (16.28) \quad (-7.32) \quad R^2 = .9998$$
$$\text{SSE} = .004797 \quad \text{D-W} = 2.12 \quad \text{LM} = 4.20 \quad \text{GQ} = 1.09 \quad n = 55$$

There is strong statistical support for the specification of this model – high R^2, adequate ts, and no evidence of autocorrelation. LM is the Lagrange multiplier test for general serial correlation; its Box–Pierce Q is 4.20 and has a chi-square distribution under the null hypothesis of independence with degrees of freedom equal to the number of lagged error terms considered ($m=10$) (Spanos, 1986, pp. 518-521). Because the critical $\chi^2(10)$ is 18.305, the above results are quite consistent with independence and proper model specification. A coefficient of determination, R^2, of 99.98% could not reasonably be expected to be higher unless one enjoys estimating identities (the adjusted R^2 remains quite high, 99.97%).

All estimated coefficients have the expected signs and fall within the ranges imposed by BIH. The coefficients on lagged consumption are both within the necessary bounds; recall that coefficients are $\alpha_1 + \rho$ and $-\rho\alpha_1$ for C_{t-1} and C_{t-2}, respectively.[6] And, as expected, contemporary disposable income has a positive effect on consumption while lagged consumption has a negative effect. Some readers may question why the coefficients on the lagged independent variable have the opposite signs as their contemporaneous values. Typically, when economic processes take time to adjust they can be expressed by functions of multiply lagged independent variables with declining coefficients of the same signs. However, the observed pattern seen in equation (6.7) is a direct implication of BIH. A more detailed specification of the implicit dynamic structure of BIH is

tested below by equation (6.9). It may be interesting to note that this
structure of dependence of consumption on lagged values of income
underscores the difference of BIH from Friedman's permanent income
hypothesis using adaptive expectations. In this case, the permanent income
hypothesis would have a similar form to (6.7) but without lags in income –
see, for example, Gujarati (1988).

Nor is there any reason to suspect heteroskedasticity by any of the usual
tests. The Goldfeld–Quandt test (see G–Q above) finds no evidence of
heteroskedasticity. It is distributed $F_{17,17}$ because the chosen sub-periods
were 22 years in length. However, linear representations of the
consumption function typically exhibit heteroskedasticity. For example, the
linear specification of (6.7) yields:

$$\hat{C}_t = -1.952 + 1.028\ C_{t-1} - .107\ C_{t-2} + .604\ Y_t - .523\ Y_{t-1} \qquad (6.8)$$
$$\quad\quad (8.84) \quad\ (-1.29) \quad\quad (9.21)\ \ (-5.85)$$
$$R^2 = .9996 \qquad\qquad\qquad D\text{-}W = 1.996$$

Although the above statistical results are quite good, the Goldfeld–
Quandt, Bresch–Pagan and White tests all indicate heteroskedasticity in the
simple linear consumption function at the .01 level (G–Q = 6.32; BP =
10.63; W = 23.07). The Breusch–Pagan test used only time^2 as an
independent variable and is thus distributed $\chi^2(1)$. And, White's
asymptotically equivalent test for general heteroskedasticity is $\chi^2(5)$.
(White, 1980, Spanos, 1986). In remaining tests, the Goldfeld–Quandt test
willl be used where possible because it proved to be more sensitive in these
applications.

To correct for heteroskedasticity, most empirical studies of consumption
use logarithmic functional forms. Although from the orthodox perspective,
these logarithms are largely *ad hoc*, behavioral inertia furnishes a rather
natural explanation of the log-linear statistical specification of consumption.
If inertia decays exponentially, equations (6.1) and (6.2) have a
multiplicative form. That is, if the memory of a given standard of living
fades and if its change adjusts by a constant proportion over time, we would
expect $C_t = \alpha_0\ C_{t-1}^{\alpha_1} \eta_t$ and $\eta_t = X_t^{\beta}\ \eta_{t-1}^{\rho}\ \varepsilon_t$. Taking the natural logarithm of
these equations gives the same relations as before, equations (6.1) and (6.2),
with the exception that all variables are natural logs and thus leads to the
empirical specifications estimated by equations (6.7) and (6.9).

A potential problem in the specification of equation (6.7) is that the
variables are measured as levels, logarithms of levels, but levels
nonetheless. When economic time series variables are expressed as levels,
nonstationarity is a real possibility and leads to spurious findings (Granger
and Newbold, 1975).[7] Using such levels and logs of the independent

variables may also cause a high degree of multicollinearity in the above estimated relation and a concomitant unreliability of the individual coefficients. More importantly, equation (6.7) does not reflect all of the theoretical information contained in the postulated stochastic dynamics. Specifically, BIH restricts the coefficients on Y_t and Y_{t-1} to have the same magnitude but opposite signs, and when $\alpha_1 = 1$ the coefficients of C_{t-1} and C_{t-2} should sum to one. These restrictions produce equation (6.6) and are estimated as:[8]

$$dln\hat{C}_t = .00655 + .177\ dlnC_{t-1} + .595\ dlnY_t \qquad R^2 = .872 \qquad (6.9)$$
$$(3.84) \qquad\qquad (15.83) \qquad\qquad SSE = .005306$$
$$h = -1.18 \qquad LM = 7.11 \qquad G\text{-}Q = 1.15 \qquad n = 55$$

This restricted linear model appears to be well specified by conventional goodness of fit criteria as well as tests of independence – recall that Durbin's h has a standard normal distribution. R^2, though smaller, is still quite respectable. Because we have changed the definition of the dependent variable, the coefficient of determination is no longer comparable. Change is always much harder to explain than the level of an economic variable. Figure 6.2 illustrates the 'goodness of fit' of this model by using the within-sample predictions 1929-1991 to trace the actual movements of consumption. The F-test for BIH's restrictions yields a value of 2.65 compared to a critical value of 3.20 ($\alpha = .05$ and degrees of freedom are 2 and 50).[9] Therefore, we may accept BIH's postulated behavioral dynamics.

The econometric analysis undertaken here is intentionally elementary. Often the conventional reliance on mathematically sophisticated estimation techniques suffers from the illusion of technique. Although robust, generalized, and less parametric methods have their place, it is far more important to estimate the correct model simply than to estimate a misspecified model more 'efficiently'. In many cases, sophisticated econometric analyses do not lend themselves readily to specification testing, which is the centerpiece of the methodology advocated and applied here. Because these techniques are designed to remedy some specific problem, the researcher who uses them is lulled into the false belief that they solve all relevant problems of specification. In contrast, ordinary least squares (OLS) is both transparent and robust, when correctly specified, and quick to reveal its misspecification, when not. Like BIH, alternative models are expressed simply and estimated without the data-mining that accompanies VAR or general-to-specific modelling.

Although BIH superficially resembles VAR or general-to-specific modelling, it is neither. Because BIH relies upon one specific dynamic structure, the biases of specification searches can be avoided. As a result, Granger-causation testing is not needed either. Granger-causation testing could be added as yet another specification test, but to do so adds the unavoidable additional risks of data-mining and pretest biases. Such testing would better be used by independent researchers to replicate or falsify these findings so that the associated lag-fitting cannot be used to specify the model and thereby contaminate its evaluation.

FORECASTING CONSUMPTION AND RECESSION

It is a test of true theories not only to account for but to predict phenomena.
　　　　　　　　　– W. Whewell, *Philosophy of Inductive Science* (1840, p. 39)
Prediction is very difficult, especially about the future.
　　　　　　　　　　　　　　　　　　　　　　　　　– Niels Bohr

In practice, prediction represents the most demanding empirical test of a model. Predicting within the sample, however, gives an overly generous view of a model's actual explanatory power. Because conventional econometric practice gives great freedom for specification searches, high predictive power over the sample is nearly guaranteed. Thus, econometricians are unlikely to be surprise to find that BIH predicts so accurately within the estimation sample – see Figure 6.2 which compares actual vs. predicted consumption expenditures 1929-1991 from equation (6.9). Out-of-sample forecasting presents a more realistic challenge. Towards this end, equation (6.9) is re-estimated for the period 1929-1985 and then used to predict consumption in 1986-91.

The results are given in Table 6.1 and Figure 6.3 and compared to the simple linear per capita consumption model used by Friedman (1957) and Stock (1988), (FS), and used here as a benchmark – see equation (6.11) for more detail. Stock (1988) argues that per capita consumption and income are cointegrated; thus, their simple OLS regression estimates will be superconsistent. That is, the estimated regression coefficients will converge much faster to their true values than the usual classical regression model.

The striking feature of Table 6.1 and Figure 6.3 is the incredible accuracy of this model of behavioral dynamics. These out-of-sample forecasts are off by about one-half of one percent for the period 1986-1991, *i.e.*, MAPE (mean absolute percent error) is .56%. Recall that this period includes both recovery and recession. Regardless of the competition, these are very accurate econometric forecasts. For comparative purposes, notice

Figure 6.2: Within-Sample Predictions of BIH (6.9)

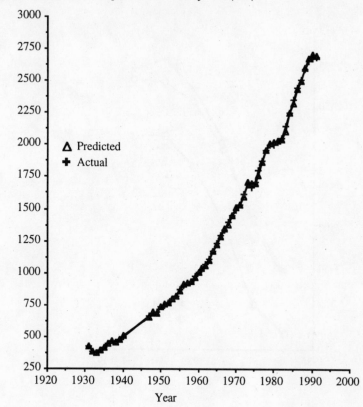

Table 6.1: Out-of-Sample Forecasting Accuracy

Year	Actual C_t	BIH Eq. (6.9)	FS Eq. (6.11)
1986	2446.4	2441.7	2370.3
1987	2513.7	2503.1	2407.0
1988	2598.4	2608.7	2509.5
1989	2656.8	2674.1	2576.5
1990	2681.6	2710.7	2615.8
1991	2684.8	2699.3	2615.8
	MAD	14.4	82.48
	MAPE	.56%	3.18%

Figure 6.3: Forecasting Consumer Expenditures 1986-1991

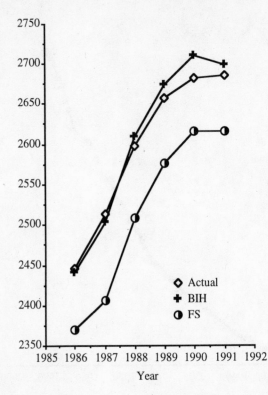

that the simple linear model, FS, has a mean absolute error (MAD) of $82 billion or over 3%. Even if one were not constrained to any given approach and used intensive data-mining, a significantly more accurate predictor of consumption would be difficult to find.

A still more rigorous test of the predictive accuracy of BIH is to attempt to forecast quarterly consumer expenditures during the recession of 1990-1991. Forecasting economic recessions is particularly challenging, because they are by definition periods that break trend. By confining our focus to a recessionary period, we have no recourse to improving forecasts that an inertial model of recovery usually entails. The reduction in consumer expenditures during the last recession received considerable attention by the popular press; this recession was broadly cited as a major factor in the 1992 presidential election. Because BIH is estimated using annual data, making accurate *quarterly* predictions represents an additional challenge.

Table 6.2: Forecasting the 1990-1991 Recession

Quarter	Actual C_t	Predicted BIH (6.9)
1990-I	2677.3	2709.3
1990-II	2678.8	2682.8
1990-III	2696.8	2694.9
1990-IV	2673.6	2702.0
1991-I	2663.7	2656.3
1991-II	2680.5	2666.3
1991-III	2705.3	2702.0
1991-IV	2689.5	2727.1
	MAD	16.1
	MAPE	.60%

Figure 6.4: Forecasting the 1990-1991 Recession

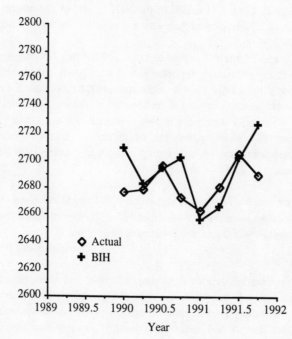

Out-of-sample forecasts of quarterly consumption expenditures, 1990-1991, are presented in Table 6.2 and Figure 6.4.[10] These forecasts of consumer spending during the past recession have an average error of less that 1 percent and are almost as accurate as the previous annual forecasts. BIH's quarterly forecasts are comparable to the accuracy of the internal 15 and 45 day estimates of the national income and product accounts (King, 1982, pp. 12-13). Because the preliminary estimates of GNP (which have an average error of 1 and .6 percent for the 15 and 45 day estimates, respectively) are deemed 'reliable' (King, 1982), so must BIH's quarterly *forecasts*.

To make this prediction test as realistic as possible, one might demand that only past values of the explanatory variables be substituted into equation (6.9) because only these values could be known by the economist at the time that a real world forecast is required. The change in disposable income may be predicted from its own past values. GNP is well known to possess a stable time series representation, AR(2). Or similarly, BIH may be employed, Chapter 2. Using BIH, the change in disposable income may be predicted from past changes in disposable income and interest rate. To allow for more psychological aspects of consumer behavior, the change in the index of consumer sentiments, collected by the University of Michigan's Survey Research Center, is added to the BIH model of consumption along with the change in the interest rate which represents the opportunity cost of current consumption.[11]

Table 6.3 and Figure 6.5 report forecasts of the last US recession about as accurate as my previously reported forecasts. Given that all information used here could have been known at the time, these forecasts of a recession are as accurate as anyone could reasonably expect – again less than 1 percent off. The only weakness in this approach is that turning points are rarely anticipated. However, models, which are quick to recognize turning points (if such a method exists), would also be quick to mistake noise for the message.

> But any method that responds to sudden changes in trend also responds strongly to large random events. Makridakis and Hibon (1984) noted that the methods that best spot turning points also make more large errors.
>
> – Pant and Starbuck (1990, p.442)

Because inertia and caprice dominate economic and financial time series, one entirely random, but sizable, event can generate the appearance of a recession or a boom. That is, random processes can create spurious cycles, reinforced by inertia and indistinguishable from genuine recessions or prosperity.[12]

Table 6.3: Forecasting the 1990-91 Recession Using Only Past Information

Quarter	Actual C_t	Predicted BIH
1990-I	2677.3	2713.7
1990-II	2678.8	2688.0
1990-III	2696.8	2692.7
1990-IV	2673.6	2707.8
1991-I	2663.7	2665.5
1991-II	2680.5	2682.6
1991-III	2705.3	2706.4
1991-IV	2689.5	2736.8
	MAD	17.0
	MAPE	.63%

Figure 6.5: Forecasting the 1990-1991 Recession with Past Information

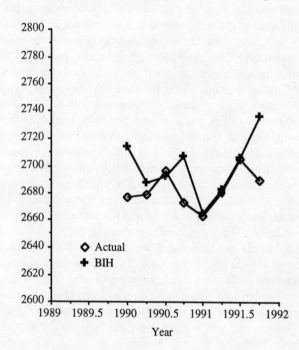

To demand that an explanatory model accurately identify turning points
– regardless of how profitable that might be – is a misunderstanding of
economic and financial time series. Such a demand would be particularly
inappropriate if directed at BIH. This behavioral inertia model of
consumption may be interpreted an entirely driven by randomness and
inertia. Recall that even the effect of disposable income growth may be
viewed as random expenditures in a changing consumption space.

> Assume that you cannot identify turning points, that you can distinguish a
> significant change from random perturbation only in retrospect. Any forecasting
> technique that tries to pick out turning points while they are occurring has to
> draw strong inferences from very recent events. Such a technique has a high
> likelihood of drawing strong inferences from unusual random events.
>
> – Pant and Starbuck (1990, p.455)

In this application, it is virtually impossible to say definitively whether
the downturns seen in US consumption expenditures in the fourth quarters
of 1990 and 1991 (which BIH failed to anticipate) represent a genuine
'consumer recession' or any other economic message. Because these
downturns were so quickly reversed and are well within two standard errors
of BIH's forecasts, they cannot be distinguished, *even in hindsight*, from
pure randomness. The 1990-1991 US recession presents a considerable
puzzle to both business and academic economists. Its cause and persistence
are still quite perplexing. Yet, this slump is accurately traceable by the
simple dynamics of inertia and caprice, turning points notwithstanding.

The advantage of this simple approach to behavioral dynamics is that it is
both more general and more parsimonious than more conventional
approaches. The *change* in an economic variable may be modelled in
almost any sensible manner. Its simplicity follows from the elementary
notion of inertia and change. Inertia is a much clearer and more efficient
explanation of economic dynamics than the conventional combination of
optimization and equilibrium adjustments or the arbitrary use of VAR and
other time series methods. It 'explains much by little'.

Simple inertia and changes in the economic background are entirely
sufficient to explain all the dynamics of consumption; that is, to explain all
the nonrandom movements in consumption expenditures. They give rise to
the second order autoregressive processes often found in economic time
series, recall equation (6.3). BIH's dynamic structure is consistent with
AR(2) models but not with any lagged structure. A more complex
equilibrium solution to the dynamics of economic time series is
unnecessary. Nor must we employ the full array of univariate and
multivariate time series methods to capture the dynamic structure of

economic time series and thereby take a real risk of accepting spurious pattern as 'explanation'. Inertia and caprice are the double-edge of Occam's Razor.

AIN'T MISBEHAVIN': EXPLAINING THE CONSUMPTION PUZZLE

Inertia in social systems makes it extremely easy to discover high correlations between historical series that do not arise from direct causal relations. Confirmatory strategies make scientists likely to see what they expect to see.

– (Pant and Starbuck, 1990, p.457)

Returning to the initial 'consumption puzzle' identified by points (1)-(4) and following Spanos (1989), it can be argued that these 'stylized facts' are not facts because they are based upon misspecified models. The 'consumption puzzle' does not arise when correctly specified empirical models are employed; thus, the paradox disappears. Although the logic of this argument is straightforward, some readers may find it less than satisfying. Therefore, we shall provide a more detailed assessment of the relation of our model to the 'consumption puzzle' and previous findings.

To illustrate the properties of BIH in the most transparent terms, let us focus on the functional dependence of the level of consumption, not its change or logarithm. By solving for C_t recursively and eliminating terms of Y_{t-1}, the logarithmic equivalent of equation (6.6) gives

$$C_t = [\alpha_0 (1-\rho)]^2 (C_{t-2}/Y_{t-2}^{\beta_1})(C_{t-1}/C_{t-3})^\rho \; C_{t-2}^\rho \; Y_t^{\beta_1} \varepsilon_t \varepsilon_{t-1}$$

and

$$\begin{aligned} E_t(C_t) &= [\alpha_0(1-\rho)]^{t+1} (C_0/Y_0^{\beta_1}) (C_{t-2}/C_0)^\rho \; Y_t^{\beta_1} \\ &= k \, [\alpha_0(1-\rho)]^{t+1} \; C_{t-2}^\rho \; Y_t^{\beta_1} \end{aligned}$$

(6.10)

Where C_0 and Y_0 are consumption and disposable income at time 0, k is a positive constant and E_t is the expected value taken at time t and conditional on the available information. In consumption–income space, the expected consumption curve 'shifts' over time and as past consumption, C_{t-2}, grows. This is illustrated in Figure 6.6 by a movement of the consumption function from AB to AC to AD, each corresponding to a particular value of C_{t-2} and time.

With this phenomenon in mind, the observed 'ratchet effect' is more readily understood. Figure 6.6 shows a similar pattern among short run consumption relations as in Figure 6.1. Next, imagine how a random scatter of observations around one of the curves in Figure 6.6 would be estimated by a simple linear consumption function. If such linear estimation is repeated for different short run time series, a number of less steeply sloped relations would emerge, just as in Figure 6.1. This is a phenomenon analogous to Duesenberry's relative income hypothesis – a higher previous standard of living, C_{t-2}, stimulates an even higher present consumption schedule.

Figure 6.6: Explaining the Consumption Puzzle

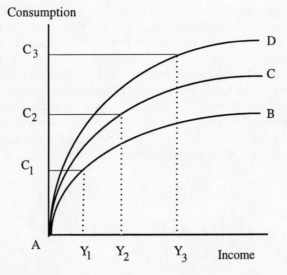

Although Figure 6.6 represents the expected relations for a given moment in time, the same effect would result if we were to construct 'long run' relationships by allowing C_{t-2} and time to vary. Such longer run consumption functions would resemble the curves depicted in Figure 6.6 but more steeply sloped – one point chosen from each static consumption function. The greater the passage of time or the larger the past consumption, C_{t-2}, the more sensitive current consumption is to current income. It is the shifting (or rotation) of these relationships over time that can cause the observed 'consumption puzzle'.

It is interesting to note that our specification of the consumption function implies that the income elasticity of consumption depends on lnY_t.[13] This, in turn, means that MPC will grow larger relative to the APC as the economy expands (recall that elasticity is also equal to MPC/APC). The BIH specification of the consumption function suggests that the sensitivity of consumption to income will increase as the economy grows. This finding is consistent with the previous research which concluded that 'the savings ratio is not a constant, but is on a *declining* trend' (Klein and Kosobud, 1961). Thus, BIH can also explain, at least in part, the observed fall in savings experienced in recent decades.

COINTEGRATION, ERROR CORRECTION, AND THE PERMANENT INCOME HYPOTHESIS

(A)n empirical econometric model which explains why and how other empirical studies have reached the conclusions they did is invaluable.

– (Spanos, 1986, p.670)

Reexamining the Permanent Income Hypothesis

Complicating the above, straightforward interpretation and solution of the 'consumption puzzle' are recent findings concerning the most generally accepted solution – Friedman's permanent income hypothesis (PIH). First of all, PIH can be seen as a statistical proposition. Because income is measured imperfectly (errors-in-variables), the ordinary least squares (OLS) estimation of the simple linear consumption function will contain biased estimates of both the intercept and slope coefficients (Friedman, 1957, pp.31-32, Kmenta, 1971, Stanley, 1986a, 1988, 1989, Stock, 1988). Errors-in-variables bias is of the correct type and magnitude to account for the observed stylized facts (2)-(4), and it implies 'true' and estimated relations exactly as depicted in Figure 6.1. Thus, the 'consumption puzzle' may also be reconciled as the statistical artifact that results from using stochastic independent variables in OLS regression (Stanley, 1989).

However, Stock (1988) offers a twist to this concise interpretation of PIH. In his reexamination of PIH, Stock shows that OLS estimation of the consumption function involves only small sample biases that soon evaporate with larger samples. Thus, the routinely observed differences among short run and long run marginal propensities to consume that are the source of much of the consumption controversy can be seen as the melting of statistical bias in the sunlight of additional information. The source of Stock's result is the cointegration of income and consumption and the resulting 'superconsistency' of OLS estimators (Stock, 1987). Though they may still contain small sample bias due to the problem of errors-in-variables, this bias dissipates rapidly with larger samples – at a rate faster than that with which classical regression estimators converge to their true parameters. Stock's contribution to the debate is to show that OLS provides *consistent* estimates of the marginal propensity to consume even in the presence of errors-in-variables. He concludes, 'These results suggest that although Friedman's PIH provides an empirically consistent explanation of the APC–MPC puzzle, this explanation is more in keeping with Friedman's informal notion of errors-in-variables "bias" than the formal "inconsistency" argument of the early econometricians' (Stock, 1988, p.407).

However, there are a number of potentially misleading aspects of Stock's reinterpretation of Friedman's PIH. Most importantly, it does not imply that observational errors or the errors-in-variables bias can be safely ignored in typical econometric applications. Quite the contrary; if Stock's interpretation is correct, then it is this small sample bias of errors-in-variables that caused the most famous empirical puzzle in econometric history. The 'superconsistency' property, though desirable, gives no guarantee that estimation in practical samples will be usefully accurate. Convergence may begin at very large samples, well beyond what is practically feasible. Furthermore, there are statistical reasons to doubt Stock's interpretation. The simple linear consumption function upon which Stock's analysis is in part based is statistically misspecified. Using more recent data, 1929-1991, and omitting the Second World War,[14] we find:

$$Cp_t = .176 + .894 \, Yp_t \qquad R^2 = .997 \qquad (6.11)$$
$$(127.5) \qquad \text{D-W} = .37 \quad n=57$$

where Cp is per capita consumption, Yp is per capita income. Although casual inspection of these statistical results suggests that there is a very good fit ($R^2 = 99.7\%$ and a t-value of 127!),[15] the Durbin–Watson gives a clear indication of significant positive autocorrelation. Recall that the above model, previously referred to as FS, serves as a benchmark for BIH's forecasts presented in Table 6.1 and Figure 6.3.

As is well known, the Durbin–Watson statistic may be used to detect model misspecification. Although autocorrelation is often found in cointegrated regressions, the Durbin–Watson may still be used as a specification test. When residuals are nonstationary, the Durbin–Watson statistic will approach zero. If, on the other hand, the variables are in fact cointegrated, the residuals must be stationary and the Durbin–Watson statistic should be significantly greater than zero. The cointegrating regression Durbin–Watson test (CRDW) exploits this relation between the

Durbin–Watson statistic and stationarity of the residuals. In the case of per capita consumption and income, the above Durbin–Watson statistic is less than the critical value, .78 (Engle and Yoo, 1987), consistent with nonstationary residuals and indicating that per capita real consumption and per capita real disposable income are not, in fact, cointegrated. Engle and Granger (1987) find that CRDW is the most sensitive cointegration test for detecting cointegration, but it is not as robust as some others are. Yet other tests, the Dickey–Fuller test ($t=-2.25$) and the augmented Dickey–Fuller test ($t=-1.84$), are also consistent with unit root of the residuals and the noncointegration of per capita consumption and income.[16]   Because Stock's explanation depends upon the cointegration of per capita consumption and income, more recent data cast doubt on Stock's resolution of the consumption puzzle and his consumption model. Further evidence of the misspecification is supplied by Spanos (1989). Spanos subjects the linear consumption model to a whole battery of specification tests for both historic and contemporary data sets, finding evidence of misspecification in almost every possible sense.

Recent empirical evidence questions the validity of PIH altogether (Mankiw, 1981, Shapiro, 1984). 'There is by now substantial evidence that US consumers do not in practice act fully as life-cycle-permanent-income consumers' (Dornbusch and Fisher, 1990, p. 286). Specifically, there are the problems that consumption is too 'sensitive' and too 'smooth' (depending on your choice of perspective) (Flavin, 1981, Campbell and Deaton, 1989, Campbell and Mankiw, 1990). That is, consumption systematically responds too much to changes in observed income, and the standard deviation of the change in consumption is too small (Campbell and Deaton, 1989). The problem is that consumption is excessively sensitive to innovation (or 'caprice') in observed income (Flavin, 1981) and that the change in consumption has too little variance (Campbell and Deaton, 1989, Cushing, 1991).

Although there appears to be sufficient evidence against PIH, several studies attempt to restore its empirical integrity. Campbell and Mankiw (1990) show that a more general model in which half of the consumers behave in accordance with PIH and the other half conform to the simple, 'Keynesian', linear consumption function remains consistent with the data. Thus the permanent income hypothesis may be half-right. Christiano et al. (1991) claim to the contrary, they report rather strong evidence against PIH even after allowance is made for continuous time consumption.[17] Quah (1990) uses rational expectation and the distinction of permanent and transitory movements in labor income to explain the excess smoothness of consumption. Nonetheless, he clearly recognizes that PIH is refuted by the empirical data. 'Aggregate consumption is not a martingale, and so the PIH would be rejected' (Quah, 1990, pp.472-473).

Correcting the Error of Error Correction Models

Exploiting recent developments in time series analysis, error correction models (ECM) and cointegrated variables have been widely used to study the dynamics of the consumption function – for example, Davidson, Hendry, Srba, and Yeo (1978) and Stock (1988). Others, notably Engle and Granger (1987), have related ECM explicitly to cointegrated variables. They prove that if two variables are cointegrated there must be an ECM representation, and conversely. Error correction models postulate an equilibrium adjustment mechanism and can be formulated to portray most theories, orthodox or otherwise. These models may be derived from general autoregressive distributive lag or partial equilibrium representations. It is their adjustment mechanisms, however, that are largely responsible for the dynamic properties of ECM and for their considerable econometric successes. ECM have much in common with the approach taken here. Both BIH and ECM focus on the *change* in the phenomenon of interest using lags and changes in the explanatory variables. However, BIH may be interpreted as a partial adjustment of the *change* in the dependent variable, whereas ECM adjusts towards equilibrium levels. In fact, inertia and caprice in economic behavior can explain why error correction models have been so statistically successful in representing economic time series. These empirical economic frameworks are quite similar but they derive from different hypotheses about behavior. A serious limitation in the empirical evaluation of ECM is that many alternative forms of ECM have been offered in the literature. To attempt a fair survey and to capture the breath of ECM, three different approaches are investigated below.

First, Stock (1988) applies a Granger vector error correction model to adjust for the bias in the usual OLS estimates of the MPC. According to Stock (1988), a consistent estimate of the MPC may be found by taking the negative ratio of the estimated coefficients of Yp_{t-1} to Cp_{t-1} in

$$dCp_t = \gamma_0 + \gamma_1\, dCp_{t-1} + \gamma_2\, dYp_{t-1} + \gamma_3\, Cp_{t-1} + \gamma_4\, Yp_{t-1} + \varepsilon_t \qquad (6.12)$$

Note the similarity to the previously discussed BIH model (6.9). The change in consumption is explained using both the lagged change in consumption (though in per capita terms) and the change in disposable income (also in per capita terms). The difference is that Stock uses the lagged change in disposable income along with the error correction terms, $\gamma_3 Cp_{t-1}$ and $\gamma_4\, Yp_{t-1}$.

Using more recent data, 1929-1991, and omitting WWII, the estimates of (6.12) are:

$$d\hat{C}p_t = -.0149 + .454\ dCp_{t-1} - 0.52\ dYp_{t-1} + .0138Cp_{t-1} - .00524Yp_{t-1} \quad (6.13)$$
$$\quad\quad (2.45) \quad\quad\quad (-.36) \quad\quad\quad (.10) \quad\quad\quad (-.04)$$
$$R^2 = .252 \quad D\text{-}W = 1.76 \quad\quad h = \text{undefined} \quad\quad n = 55$$

Compared to the previously reported results, Stock's ECM does not seem very adequate. Many of the explanatory variables are not statistically significant, and together they explain only 30 percent of the change in per capita consumption.[18] The status of this model is little improved if the logarithm of aggregate levels replaces per capita terms. The consistent estimate of the MPC is –(–.00524)/ .0138= .38 and is quite different from the magnitude reported by Stock (1988) for the 1897-1949 period (p.406). Because the coefficient in the numerator is known to be significantly insignificant, this estimate of the MPC cannot be trusted. Stock further adjusts his estimate of MPC for its small sample bias (approximately .15) to find both the MPC and the APC to be approximately equal and around .90. However, the much smaller estimate of MPC found for 1929-1991 calls into question Stock's approach. Surely, such a large difference cannot be attributed to differences in small sample bias alone. If so, what practical value does super-consistency have? These results confirm the finding that per capita consumption and income are not, in fact, cointegrated.

Incidentally, it is interesting to note that the above results offer evidence against PIH. The random walk implications of PIH (Hall, 1978) imply that all the regression coefficients in (6.13) should be zero (Stock, 1988, pp. 406-407).[19] However, the F-test clearly rejects the joint hypothesis that all these coefficients are zero ($F = 5.17$; $p<.01$). Although Stock is quick to point out that either the nonconstancy of interest rates or temporal aggregation bias may be responsible for this apparent rejection of PIH (Stock, 1988, p.407), empirical evidence from other studies casts doubt on PIH even after adjustments are made for these complications (Christiano *et al.*, 1991, Mankiw, 1981, Shapiro, 1984).

A more popular approach to error correction modelling, especially when applied to consumption, is attributable to Hendry. In this context, an ECM may be expressed as:

$$dlnC_t = \alpha + \beta\ dlnY_t + \gamma(lnC_{t-1} - lnY_{t-1}) + \varepsilon_t \quad\quad\quad (6.14)$$

(Gilbert, 1990, Alogoskoufis and Smith, 1991).[20] This version of ECM gives a considerably improved statistical representation of the change in aggregate consumption. The estimates are:

$$dln\hat{C}_t = -.000386 + .676dlnY_t - .160\,(lnC_{t-1} - lnY_{t-1}) \qquad (6.15)$$
$$(19.60) \qquad (-3.57) \qquad\qquad R^2 = .883$$
$$\text{D-W} = 1.89 \qquad \text{LM} = 4.23 \qquad \text{G-Q} = 1.44 \qquad n = 56$$

for 1929-1991 and omitting WWII. This error correction model passes all specification tests and is comparable to the previously reported BIH model (6.9).

Hendry's ECM specification also forecasts the 1986-1991 period quite well, see Table 6.4, only slightly less accurate than BIH. However, ECM does not forecast the lackluster consumer expenditures during the last US recession very well, Table 6.5 and Figure 6.7. Over the recession, BIH clearly outperforms ECM, which has errors over twice as large of BIH whether computed on past information alone or with contemporaneous information. Also notice that ECM continually over-predicts consumer expenditures throughout the recession. To be fair, BIH also over-predicts consumption in those periods when it first turns down, but it is better able to compensate in following quarters. Perhaps this is to be expected, because error correction models are long run equilibrium models and this period of US economic history is clearly one of 'disequilibruim', or at least, of great uncertainty. In each period during the recession, the error correction term, $lnC_{t-1} - lnY_{t-1}$, tends to dominate reductions in disposable income, causing predicted consumption to remain too large.

Table 6.4: Forecasting Consumer Expenditures 1986-1991 (ECM)

YEAR	Actual	BIH: Predicted by eq. (6.9)	ECM: Predicted by eq. (6.15)
1986	2446.4	2441.7	2433.1
1987	2513.7	2503.1	2492.6
1988	2598.4	2608.7	2603.6
1989	2656.8	2674.1	2666.7
1990	2681.6	2710.7	2707.8
1991	2684.8	2699.3	2701.1
	MAD	14.4	15.3
	MAPE	.56%	.59%

Table 6.5: Forecasting the 1990-1991 Recession

Quarter	Actual	BIH: Predicted by (6.9)	ECM: Predicted by (6.15)
1990-I	2677.3	2709.3	2731.9
1990-II	2678.8	2682.8	2713.1
1990-III	2696.8	2694.9	2723.8
1990-IV	2673.6	2702.0	2726.2
1991-I	2663.7	2656.3	2688
1991-II	2680.5	2666.3	2694.8
1991-III	2705.3	2702.0	2725.1
1991-IV	2689.5	2727.1	2748.5
	MAD	16.1	35.7
	MAPE	.60%	1.33%

Figure 6.7: Comparing Forecasts of the 1990-1991 Recession

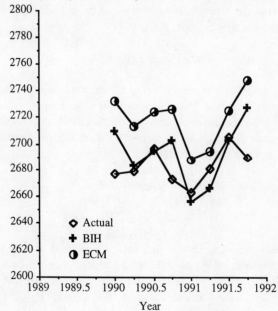

The error correction term mistakenly expects consumption to rebound in the period following a low APC (note that the error correction term is the logarithm of the average propensity to consume). As opposed to ECM, BIH expects trends in consumption movements to linger rather than to be immediately self-correcting. By viewing change as partially adjusting, the behavioral inertia hypothesis better forecasts the economy during recession.

Nonetheless, my model of behavioral dynamics and Hendry's ECM are closely related. Each employs the same dependent variable, and one of two independent variables are identical. Only the second term is different, but not entirely so. The error correction term, $lnC_{t-1} - lnY_t$, and the lagged dependent variable in equation (6.9) have lnC_{t-1} in common. Both model the change in economic time series and are capable of reflecting the inertia of economic behavior. Hendry, *et al.* (1984) consider inertia as a 'quasi-theoretical basis for dynamic models' (pp. 1037-8). They also suggest that economic agents may 'use simple adaptive decision rules rather than optimal ones' (Hendry *et al.*, 1984, p.1038). The salient difference is that BIH and ECM involve different dynamics and impose different restrictions on the model's coefficients. 'A vector autoregression in differenced variables is incompatible with these representations (ECM) because it omits the error correction term' (Engle and Granger, 1987, p. 274).

These alternative restrictions can be tested by imbedding both models into a more general specification,

$$dlnC_t = \delta_0 + \delta_1 dlnC_{t-1} + \delta_2 dlnY_t + \delta_3 dlnY_{t-1} + \delta_4(lnC_{t-1} - lnY_{t-1}) + \varepsilon_t \quad (6.16)$$

This general model is chosen such that all the explanatory variables are stationary, thus ensuring that OLS estimates will possess all of the conventional properties, at least in large samples. BIH implies that $\delta_3 = 0$ and $\delta_4 = 0$, while Hendry's ECM imposes the restrictions that $\delta_1 = 0$ and $\delta_3 = 0$. The estimated general model is:

$$dln\hat{C}_t = -.00128 + .203 dlnC_{t-1} + .623 dlnY_t - .079 dlnY_{t-1} - .104(lnC_{t-1} - lnY_{t-1})$$
$$\quad\quad\quad (2.74) \quad\quad (16.34) \quad\quad (-1.38) \quad\quad (-2.17) \quad\quad\quad (6.17)$$
$$R^2 = .885 \quad\quad D\text{-}W = 2.23 \quad\quad SSE = .004757 \quad\quad n = 55$$

Comparing the sum of squared errors in equation (6.9) with (6.17) above implies that the restrictions on BIH are consistent with the data: $F_{2,50} = 2.88$ (critical F is 3.15). Likewise, comparing Hendry's ECM equation (6.15) to the unrestricted model, equation (6.17), yields $F_{2,50} = 4.14$ and leads to the rejection of ECM's restrictions ($\alpha = .05$).[21] Thus, there are empirical reasons to reject Hendry's ECM of US consumption expenditures.

Not only does this long run approach fail to track some of the short run patterns; its parameter restrictions are rejected by the data.

Third, Engle and Granger (1987) take a slightly different approach to error correction modelling. Their two-step method utilizes the consistency of OLS estimation in the cointegrating regression to provide an estimate of the error correction term, $\hat{Z}_{t-1}$. In the second step, this estimate of the lagged error correction term is added to a Granger ECM and estimated using OLS. Engle and Granger (1987) prove that the resulting estimates of their ECM will be consistent and asymptotically normal.[22] Given our data, the Engle–Granger two-step method yields

$$dln\hat{C}_t = .016 + .312 dlnC_{t-1} + .138 dlnY_{t-1} + .104\, \hat{Z}_{t-1} \qquad (6.18)$$
$$\phantom{dln\hat{C}_t = .016 +} (1.71) \qquad\quad (.94) \qquad\qquad (.69) \qquad R^2 = .27$$
$$\text{D-W} = 1.99 \qquad h = \text{undefined} \qquad \text{SSE} = .03025 \qquad n = 55$$

Overall, this error correction model is quite disappointing, relative to both BIH and Hendry's ECM. It explains less than one-third of the variation of the percentage change in consumption while BIH accounts for nearly 90 percent. Neither lagged income nor the equilibrium adjustment, $\hat{Z}_{t-1}$, helps to explain consumption. If the ECM is correctly specified, all independent variables are I(0), i.e, integrated of order zero or stationary, and conventional testing is valid. It is unlikely that this poor fit can be attributed to small sample bias, which is inversely proportional to the R^2 (99.9%) of the first step (Muscatelli and Hurn, 1992, n.18).

If one is prepared to invoke the weak exogeneity of income, a contemporaneous effect may be added to the Granger ECM.

$$dln\hat{C}_t = .0064 + .25 dlnC_{t-1} + .619 dlnY_t - .102 dlnY_{t-1} + .104\, \hat{Z}_{t-1} \qquad (6.19)$$
$$\phantom{dln\hat{C}_t = .0064 +} (3.4) \qquad (16.23) \quad (-1.68) \qquad\quad (1.98)$$
$$R^2 = .884 \quad \text{D-W} = 2.29 \qquad h = -1.29 \quad \text{SSE} = .004828 \qquad n = 55$$

Clearly, contemporaneous income dramatically improves the statistical explanation of consumption. But it is no improvement over BIH. In this formulation, ECM is the same as BIH with the addition of two independent variables, lnY_{t-1} and $\hat{Z}_{t-1}$. Therefore, equation (6.19) may be considered a generalized version of BIH, equation (6.9). The restrictions imposed by BIH may then be tested in the usual manner, $F_{2,50} = 2.47$. Thus, BIH's restrictions are accepted by the data, implying that the error correction term and lagged income growth do not contribute to the explanation of consumption expenditures. Unsurprisingly, forecasts based on BIH, equation (6.9), or ECM, equation (6.19), are largely the same, confirming their close association. Engle–Granger two-step ECM with contemporaneous effects is more accurate in forecasting annual consumption expenditures (1986-1991), MAD = $10.5 billion (or .4%) and a little less accurate forecasting quarterly consumption during the last recession, MAD = $17.9 billion (or .67%).

However, there are reasons to suspect the long equilibrium approach altogether. Testing for cointegration is also a test of the presence of a long run equilibrium relationship (Muscatelli and Hurn, 1992, p.3). Both the Dickey–Fuller test (t=–2.39) and the augmented Dickey–Fuller (t=–2.63) are consistent with the unit root of the residuals to the logarithmic aggregate consumption function and thereby disconfirm cointegration. Further confirmation that aggregate income and consumption are not cointegrated is provided by the CRDW test, cointegrating regression Durbin–Watson. The simple regression of the log of aggregate consumption on the log of aggregate disposable income gives a Durbin–Watson statistic of .46, which is less than the critical value of .78 needed to confirm cointegration (Engle and Yoo, 1987).[23] Because ECM are equivalent to cointegrated regression models, disconfirming evidence of cointegration is equally applicable to the ECM representation of consumption and its notion of long run equilibrium.

Exceptional Consumption: BIH and the War

My approach has the added advantage of being able to account for the influence of exceptional periods, i.e., the Second World War (WWII) and the Great Depression. Conventional practice is to omit such periods from the analysis altogether, thus implicitly admitting the failure of one's model of reality. In fact, it is common practice to discard any historical period that produces unacceptable outliers relative to the chosen model. Of course, forced rationing and the diversion of a large proportion of US resources to the war effort during the Second World War had a profound effect on consumer behavior, an effect that is not likely to be repeated in less exceptional circumstances. However, a model that correctly accounts for consumption dynamics should also be able to accommodate the influence of rationing and war.

When exceptional periods are not eliminated from the analysis, conventional econometric practice adds dummy variables to the model. Adding a modified dummy variable and interaction term to BIH yields the following estimated regression.[24]

$$dln\hat{C}_t = .00798 + .279 dlnC_{t-1} + .501 dlnY_t + .049 WWII - 1.127 dlnYxWW$$
$$\qquad\qquad (3.96)\qquad (8.99)\qquad (3.26)\qquad (-6.03)\qquad (6.20)$$
$$R^2 = .712 \qquad h = .68 \qquad n = 61 \qquad SSE = .0143$$

where *WWII* reflects the Second World War, and *dlnYxWW* is an interaction term that allows for a differential propensity to consume during war. Even though equation (6.20) adds two significant variables and six observations, its statistical fit is not as good as BIH, equation (6.9), by conventional criteria. Worse still is the unacceptable estimate of a significant negative effect for income during the height of WWII $(.501 - 1.127 = -.626)$.[25]

However, if the framework implied by the behavioral inertia hypothesis is correct, then it should be the *change* in the war status which has explanatory power, neither its presence nor absence.

$$dln\hat{C}_t = .00655 + .177 \, dlnC_{t-1} + .595 \, dlnY_t \, -.143 \, dWWII \qquad (6.21)$$
$$\qquad\qquad (4.36) \qquad (15.69) \qquad (-13.19) \qquad R^2=.785$$
$$h = -.99 \qquad \text{G-Q} =1.01 \qquad \text{LM}=8.86 \qquad n = 61 \qquad \text{SSE}=.006144$$

Where *dWWII* represents the change in war status $(WWII_t - WWII_{t-1})$. As before, this version of BIH is well specified passing all statistical tests. The estimated values of the coefficients lie well within expected bounds, and BIH's parameter restrictions are acceptable while ECM's are not.[26] The coefficient of determination and the standard error of the estimate reveals a much better fit than the traditional dummy variable approach, and this version of BIH likewise forecasts the past recession quite well, MAD= 16.2; MAPE = .60% .

BIH's approach to the war years also resolves the stylized fact (2) of the consumption puzzle, concerning the underprediction of postwar US consumption. The misspecification of early consumption functions and the attendant 'ratchet effect' can explain the existence and direction of this historic underprediction of postwar consumption but not its full magnitude. In 1946, the effect of 'pent-up' demand was unprecedented, increasing consumption by approximately 10 percent. Only a measure of the war's effect and its cessation can explain the surge of spending just after the Second World War. The estimated coefficient of *dWWII* in equation (6.21) implies that the full return to a normal economy (i.e., $dWWII = -1$) would induce a one time increase in consumption by 15 percent. This effect is symmetric with the forced decrease in consumption that rationing caused at the beginning of the war. It is the addition or removal of consumption constraints (i.e., *dWWII*) which affects consumption, not their presence or absence as modelled by conventional practice.

The invariance of BIH to large policy interventions during both the Great Depression and the Second World War is a corroboration of its causal explanatory power (Hoover, 1990). Oral tradition unabashedly reconciles this historic economic episode by *ad hoc* reference to 'pent-up' demand. From the perspective of BIH, pent-up demand is not *ad hoc*, but merely the opposite side of the imposition of consumption constraints demanded by the war. Inertia and caprice, which by the law of large numbers alone, can predict the observe behavior of consumption during and just after the Second World War. BIH resolves the most notorious failure in the history of econometrics. It is the exception that proves the rule.

Error Correction or Behavioral Inertia?

Although there is a great deal of similarity between the behavioral inertia hypothesis and error correction models, the specific dynamic structure of BIH is more consistent with US consumption data. Recall that, 'A vector autoregression in differenced variables is incompatible with these representations (ECM) because it omits the error correction term' (Engle and Granger, 1987, p. 274). Yet, in the language of Engle and Granger, BIH is just such a vector autoregression in differenced variables. As shown above, either the error correction term does not add significantly to the explanation of consumption or ECM representations actually worsen the fit over the simple BIH model. The behavioral inertia hypothesis can explain both the past successes of ECM models and their failures. What they contain in common, changes in current independent variables and the past change in the dependent variable, is statistically responsible for almost all of ECM's explanatory power. ECM's failures may be attributed to the error correction term and the associated unnecessary or incorrect dynamics. Equilibrium and error correction are an unnecessary theoretical pretense forced upon the data. Habit and randomness are entirely sufficient to explain observed consumer behavior. So why demand more?

SUMMARY: PARSIMONY OR THE POMP OF RATIONALITY?

> We are to admit no more causes of natural things than such as are both true and sufficient to explain their appearances. To this purpose the philosophers say that Nature does nothing in vain, and more is in vain when less will serve; for Nature is pleased with simplicity, and affects not the pomp of superfluous causes.
>
> – Sir Isaac Newton, _Principia_

To review, the simple model of the behavioral dynamics (BIH) presented here explains:

- The consumption puzzle.
- The recent (1990-1991) US consumer recession.

- Consumer behavior during the Second World War.
- Both the past successes and failures of error correction models.

In particular, predicting the quarterly movement of consumption expenditures during recession with a model estimated from annual data before the recession represents a severe challenge. According to some philosophers of science, 'Confirmations should count only if they are the result of *risky predictions*' (Popper, 1963, p. 36). Such a challenging test, when successfully passed, represents an example of what philosopher Imre Lakatos described as 'corroborated excess empirical content' and confers the label 'progressive' on the research programme achieving it (Lakatos, 1970).

Our resolution of the consumption puzzle is entirely independent of utility theory. Habit and random buying are sufficient to explain all of the empirical regularities found in the aggregate consumption expenditures. Utility theory and hence conventional consumer theory are simply unnecessary and irrelevant. In short, utility maximization has no explanatory power. If, as economic rhetoric repeatedly asserts, the simplicity of an explanation has value, then the behavioral inertia hypothesis is the clear choice, and consumer theory may be freed from the unnecessary constraint, and accompanying ideological bias, of individual utility maximization.

BIH also predicts the pervasive autocorrelations that are routinely found in most empirical econometric studies. This excess empirical content follows, in part, from the logarithmic form of the consumption relation. Whenever one attempts to estimate a curve with a linear relationship, positive autocorrelation often results. However, the behavioral dynamics of BIH suggests an even more pervasive autocorrelation. Notice the inertia of equation (6.2) and the error terms of equation (6.9). If one eliminates the C_{t-1} term through substitution (because it can contribute to the first-order autocorrelation), the error term becomes $\varepsilon_t \varepsilon_{t-1} \varepsilon_{t-1}^\rho$ implying a first-order autocorrelation of $(1+\rho)^2/(2+\rho)$. From our estimate of ρ in equation (6.8), a logarithmic simple consumption function should produce an autocorrelation coefficient of .64 , and this is consistent with regression results for the logarithmic consumption function.[27] In general, regressions on nonstationary variables, as implied by BIH, give low Durbin–Watson values. The ubiquitous empirical finding of autocorrelation in the traditional consumption models, whether linear or logarithmic, is yet another corroboration of the excess empirical content of BIH.

The advantage of our simple approach to behavioral dynamics is that it is both more general and yet more parsimonious than the error correction modelling framework. Its generality ensues from the flexibility permitted in modelling change; $X_t\beta$ may be specified in whatever manner is empirically defensible. The change in an economic variable can be modelled in almost any manner. Its simplicity follows from the basic, commonsense notion of inertia and change. The only restriction that BIH places on economic time series is in the structure of its dynamics.

Hendry also gives parsimony an important role in his methodology (Gilbert, 1990). Aside from practical considerations of degrees of freedom,

> Complexity permits *degenerate* research programmes to defend their central propositions by a *protective belt* of auxiliary hypotheses (Lakatos, 1970). These auxiliary hypotheses may be correct, but it is more plausible to suppose that vested professional interests are being protected. Parsimony, on this view, forces scientific honesty.   –Gilbert (1990, p.295)

This is why it is imperative to cut through the abstruse thicket of technical methods that describes modern econometrics. Have we not already devoted sufficient resources to the defense of individual utility maximization from its countless empirical anomalies? Surely the returns to yet another epicyclical adjustment of neoclassical theory have diminished beyond any practical significance. Need our empirical methods presume optimization and equilibrium?

When one is confined to the 'Newtonian deterministic', neoclassical framework, observed consumption expenditures might well appear to be misbehavin'. However, a more dynamic and stochastic view quite easily explains the time series properties found in consumption as well as other economic phenomena. This empirical investigation begins with a theory of consumption dynamics that has the same general form as an explanation of GNP's puzzling empirical behavior – Chapter 2. BIH is meant as a general framework for modelling time-dependent and stochastic economic phenomena. Inertia is the simplest form of time-dependence. Although inertia and randomness may, at first, seem antithetical, they are quite complementary. According to the 'new science' of nonlinear dynamics, chaos theory, 'Only when a system behaves in a sufficiently random way may the difference between past and future, and therefore irreversibility, enter its description' (Prigogine and Stengers, 1984).

This approach can also clarify more recent problems found with the PIH. Because BIH does not possess the filter of permanent income, we expect consumption to be sensitive with respect to changes in measured income. As previously discussed, this sensitivity increases with the growth of the economy. And, inertia causes consumption to change less than it might otherwise, predicting that consumption is too 'smooth'. In fact, Campbell and Deaton (1989) state quite clearly that one explanation for the inadequacy of PIH is 'that consumers adjust slowly through inertia or habit formation' (p.372). If one employs our simple model of behavioral dynamics, it is not necessary to resort to the rather *ad hoc* pasting of the simple linear Keynesian model back onto PIH, as do Campbell and Mankiw (1990).[28] Although orthodox consumption theories still exhibit puzzling empirical behavior, the model of capricious consumption presented here 'just ain't misbehavin''.

NOTES

* From the *Journal of Post Keynesian Economics*, **16**, 1993, 249-267.

1 An exception is the errors-in-variables interpretation of Friedman's permanent income hypothesis (Friedman, 1957, Stock, 1988). By this view, the permanent income hypothesis is not a different economic theory but rather the recognition that the 'consumption puzzle' is a statistical artifact.

2 The notation used in this chapter is superficially the reverse of what is introduced in Chapter 2. Because standard economic convention uses C for consumption and Y for income, these letters take on the opposite role to their role in Chapter 2 where C represents the caprice and is associated with the independent variables and Y represents the dependent variable. However, the dynamic structure and explanatory framework of BIH remains unchanged throughout this book.

3 In fact, utility theory has less explanatory power than purely random consumer behavior. As is well known, utility does not predict an inverse relation of consumption expenditures to price nor a positive association with income. From utility theory anything is possible; hence it is exegetically empty.

4 Interest rate change has a marginal effect on consumption, as does the index of consumer sentiments. Prices were also investigated, but they exhibit no significant effect on real consumption. The influence of these additional variables fits nicely within the BIH framework but does not materially affect the discussion. For clarity of exposition and consistency with rival econometric models, only the effects of income are presented here.

5 The data are from *The National Income and Product Accounts of the United States, 1929-82* and the *Survey of Current Business*. The results reported here are slightly different from those in Stanley (1993b). The difference is that the interest rate and 1941 are omitted. The interest rate is omitted to be directly comparable to alternative approaches (i.e., error correction models and cointegrated variables). Keeping 1941 in the data creates an outlier regardless of the model chosen. Although the US did not officially enter the war until nearly 1942, the military buildup and allied assistance program were already well under way by 1941. This outlier was left in previously because I sought to use minimal model selection in order to lessen the possible biases and misrepresentation that

specification searching can induce. BIH is also compared to alternative specifications and used to explain consumption expenditures during the Second World War – see later sections of this chapter.

6 BIH's restrictions are more formally tested later.

7 Typically, regression on nonstationary variables produces biases, inconsistency and nonstandard distributions for OLS estimates. However, the potential for spurious regressions can be turned into an advantage if the independent and dependent variables are cointegrated. Stock (1987) shows how conventional estimates from cointegrated variables are 'superconsistent', converging to their true values much faster than the rate at which classical regression estimates converge. A detailed exploration of the role of cointegration in the estimation of the consumption function is given later in this chapter.

8 Estimated regression equations reported below use the same data time period unless otherwise stated, 1929-1991 and excluding the Second World War.

9 Because the explanatory variables are nonstationary, this F-test may not be strictly valid. However, if the restrictions implied by BIH are correct, then the F-test will be valid, and the F-test may be approximately valid in any case. Stock and Watson (1988) demonstrate that conventional tests and distributions remain valid even when the independent variables are nonstationary, provided that the coefficients in question can be written as coefficients on stationary variables. When both C_t and Y_t are integrated of order one, I(1), the difference between successive lags is stationary, and BIH implies that this relation can be written in a difference form. Otherwise, when consumption and income are cointegrated, the unrestricted regression, equation (6.7), can be written approximately in the form of stationary regressors because the difference between cointegrated variables is also stationary (Stock and Watson, 1988). If BIH is valid, this F-test should have the correct large sample properties; if it is not, the nonstandard terms should make rejection all the more likely and the test of BIH's restrictions all the more powerful.

10 As discussed in Chapter 2, the intercept is reduced to one fourth of its annual value to adjust for the expected difference in quarterly dynamics.

11 Using annual US data 1953-1991 because ICS was first collected in 1953, the estimated model is:

$$d\hat{C}_t = 8.882 + .272\, dC_{t-1} + .530\, dY_t + 1.225\, dICS_t - 6.268\, di_t$$
$$\quad\quad\quad (2.76)\quad\quad (6.69)\quad\; (3.84)\quad\quad\; (-2.53)$$

$R^2 = .856$ $S = 12.1$ $h = -1.80$ $LM = 12.27$ $G\text{-}Q = 2.78$ $n = 39$

Where S is the standard error of the estimate. This model passes all statistical tests. Interest rate (i_t), Moody's Aaa bond yields, can be both a direct cost of consumption when consumer credit is used and the opportunity cost of not saving. Wilcox (1990) demonstrates that nominal interest rates are more appropriate for consumption than the 'theoretically correct' real rate of interest.

12 This is also the reason that annual data is used here. Annually estimated models should contain approximately half the random variation (as measured by the standard error of the estimate).

13 Recall the log-linear specification in (6.9). From these estimates, the long run response of $dlnC_t$ to changes in $dlnY_t$ is $\beta_1/(1-\rho) = .595/(1-.177) = .723$. However, this is not yet equal to the income elasticity of consumption, as you might expect, because both variables are already expressed as changes. Rather, $d^2lnC_t/d(lnY_t)^2 = \beta_1/(1-\rho)$. To find the elasticity, we must integrate this expression over lnY_t, giving $\eta = \int [\beta_1/(1-\rho)]dlnY_t = K_0 + [\beta_1/(1-\rho)] lnY_t$, for K_0 as a constant of integration.

14 Misspecification of Stock's model does not depend upon the time period or data set chosen. It is found also in the data that Friedman (1957) used and in the data used by earlier consumption studies (Spanos, 1989). Stock (1988) also reports a more sophisticated error correction model that is discussed later.

15 When variables are cointegrated, OLS estimates do not have a normal distribution, and conventional inference using t-tests is no longer appropriate.

16 The Engle–Granger distribution is used with critical values provided by MacKinnon (1991). For our sample, the critical value is -2.917, $\alpha = .05$.

17 This is clearly shown in their Tables I and III when one focuses on the entire sample period and disposable income with nondurable consumption. Quah also interprets Christiano *et al.* (1991) as lending support to the empirical refutation of PIH.

18 Usually, the t-values for nonstationary variables have nonstandard distributions, and conventional inference does not apply. However, when these variables, Cp_{t-1} and Yp_{t-1}, are cointegrated, the coefficient on Yp_{t-1} can be written as a coefficient for a stationary variable and hence its estimate has all the conventional properties (Stock and Watson, 1988).

19 (R)andom walk behavior of macroeconomics aggregates is something quite general which need have little relation to the optimizing behavior of individual agents' (Orszag and Staroselsky, 1993, p.145). BIH may also give the appearance of a random walk when ρ is small.

20 Note that this specification implicitly assumes that the cointegrating coefficient is one and hence that the consumption function has unitary elasticity. It is this assumption that makes Hendry's ECM estimable by OLS.

21 To be entirely compatible with the general model and fair to Hendry's ECM, the first observation must be removed in the estimation of Hendry's ECM, SSE=.005544. If we drop the $dlnY_{t-1}$ term, BIH's restrictions are again accepted (F=3.91) while ECM's are not (F=6.54).

22 A limitation of the Engle–Granger two-step method is that it does not provide an estimate of the long run effect that has a conventional statistical distribution. However, the 'two-step' estimates for the ECM parameters do allow conventional inference, at least in large samples – see Theorem 2 of Engle and

Granger (1987). Engle and Yoo (1991) have developed a three-step method to provide conventional (FIML) estimates of the long run effect.

23 The estimates of the first step of Engle–Granger two-step method are:

$$ln\hat{C}_t = .0064 + .96 \, lnY_t \quad R^2 = .999 \quad \text{D-W} = .46$$
$$(206.8) \quad \text{SSE} = .02733 \quad n = 57$$

24 Because the involvement of the US in the Second World War did not begin or end sharply with calendar years, an adjusted, nondichotomous dummy variable, *WWII*, is used here. The war ended midway through 1945 and resources had begun to be redirected; thus $WWII_{1945} = .5$. Even though the US did not become officially an active participant until the very end of 1941, the military build-up and support of the Allied effort was well under way throughout 1941. To account for this in an adequate manner, the war variable, *WWII*, is set equal to the proportion of the armed forces in 1941 compared to the average size of the armed forces throughout the remainder of the war, .226. This modified dummy variable is better than the usual dichotomous variety because it eliminates outliers at the beginning and end of the war. This adjusted definition improved the statistical fit regardless of which model is used. The following statistical results are not materially affected by the chosen definition of *WWII*. A simple dichotomous definition yields the same relative judgments for BIH vs. ECM models but improves their overall fits.

25 This negative effect of income for the conventional approach does not vanish if interactions for the other independent variables are included in the estimating model. Nor does the definition of *WWII* matter. This negative income effect persists when the war years are represented by a more conventional dichotomous dummy variable.

26 When equation (6.21) is compared to an unrestricted version analogous to equation (6.17), $F_{2,55} = 2.59$. BIH's restrictions are accepted by the data. On the other hand, adding *dWWII* to the Hendry ECM model and comparing it to this same unrestricted model rejects its restrictions, $F_{2,55} = 14.16$. Also, the error correction term is not statistically significant. Or, when this BIH model is embedded in a more general model representing the Engle–Granger two-step model with contemporaneous effects, BIH's restrictions are again accepted, $F_{2,55} = 2.14$.

27 A 95 percent confidence interval for this first order autocorrelation coefficient is (.604, .965). Although others have used nonlinear functional forms to explain the empirical problems of the consumption function (Malinvaud, 1980), it is the dynamics of BIH that explains its success. However, if empirical success could be ascribed solely to the logarithmic nature of the consumption function, then a simple logarithmic consumption function would be statistically adequate. It is not; the extent of its misspecification is predicted by BIH.

28 The approach taken here is, in any case, a statistical improvement on the explanation found in Campbell and Mankiw (1990). The model which they utilize is a simple linear regression between the change in consumption and the change in income. Their approach may be an improvement over a number of alternative consumption studies, but the empirical results reported here clearly confirm BIH's use of past changes in consumption as well as other changes.

7. Prices, Inflation, Unemployment, and Okun's Law

(E)mpirical attempts by Robert Barro (1978) and others to validate the new classical proposition of policy ineffectiveness have failed, running aground on the bedrock that inflation inertia exists. . .

– Gordon (1997, p. 19)

INTRODUCTION

Aside from consumption, few if any economic subjects have been so well studied or remain as controversial as inflation. There have been thousands of papers written about inflation, stimulating hundreds of empirical studies. Yet the most widely accepted theory, the natural rate hypothesis, is empirically indefensible.[1] After centuries of economic inquiry, the causes of inflation or its relation to unemployment remain in dispute.

The Phillips curve, though once widely accepted, has been in great disrepute for at least two decades. The conventional alternative, the natural rate hypothesis (or, alternatively, the nonaccelerating inflation rate of unemployment – NAIRU), has been largely falsified by the great volatility of NAIRU and the inexplicably high unemployment rates found in Western Europe over the recent years. What then explains inflation and its relation to unemployment? Can any economic theory withstand the rigors of genuine empirical testing?

The purpose of this chapter is to investigate whether behavioral inertia can also explain inflation. Modelling inflation in nearly an identical manner as consumption corroborates BIH and, in the process, uncovers a few insights into the mechanism that generates and perpetuates inflation. Specifically, it is found that the link between inflation and unemployment operates more indirectly than is usually conceived, through Okun's law, and that a significant asymmetry exists between the effects of excess demand growth and supply shocks. My BIH model also explains the apparent successes and eventual failures of the 'expectations augmented' Phillips curve and thereby serves as a falsifying hypothesis for the natural rate hypothesis.

114

INFLATION AND UNEMPLOYMENT

Prices and their movements have always been a central concern of economists. The theory of value (which is primarily a theory of prices) was the main theme of classical economics, from Adam Smith through Karl Marx to the marginalists. Nor has its pivotal importance been diminished by modern economic analysis though the interests of economists have broadened.[2] Inflation's damaging effect on real economies, especially in the twentieth century, has only served to heighten academic and policy interest. In fact, a general evaluation of modern economics itself depends more critically upon the success or failure of economic theory in explaining inflation and price movements than any other economic phenomena. Economists might be excused for having disparate and unrealistic views on genuinely difficult topics, such as the effects of deficit spending or the proper role of monetary and fiscal policy. But should the public be so forgiving when orthodox theories cannot adequately explain inflation and price movements?

The modern era of inflation theory began with Phillips (1958) who found a stable empirical relationship between wage growth and unemployment in Great Britain, 1861-1957. Subsequent empirical applications and theoretical extensions have focused primarily upon the connection of the rates of inflation and unemployment. During the heyday of Keynesian economics, these models of an inverse relationship between inflation and unemployment were generally accepted, and their policy implications widely discussed. However, the simultaneously high rates of inflation and unemployment observed among industrial nations during the 1970s convincingly discredited this simple Phillips curve. Thus, extensions and adjustments, which might explain the existence of 'stagflation', were sought. Enter the natural rate.[3]

Since the late 1970s, the conventional story of inflation augments the Phillips curve with rational expectations and the natural rate of unemployment.

$$\pi_t = \pi_t^e + \gamma(u_t - u^*) \tag{7.1}$$

where

π_t is inflation rate at time t

π_t^e is the expected inflation, formed at time $t-1$ about t[4]

u_t is the unemployment rate

u^* is the natural rate of unemployment or NAIRU

(Frisch, 1983). Such an 'expectations-augmented' Phillips relationship allows for shifts in short run curves with changing expectations, π_t^e, but implies a stable, vertical relation in the long run when expectations are formed 'rationally'.

Various theoretical versions and empirical specifications of the natural rate hypothesis have dominated inflation research over the past two decades. However, all such models have had major empirical difficulties. First, the constancy of NAIRU cannot be seriously maintained in the face of the recent economic history of the developed western nations. As one supporter of NAIRU admits, 'Today, there is general recognition that if a NAIRU exists, it must be changing over time' (Stiglitz, 1997, p.6). When NAIRU is allowed to vary, the natural rate hypothesis and equation (7.1) threaten to be reduced to a tautology incapable of *explaining* anything. Because no independent empirical referent to NAIRU exists, some circular, self-confirming estimate must be invented. For example, a fully time-varying estimate of NAIRU could make u_t^* equal to whatever gap remains in the current unemployment rate's ability to explain the unexpected inflation: $u_t^* = u_t - (1/\gamma)(\pi_t - \pi_t^e)$. Although supporters of NAIRU do not seriously advocate such a procedure, the currently fashionable method of 'stochastic time-varying parameter regression' may be viewed as an arbitrary weighted average of fully time-varying and unvarying estimates of NAIRU. Can a weighted average of two unacceptable estimates thereby become more acceptable?

By this point, it has become quite difficult to defend the natural rate hypothesis (Stiglitz, 1997, Galbraith, 1997), and there is no defense for the view that predicts an accelerating inflation whenever the unemployment rate falls below some predetermined value, say 6 percent. If the standard textbook version of the natural rate hypothesis is wrong, what does explain observed inflation dynamics and its relation to unemployment?

BEHAVIORAL INERTIA IN PRICES AND INFLATION

The price of any good is likely to be the same today as yesterday absent disturbing forces. In fact, consumers would likely go elsewhere seeking a 'fair' or 'competitive' price if they believed that the price was raised without sufficient justification. Although such an obvious statement about price inertia seems innocuous and true enough, it has profound empirical implications when combined with an equally obvious structure of price change. If the memory of a price fades and its innovation partially adjusts by a constant proportion,

$$P_t = \alpha_0 P_{t-1}^{\alpha_1} \, \Delta_\tau \qquad (7.2)$$

$$\Delta_\tau = \Delta_{t-1}^{\rho} \prod_{j=1}^{K} X_{f_t}^{\beta_j} \, e_t \qquad (7.3)$$

where

P_t	is the price at time t
P_{t-1}	is the price at time $t-1$
$\alpha_1 \leq 1$	is the price inertia coefficient
Δ_τ	is everything that might cause price to change, the 'caprice' or 'innovation'
X_{jt}	is an explanatory variable related to the change in prices
β_j	is a parameter and a regression coefficient for $dlnX_{jt}$
e_t	is the irreducibly random part of the 'innovations'
$\rho \leq 1$	is the autoregression coefficient for 'innovation', reflecting the persistence of (or adjustment to) change.

Recall that the structure of these equations defines the behavioral inertia hypothesis (BIH) (Chapters 2 and 6). α_1 is expected to be quite close to one; however, it may be somewhat less to allow for some decay of memory or discipline. X_{jt} is a predictor of the *change* in prices; therefore, it often takes the form of a first difference or a ratio of the current value of some economic variable to its lagged value. The multiplicative version of BIH, equations (7.2) and (7.3), is employed because it directly leads to a well-specified regression model of inflation.

To simplify and to derive a testable model, first take the logarithm of equations (7.2) and (7.3). Next, combine the result and eliminate the unobservable Δ_{t-1} by using the fact that $ln\Delta_{t-1} = lnP_{t-1} - ln\alpha_0 - \alpha_1 lnP_{t-2}$ from (7.2), thereby obtaining

$$lnP_t = (1-\rho)ln\,\alpha_0 + (\alpha_1 + \rho)lnP_{t-1} - \alpha_1\rho\,lnP_{t-2} + \sum_{j=1}^{K} \beta_j lnX_{jt} + lne_t \quad (7.4)$$

Assuming $\alpha_1 = 1$ greatly simplifies the dynamic price structure to:

$$\pi_t = \beta_0 + \rho\pi_{t-1} + \sum_{j=1}^{K} \beta_j lnX_{jt} + \varepsilon_t \qquad (7.5)$$

where $\pi_t = lnP_t - lnP_{t-1}$, $\beta_0 = (1-\rho)\,ln\alpha_0$, and $\varepsilon_t = lne_t$. Furthermore, ε_t is assumed to be independently and identically distributed as an essential part of the BIH representation. Thus, all necessary assumptions about regression error terms are satisfied, and equation (7.5), if true, defines a well-specified regression relation.   Note that this regression model, equation (7.5), expresses the inflation rate, π_t, in terms of its past value and other explanatory variables. Price inertia, which allows for the partial adjustment of innovation, leads quite naturally to an econometric model for inflation with a familiar autoregressive structure. All that remains for this theory of inflation to be fully specified is to identify X_j.[5]

Both the restricted version of BIH, equation (7.5), and the unrestricted version, equation (7.4), impose structure upon the price-inflation dynamics. In particular, note the magnitude of the coefficients in equation (7.4). First, the twice-lagged price term has a negative coefficient, the opposite of what some adjustment models imply. Furthermore, the coefficient on lagged prices exceeds one and the amount by which it does so should be approximately equal to the magnitude of the twice-lagged price coefficient.[6] Such demanding restrictions, of course, beg empirical testing.

It is interesting to note that this BIH model of inflation is quite similar to the better-known triangle model of Robert Gordon. For over twenty years, Gordon has advanced and tested a Keynesian model of inflation and unemployment that is consistent with the problematic 'stagflation' of the 1970s (Gordon, 1977, 1997). He calls this model the triangle model and expresses it as:

$$\pi_t = a(L)\,\pi_{t\text{-}1} + b(L)\,D_t + c(L)\,z_t + \varepsilon_t \qquad (7.6)$$

Where:

π_t is the inflation rate at time t, measured as the first difference in the logarithm of the price level

D_t is an index of excess demand

z_t is a vector of supply shocks, expressed in first differences of logarithms

$a(L)$, $b(L)$, and $c(L)$ are polynomial lag operators.

Empirical testing and historical events give support to the triangle model (Gordon, 1982, 1997), leading others to call it 'state-of-the-art specification of the reduced-form Phillips curve' (Blanchard and Katz, 1997, p.61). BIH enjoys many similarities with Gordon's triangle model. Both explicitly recognize the importance of lagged inflation (hence persistence) and the role of other explanatory variables. Like the triangle model, the forces of supply and demand are considered to be prime candidates for choosing BIH's X_js. Thus, this behavior inertia model of inflation fits into the mold cast by Gordon's triangle model.

TESTING THE EXPLANATORY POWER OF THE BEHAVIORAL INERTIA HYPOTHESIS

An examination of the data on inflation and unemployment in a wide range of Western countries over the past forty years tells a story which is different from the Phillips curve, both in its original form and in it current guise, augmented with rational expectations. Analysing the data with none of the orthodox preconceptions . . . allows us to identify the true relationship between inflation and unemployment.

– Ormerod (1997, p.127)

First, the growth in real GNP, $dlnY_t$, and the change in the unemployment rate, $du_t = u_t - u_{t-1}$, are selected as the explanatory variables, X_j, to complete the specification of the restricted BIH model, equation (7.5).[7] Such a specification corresponds to the innovation equation:

$$\Delta_\tau = \Delta P_{t-1} \, (Y_t/Y_{t-1})^{\beta_1} \, exp[\beta_2(u_t - u_{t-1})] \, \varepsilon_t$$

Estimating BIH, equation (7.5), with US data 1929-1996 gives: [8]

$$\hat{\pi}_t = .0227 + .706 \, \pi_{t-1} - .0168 \, du_t - .427 \, dlnY_t \qquad R^2 = .740 \quad (7.7)$$
$$\phantom{\hat{\pi}_t = .0227 +} (10.98) \qquad (-7.05) \qquad (-5.03) \qquad SSE = .02941$$
$$h = 1.59 \qquad LM = 8.59 \qquad G\text{-}Q = 1.64 \qquad n = 66$$

The restricted version BIH fits the US inflation quite well without omitting difficult periods such as the Second World War or the Great Depression. All conventional statistical tests are significant, and all specification tests are passed. A Lagrange multiplier test for higher orders of autocorrelation (the number of lags is 5) also accepts the null hypothesis of no autocorrelation; its Box–Pierce Q is 8.59 and is distributed χ^2 with 5 degrees of freedom. From past experience with consumption (Chapter 6), heteroskedasticity tends to be more problematic. However, no indication of it can be found in this BIH model of inflation. After ordering the data chronologically because time shows the greatest connection to the regression residuals, the Goldfeld–Quandt F = 1.64 (21 and 21 degrees of freedom) exhibits no signs of heteroskedasticity. Unsatisfied with the positive results of only one test for heteroskedasticity, many additional Breusch–Pegan tests were conducted using third degree polynomials for each of the explanatory variables, GNP, the real money supply, and the federal deficit. None exhibits statistical evidence of misspecification; however, using the deficit produces the largest the Breusch–Pegan $\chi^2(3) =$

4.17.   Finally, BIH also passes a Ramsey's RESET test for general misspecification, including simultaneous equation bias, $F_{2,60} = .39$.

Some might wonder whether these remarkable results are nothing more than statistical artifact.   Recall that spurious regressions are the expected outcome of nonstationary time series.   However, in this case, we can reject the nonstationarity of the annual US inflation rate – the Dickey–Fuller t = –3.40 compared with a critical value, –2.91 (MacKinnon, 1991).   Needless to say, the logarithms of prices are nonstationary, Dickey–Fuller t = 2.55; hence, caution needs to be exercised when interpreting any regression of the levels or logarithms of prices.

Clearly, the restricted BIH model comfortably passes all specification tests and thus provides a sound statistical explanation of inflation.   But is BIH's dynamic structure mirrored in the data?   Recall that BIH imposes constraints upon the coefficients of a more general VAR representation, $lnP_t = \beta_0 + \lambda_1 lnP_{t-1} + \lambda_2 lnP_{t-2} + \beta_1 u_t + \beta_2 u_{t-1} + \beta_3 lnY_t + \beta_4 lnY_{t-1}$.   In particular, the coefficients on the lagged price terms should sum to one, $\lambda_1 + \lambda_2 = 1$, while the coefficients on the contemporaneous and lagged values of each independent variable should sum to zero, $\beta_1 + \beta_2 = 0$ and $\beta_3 + \beta_4 = 0$.   To test these restrictions, the previous results, equation (7.7), need to be compared with the unrestricted regression,

$$ln \hat{P}_t = -.26 + 1.63 lnP_{t-1} - .67 lnP_{t-2} - .015 u_t + .017 u_{t-1} - .40 lnY_t + .45 lnY_{t-1} \quad (7.8)$$
$$(20.93) \quad (-8.81) \quad\quad (-6.18) \quad (7.02) \quad (-4.67) \quad (5.31)$$
$$SSE = .026214 \quad\quad D\text{-}W = 1.80 \quad\quad R^2 = .9993 \quad\quad n = 66$$

Those seeking high R^2s will be pleased by this unrestricted version of BIH that explains 99.93 percent of the variation in the log of prices.[9]   But of course, this apparent difference between the explanatory powers of models (7.7) and (7.8) is illusory; it is entirely attributable to the distinction between how the dependent variables are defined.

Note the magnitudes of the estimated coefficients.   The coefficient of the first lag of price exceeds one, and the amount by which it does so is almost exactly the same as the amount by which the coefficient on the twice lagged price term is less than zero, just as anticipated by BIH.   Furthermore, the lags for both the logarithms of GNP and the unemployment rate have coefficients that are approximately the same magnitude but the opposite sign as their contemporaneous coefficients.   Note further that any variation from the anticipated pattern set by BIH is well within the corresponding standard errors.   Comparing the restricted and the unrestricted versions directly yields an $F_{3,59} = 2.40$, accepting BIH restrictions.   Again, BIH is corroborated.

Still some may question whether the unrestricted model (7.8) is correctly specified. Is there nonstationarity or multicollinearity? The nonstationarity or cointegration of equation (7.8) is of little importance to the interpretation of the BIH model of inflation. The restricted version, equation (7.7), is the more faithful representation of BIH, and all of its variables are stationary. The unrestricted version, equation (7.8), is reported only to test BIH restrictions. In any case, the unrestricted version is likely to provide valid testing (Stock and Watson, 1988) and there is evidence of nonstationarity of its residuals (Dickey–Fuller t = −7.17). Multicollinearity does not bias the estimates, nor does it affect the validity of the restriction testing. If anything, it makes the closeness of the estimated coefficients to the predicted pattern all the more remarkable. Together, this series of specification tests gives powerful corroboration of the behavioral inertia hypothesis of inflation.

HYSTERESIS, OKUN'S LAW, AND THE INFLATION-UNEMPLOYMENT TRADE-OFF

> Whether the change or the level of unemployment matters, a seeming small matter of shifting one derivative, has profound implications for both economic doctrine and policy.
>
> – Gordon (1989,p. 220)

What do these empirical findings suggest about the controversial issues surrounding inflation and unemployment? How should we interpret the negative coefficient on the growth rate of real GNP? The faster the economy grows *lower* the inflation rate? Why should the *change* of the unemployment rate be related to inflation? Past research, whether new classical or Keynesian, concentrates on how the level of unemployment, rather than its change over time, is related to inflation. 'By approaching the data without the theoretical baggage of the "natural rate" concept, and seeing what the data tell us, what hypothesis is consistent with the data, we can establish a clear negative relationship between *changes* in inflation and unemployment over a forty-year period without having to invoke shifts of behaviour in any way' (Ormerod, 1997, p.132).

When the level of the unemployment rate replaces its change in equation (7.7), it is not statistically significant (t = −1.48) – nor is the lag (t = −.13) or the inverse of the unemployment rate (t = −.28). Worse yet, there are clear signs of misspecification (for example, h = 2.53). This research is not the first to find that the change in the unemployment rate is important to inflation. Lipsey (1960) uses it to explain the 'loops' around the Phillips curve, Ormerod (1997) uses it to eulogize the conventional macroeconomics, and King *et al.* (1995) find that 'inflation is better predicted by changes in the unemployment rate than by the size of the unemployment gap (the difference between unemployment and NAIRU)' (p.10). However, most studies do not find a statistically significant effect for the change in the unemployment rate, and 'no satisfying economic justification for including the rate of change of unemployment is given' (Santomero and Seater, 1978, p.508). If not 'Lipsey loops', what does explain inflation's dependence on the change in the unemployment rate?

One possible explanation might simply extend more recent developments of NAIRU research. Note the similarity of the augmented Phillips curve, equation (7.1), and BIH, equation (7.7). BIH relates π_t to its lagged value, like π_t^e, and the increase in the unemployment rate, $du = u_t - u_{t-1}$. Similarly, the natural rate hypothesis views the difference between the unemployment rate and NAIRU, $u_t - u^*$, as the principal path for inflation. Both, therefore, depend on the difference between two unemployment rates. Given the recent trend of estimating time-varying natural rates of unemployment, u_t^*, from the past unemployment record, du is not so different from $u_t - u_t^*$. They are, in fact, the same if the natural rate is allowed to adjust in one year to the actual unemployment history. Furthermore, such a misspecification of the natural rate could explain both the past successes and empirical failures of the natural rate hypothesis when the natural rate is forced to be constant.

My results are consistent with what Gordon (1989) calls 'full hysteresis'. With hysteresis, the natural rate hypothesis becomes

$$\pi_t = \alpha\pi_t^e + \gamma(1-\lambda)\, u_t + \gamma\lambda\, (u_t - u_{t-1}) + \varepsilon_t \qquad (7.9)$$

(Gordon, 1989). If $\lambda = 1$, there is 'full hysteresis' and inflation does not depend on the level of unemployment but only its change. If $\lambda = 0$, there is no hysteresis and equation (7.9) reverts to its more orthodox form. Given the previous econometric results, BIH model (7.7), we can resoundingly reject the no hysteresis hypothesis (t = -7.05), and adding the level of the unemployment rate leads to the acceptance of the full hysteresis hypothesis (t = $-.37$).[10] With full hysteresis, steady inflation is consistent with *any* level of unemployment making all levels of the unemployment rate NAIRU. With such a pluralistic notion of NAIRU, the natural rate hypothesis and its policy implications become meaningless. 'NAIRU has no meaning in an equation when only changes in the unemployment rate help predict future inflation' (King *et al..*, 1995, p.8). BIH and its implied hysteresis can explain Western Europe's recent experience, high rates of unemployment with persistent inflation, and the Great Depression. Different unemployment histories are just that– different. BIH does not require high unemployment rates to cause accelerating deflation.

With the empirical rejection of the natural rate hypothesis, the question of how to interpret *du* remains. Irrespective of the natural rate hypothesis, *du* may be seen as a proxy for the unobservable rate of change in the output gap, or excess demand, through Okun's law, 'one of the most reliable empirical regularities of macroeconomics' (Tobin, 1987, p.700). Okun's law relates the growth rate of the output gap (i.e., the difference between potential and actual GNP) to the change in the unemployment rate, $du = -\theta(dlnY_t - dlnY^*_t)$ (Okun, 1962, Gordon, 1977, Frisch, 1983, p.100). Because θ has been estimated to be somewhere between 1/3 and 1/2 (Gordon, 1977, 1997), a 1 percent reduction in the unemployment rate is associated with a 2 to 3 percent narrowing of the output gap which, in turn, may also be interpreted as a corresponding increase in excess demand.

This interpretation offers a completely sensible economic meaning for the negative coefficient on the *du* term in equation (7.7). When the output gap narrows by 2.5 percent, the unemployment rate will fall through Okun's law by 1 percent (assuming $\theta = .4$) and the inflation rate will increase by 1.7 percent (recall that $\hat{\beta}_1 = -.0168$ from equation (7.7)).[11] Increases in excess demand simultaneously increases product prices and the demand for labor.

In the absence of this Okun's law interpretation, the negative coefficient of real GNP growth ($\hat{\beta}_2 = -.427$) would be quite disturbing. The faster the economy grows the lower the inflation rate? Of course, increases in aggregate supply without corresponding expansions in demand might produce such an effect, but would anyone argue that annual US GNP growth is entirely, or even largely, the result of supply shifts, unaccompanied by rising demand? Given this Okun's law interpretation of BIH, the effect of the growth in real output, *dlnY*, need not represent supply shocks. Rather, it is an estimate of the asymmetric supply–demand effects on inflation.

To illustrate this asymmetry more clearly, consider the general form of BIH model (7.7):

$$\pi_t = \beta_0 + \rho\pi_{t-1} + \beta_1 du_t + \beta_2 dlnY_t \qquad (7.10)$$

Substituting Okun's law into the above gives

$$\pi_t = \beta_0 + \rho\pi_{t-1} - \beta_1\theta(dlnY_t - dlnY^*_t) + \beta_2 dlnY_t \qquad (7.11)$$
$$= \beta_0 + \rho\pi_{t-1} + (\beta_2 - \beta_1\theta) dlnY_t + \beta_1\theta dlnY^*_t$$

Clearly, as long as $\beta_2 \neq 0$, the effects of the growth of potential GNP, $\beta_1\theta$, are of a different magnitude than those of the growth of real GNP, $\beta_2 - \beta_1\theta$.

This differential effect is statistically significant (t = –5.03), and it is large enough to be practically important as well. Because $\hat{\beta}_2$ is significantly negative, the inflationary effect of the growth of real GNP is reduced. If we accept these parameter estimates, $\hat{\theta} = .4$, $\hat{\beta}_1 = -.0168$, and $\hat{\beta}_2 = -.427$, then a 1 percent increase in the growth of real GNP will raise the inflation rate by only one-fourth of 1 percent while an equal reduction in output capacity will raise the inflation rate by two-thirds of a percent. In both cases, the cumulative (or 'long run') price effects are much larger – by a factor of $[1/(1-\hat{\rho})] = 3.4$ – five-sixths of a percent for GNP growth and 2.29 percent for a 1 percent decrease in the full-employment level of output. In either case, supply shocks have a more powerful effect on inflation, nearly three times so, than does demand growth.

Differential effects of supply and demand are not surprising; they are consistent with various Keynesian theories. When price is a markup over cost, changes in supply would more rapidly and powerfully translate into price movements and inflation. Okun's law interpretation of BIH resolves any remaining economic suspicions about BIH's empirical estimates and gives a sensible economic meaning to all of the coefficients. Together, *du* and *dlnY* reflect both aggregate supply and aggregate demand dynamics.

Given these results, it might interesting to investigate the implied trade-off between inflation and unemployment. However, BIH is not a Phillips curve; in fact, its empirical corroboration represents a falsification of both the simple and the augmented versions of the Phillips curve.[12] A 1 percent increase in real GNP, caused by some hypothetical supply neutral policy, lowers the unemployment by .4 percent, through Okun's law, and raises the inflation rate by .245 percent over the current year and .833 percent cumulatively. Plotting these effects in the familiar inflation-unemployment space gives a short run relation with a trade-off of .6 (.6 percent higher inflation for a 1 percent reduction in the unemployment rate) and a long run trade-off of more than 2. In both cases, there is an important trade-off, although the long run relation is more vertical.

This hypothetical exercise must be interpreted with great caution. It does not suggest that there is some stable empirical relationship between inflation and unemployment, or even less likely, that there is a causal connection between the two. In fact, these trade-offs are derived on the premise that both inflation and unemployment are independently and simultaneously affected by GNP growth.

There is nothing unique about the above hypothetical scenario, and a more 'supply-side', classically friendly story is readily available. If a pure supply-side policy raises the full-employment level of GNP by 1 percent, Okun's law impels a .4 percent increase in the unemployment rate while the inflation rate drops by .67 percent (for a trade-off of 1.68 to 1) in the current year and a 2.29 percent increase cumulatively (for a trade-off of 5.73 to 1). Again, 'supply-side' policies exhibit inflation–unemployment trade-offs, though clearly less favorable ones.

Interestingly, a balanced policy (if such a thing can be designed) uncovers the Holy Grail of inflation research – a vertical inflation–unemployment relation. When both actual and potential GNP grows by 1 percent there is no effect on unemployment, according to Okun's law, and the inflation rate should fall nearly one-half of a percent (.427 percent). Balanced expansion has only positive, disinflationary effects!

So what is the actual trade-off? Both supply and demand policies exhibit inflation–unemployment trade-offs, while balanced growth gives policy makers a 'free lunch'. 'Once the true relationship between inflation and unemployment is understood, with luck and skill, a free lunch is possible' (Ormerod, 1997, p.137). However, the actual real inflation–unemployment phenomenon is quite complex and sensitive to nuances in the interaction of supply and demand shocks. However, one lesson is clear: economic growth need not be inflationary. These estimates suggest that a moderate, predominately demand-led, expansion (for example, $dlnY = 4\%$ and $dlnY^* = 1.5\%$) could reduce the unemployment by 1 percent with no inflationary impact. If this is too good to be true, what then explains our current (1996-1999) expansion?[13]

ALTERNATIVE MODELS

Behavioral inertia may fit the data well, but what about more conventional explanations of inflation? Do alternative models provide an adequate statistical explanation of the US inflation history? If inflation is a monetary phenomenon, how can monetary growth be omitted from any model purporting to explain inflation?

The simple behavioral inertia model discussed in the previous section is, of course, not unique. Several alternative BIH specifications appear to fit the data well. Adding the interest rate, Moody's AAA bond yields, improves the conventional measures of goodness-of-fit (Table 7.1), and the interest rate term, dlni, is statistically significant (t = 2.72). BIH's restrictions are accepted, $F_{4,57} = 1.59$, in this expanded model. However, there are indications of misspecification in the Goldfeld–Quandt $F_{20,20} = 2.97$. Genuine empirical analysis must take such potential misspecification quite seriously. Then there is the issue of which causes which. Is inflation passed along to interest rates through the Fisher effect? Perhaps high interest rates are directly inflationary through cost markups (Podkaminer,

1998)? Or do changes in interest rates reflect monetary movements and affect investment, savings and consumption?

If interest rate is really a proxy for monetary movements, why not incorporate monetary growth explicitly? After all, most economists believe that inflation is a monetary phenomenon. The best monetary BIH model, by conventional regression criteria, includes interest rate along with several other variables, see Table 7.1. Although the t-statistics indicate significant impacts for current monetary growth (2.95) and nearly so for lagged monetary growth (−1.92), there are clear signs of misspecification through both autocorrelation (LM = 17.33) and heteroskedasticity (G-Q: $F_{15,15}$ = 3.18). Misspecification would not be surprising with so many independent variables, several of which representing monetary factors and several others real ones.

Table 7.1: Alternative BIH Models

Variable/Statistic	Interest rate	Monetary growth
Intercept	.0230	.0302
$dlnCPI_{t-1}$	.667 (10.6)*	.568 (7.64)*
du	−.0169 (−7.45)	−.0159 (−6.54)
$dlnGNP$	−.417 (−5.14)	−.500 (−4.98)
$dlni$	.0844 (2.72)	.124 (3.88)
$dlnM_1$	-----	.209 (2.95)
du_{t-1}	-----	−.00616 (−2.51)
$dlnGNP_{t-1}$	-----	-.211 (-2.41)
$dlnM_{1t-1}$	-----	-.126 (-1.92)
$dWWII$	-----	.0404 (1.78)
R^2	76.8%	82.8%
SSE	.02624	.01942
Durbin's h	.56	1.09
LM: Box–Pierce Q	10.27	17.33
Goldfeld–Quandt F	2.97	3.18

* t statistics are in parenthesis.

Purer monetary models of inflation are easily rejected. Take either the classical quantity theory of money, with constant or random velocity, or the rational expectations Phillips curve. Both theories imply a one-to-one correspondence between inflation and monetary growth in the context of a simple regression model (Frisch, 1983). Yet, the annual US data are greatly at odds with such a characterization of inflation.

$$\hat{\pi_t} = .0175 + .277 \, dlnM_{1t} \qquad R^2 = .179 \quad n = 66 \qquad (7.12)$$
$$(3.77) \qquad\qquad\qquad D\text{-}W = .71 \quad SSE = .09565$$

Aside from this model's poor fit (much worse than inertia alone), it is clearly misspecified (D-W=.71). Worse still, the coefficient on monetary growth is not even close to one (t=−9.84). Of course, one might relax the assumption of full employment (or random variations from full employment), but to little avail.

$$\hat{\pi_t} = .0174 + .284 \, dlnM_{1t} - .0182 dlnY_t \qquad R^2 = .179 \quad n = 66 \qquad (7.13)$$
$$(3.77) \qquad\quad (-.19) \qquad\qquad D\text{-}W = .70 \quad SSE = .09559$$

Nor does adding lagged inflation correct the above misspecification (h=2.51).

Other versions of the expectations-augmented Phillips curve do little better, recall equation (7.1). Using past inflation as inflation expectations, a currently accepted practice (Gordon, 1997, Blanchard and Katz, 1997), yields:[14]

$$\hat{\pi_t} = .0225 + .626 \, \pi_{t-1} - .00126 u_t \qquad R^2 = .537 \quad n = 66 \qquad (7.14)$$
$$(6.29) \qquad (-1.57) \qquad\qquad h = 3.69 \quad SSE = .05239$$

This model is thoroughly misspecified (h = 3.69), u_t is not significant, and the restriction that the coefficient on lagged inflation be one (i.e., $\rho = 1$) is forcefully rejected ($F_{1,63} = 14.08$). Figure 7.1 makes the misspecification of the expectations-augmented Phillips curve transparent, reflecting both the autocorrelation and heteroskedasticity.

In contrast to these findings, Blanchard and Katz (1997), for example, report a seemingly acceptable expectations-augmented Phillips regression that constrains ρ to be one. Although they too use annual data, they limit their analysis to the later years, 1970-1995. However, when all the data are used this expectations-augmented Phillips relation is no better than random noise.

$$d\hat{\pi_t} = (\pi_t - \pi_{t-1}) = -.00166 + .000331 u_t \qquad R^2 = .0031 \quad n = 66 \qquad (7.15)$$
$$(.45) \qquad\qquad D\text{-}W = 1.62 \quad SSE = .0641$$

Although some judgment is unavoidable in selecting the sample period, is the selection of the best fitting third of the data defensible? 'Understanding the performance of the economy in the Great Depression of the 1930s has long been a challenge to economists. Most conspicuously, theories of inflation based on the natural rate of unemployment are unable

to account for developments after 1933. . .' (Akerlof *et al.*, 1996, pp. 43-44).
It is often suggested that the Great Depression and the Second World War
were exceptional periods and therefore should be omitted from econometric
analysis. Conventional practice is to omit such periods from the analysis
altogether, thus implicitly admitting the failure of one's model of reality. A
model that correctly specifies the dynamics of inflation should be able to
accommodate such exceptional periods. In any case, why omit the 1950s
and 1960s? One could more justly argue that it is only the 1970s which
should be omitted. The OPEC oil embargo and its aftermath is the more
unique shock, less likely to be repeated than another war or recession.
Given the large number of subsamples that are available to the researcher
and the omnipresence of spurious regressions in economic time series data,
the probability than there exists a sample that seemingly confirms any
theory is nearly one.

Figure 7.1: Expectations-Augmented Residuals

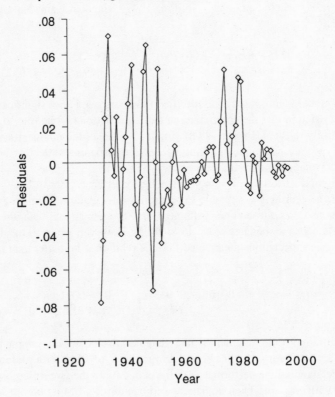

The approach taken by King *et al.* (1995) to demonstrate the misspecification of fixed and time-varying models of NAIRU is to show how unreliable their estimates truly are. For example, the conventional 95 percent confidence interval for NAIRU (December 1994) is 2.7 to 8.5 percent. 'An extreme conclusion to draw from these results would be that a natural rate does not exist. . . . A theoretical justification for such a position could be that the hysteresis . . . is present in the US economy' (Staiger *et al.*, 1997, p. 47).

The model which King *et al.* (1995) believe to be correctly specified relates the *changes* in the inflation rate to its lagged values and current and lagged values of the change in the unemployment rate, a first difference bivariate VAR. Although this specification looks quite good initially,

$$d\hat{\pi}_t = .000035 + .275 \, d\pi_{t-1} -.554 \, d\pi_{t-2} - .0079 du_t + .0032 du_{t-1} \qquad (7.16)$$
$$\quad (2.89) \qquad (-6.29) \qquad (-4.68) \qquad (2.07) \qquad n = 64$$
$$h = -.44 \quad R^2 = .531 \quad LM = 2.06 \quad G\text{-}Q = 5.89 \qquad \text{Chow} = 3.45$$

it too has some problems. First, there is heteroskedasticity (G-Q $F_{20,20}$ =5.89; p<.01) and next is the parameter instability (Chow $F_{27,27}$ =3.45, p<.01; with the sample midpoint as the *a priori* break year). Both tests seriously question the proper specification of this model. Because inflation does not appear to have a unit root, modelling the first difference of inflation is unnecessary and potentially misleading. Besides, the restriction on the dynamic structure of inflation, implicit in this first difference VAR model, is rejected ($F_{1,58}$=5.89). Relaxing this restriction brings us back to a model that employs inflation as the dependent variable with the change in the unemployment rate and lagged inflation as the independent variables. BIH returns.

Of all these alternatives, only the behavioral inertia model of inflation survives genuine empirical testing. BIH passes all specification tests using all available data and thereby reconciles the Great Depression and the Second World War with the 'stagflation' of the 1970s. As discussed previously, BIH may be interpreted as an application of Gordon's triangle model, but to do this causes problems for the 'natural rate' hypothesis. 'If the sum of the coefficients on lagged inflation variables values equals unity, then there is a "natural rate"' (Gordon, 1997, pp. 14-15). However, empirical testing strongly rejects this constraint: $F_{1,62}$ =20.92 for one inflation lag, $F_{1,60}$ =31.76 when there are two inflation lags, and $F_{1,58}$ =237.93 for three lags. Although few really believe that a fixed NAIRU exists, full hysteresis, as identified by BIH, presents a serious challenge to all versions of the natural rate hypothesis.

Furthermore, the empirical success of the behavioral inertia model (7.7) explains why the expectations-augmented Phillips relation and NAIRU, at first, seemed so appealing and empirically successful. Recall the similarity between change in the unemployment rate and the short run departure of the unemployment rate from its natural rate. During periods of a relative stability interspersed with short recessions (e.g., the 1950s and 1960s), the empirical effect of changes in the unemployment rate dampened by inertia will be much the same as the effect of variations in the unemployment rate from some fixed NAIRU. In more exceptional economic periods, the expectations-augmented Phillips relation is not successful. Especially revealing is that NAIRU researchers omit data before the mid-1950s. Because the period from the 1929 market crash through the Second World War and the economy's adjustment afterwards is more volatile, the conventional theory breaks down. The mean absolute error of the expectations-augmented Phillips curve is 3.6 percent, twice that of BIH. Thus, BIH can explain both the past empirical success and the failures of the expectations-augmented Phillips curve.

SUMMARY

The behavioral inertia hypothesis is applied to the US inflation. Allowing inertia and persistence in prices and their change accounts for the observed CPI dynamics. BIH is strongly corroborated through extensive testing of its specifications and restrictions. This corroboration of the natural rate's falsifying hypothesis serves as its empirical falsification (Chapter 5). Long before the current research, the natural rate hypothesis suffered from empirical failures or anomalies (e.g., the observed volatility of NAIRU, the inexplicably high unemployment rates in Western Europe, and the non-decelerating inflation of the Great Depression). Here a falsifying hypothesis, which explains those anomalies and the past successes of the natural rate hypothesis, is offered and corroborated.

This research also reveals that inflation is influenced by the *change* in the unemployment rate, rather than its level. The dependency of inflation on the change in the unemployment rate has profound implications for both theory and policy. There need not be any trade-off between inflation and unemployment, and the natural rate hypothesis becomes irrelevant. In conjunction with Okun's law, these findings transform the conventional views on inflation–unemployment trade-offs. A balanced expansion is deflationary without raising unemployment, and a demand-led, though supply accommodating, expansion can reduce the unemployment rate at no inflationary cost. Okun's law also helps identify a significant asymmetry between supply and demand, i.e., between the real GNP growth and the growth of the full employment level of output.

Like many successful scientific advances, BIH makes past theory a special case. The expectations-augmented Phillips relation may be derived from BIH by constraining the coefficient on lagged inflation to be one and NAIRU to adjust slowly, or not at all, to the lagged unemployment rate. Needless to say, the simple Phillips curve is a special case of the expectations-augmented Phillips relation. When illuminated by BIH's light, it is easy to understand both the misleading empirical successes and the eventual failures of the simple and expectations-augmented Phillips curves.

NOTES

1   A recent assessment of the state of research on inflation is given in the 'Symposium on the Natural Rate of Unemployment,' *Journal of Economic Perspectives*, Winter 1997 – specifically, Stiglitz (1997), Gordon (1997), and Galbraith (1997).

2   To continue in this classical metaphor, the Ricardian intensive margin for understanding inflation has not diminished, although its extensive margin may have.

3   Although the natural rate hypothesis was made by Friedman (1968) in his presidential address, its full importance and general acceptance had to wait for the OPEC oil embargo.

4   Finding an acceptable empirical correspondence to π_t^e is no simple matter. The most simple and direct measure of inflationary expectations, asking market participants and economists what they believe prices will be at some future time, is rejected by orthodox economists. Because survey-based measures of inflationary expectations are well known to be biased (Carlson, 1977a, 1977b, Mullineaux, 1978, Figlewski and Wachtel, 1981, Lovell, 1986, Lee, 1991), thus directly refuting rational expectations, they are not used to test this theory. Using lagged inflation rates has also come, gone, and come back into fashion again. Without some acceptable empirical referent to π_t^e and u^*, the natural rate hypothesis (and NAIRU) is but empty rhetoric.

5   BIH does not, in general, constrain the choice of variables in X_j; it has no political agenda. Variables may be chosen for empirical or other reasons, but the resulting model must withstand severe testing. No doubt some orthodox economists will regard my agnosticism as an admission to the absence of theoretical content. However, I regard such generality as an advantage. BIH's theoretical content lies in the structure of its dynamics, not in the source of the data's perturbations. This approach is atheoretical only if neoclassical equilibrium theory is deemed to be the *only* theory.

6 These expectations of the magnitudes of the lagged price coefficients assume a reasonably short time period, say one year or less, consistent with actual economic time series collection. In contrast, if the time between periods were a generation or more, α_1 could not be expected to be close to one. The prices of our grandparents are but dim memories to be recalled to shock our children or to illustrate the power of exponential functions to beginning students.

7 Several variations of alternative explanatory variables were also estimated. Although specification searches should be avoided because they can invalidate conventional statistical tests (Leamer, 1983, Copas, 1983), an empirical analysis of inflation would likely be dismissed if the usual suspects were not investigated. Thus, models that also include monetary growth, productivity, capacity utilization, interest rate, and the employment-to-population ratio have been estimated. Each of these variables may be found to have a statistical effect on inflation in at least one combination with some other variables. The model chosen here is the simplest and most defensible, passing a whole battery of additional specification tests. Nonetheless, more complex alternatives will be discussed in some detail in the next section.

8 The data are from *The National Income and Product Accounts of the United States, 1929-82, Business Conditions Digest*, and the *Survey of Current Business*. GNP is real (1982 base year), and prices are CPI-U (1982-1984 base).

9 Similarly, the unrestricted BIH model of consumption expenditures explains 99.98 percent (recall Chapter 6).

10 Gordon (1989) does not find evidence of full hysteresis, but then he does not use either the unemployment rate or its change in his regressions. Because he wishes to stretch the data further into the past, detrended log GNP replaces the unemployment rate.

11 Kahn (1996) estimates the long run coefficient of Okun's law to be .46 .

12 Alternative empirical models are tested and discussed in greater detail in the next section.

13 The estimates used in the above discussion of trade-offs also reconcile the most recently observed (1996-1998) *falling* unemployment rates with the observed *falling* inflation rate.

14 This practice is further confirmed in experimental markets with R^2 as high as 99 percent, see Chapter 10.

8. An Empirical Critique of the Lucas Critique

For longer than a decade, methodologists have advocated a more empirical philosophy of science ('recovery of practice') (Caldwell, 1982, 1994, McCloskey, 1983, Hausman, 1992). Although there have been many Lakatosian reconstructions, Kuhnian histories, and rhetorical analyses of various episodes of economic theory, empirical economics itself resists systematic appraisal. Recently, Goldfarb (1995) identifies additional publication biases that plague empirical economics and discusses the problems of interpreting a large empirical literature. He proposes a 'methodology of plausible inference' based on a widely used statistical technique, meta-analysis, in the social and medical sciences. Although meta-analysis has been largely ignored and under-appreciated by economists, there is a small but growing number of applications to economics.[1]

The purpose of this study is to provide a meta-analysis, or a quantitative review, of the Lucas critique (LC). LC is itself quite important to empirical economics; it represents yet another fundamental criticism of empirical economics. Recall that Lucas (1976) questions the ability of empirical economics to correctly model, test, or predict the economy based on his interpretation of the theory of rational expectations. However, unlike more philosophical and methodological criticisms of econometrics, LC is itself empirically testable. Secondly, this meta-analysis of empirical research clearly reveals how inertia plays a central role in what a researcher finds. In this chapter and the next, how a researcher chooses to handle inertia is found to have a significant effect on her results. In empirical economics nothing is more important than properly accommodating inertia.

The meta-analysis developed here provides a basis upon which to make 'plausible inferences' regarding the validity of LC. Although most studies ostensibly find support for LC, this meta-analysis reveals how the apparent applicability of LC may be attributed to misspecification and the manner in which expectations are treated. When models with questionable specification are discounted, empirical support for LC vanishes.

IS ECONOMETRIC ANALYSIS USELESS? THE LUCAS CRITIQUE

For most of this century, economics has led the social sciences in developing and applying statistical techniques, often for the expressed purpose of predicting the consequences of economic policy. The size and sophistication of some econometric models are legend. Yet, in spite of more than a half century of distinguished development, econometrics has had disappointing practical success and many visible failures.

When econometrics was at its zenith, Lucas (1976) offered a theoretical critique that could explain some of the disappointing performance of statistical analysis in economics.

> (G)iven that the structure of an econometric model consists of optimal decision rules for economic agents, and that optimal decision rules vary systematically with changes in the structure of series relevant to the decision maker, it follows that any change in policy will systematically alter the structure of econometric models . . . .
>
> – (Lucas, 1976, p.41)

LC claims that economic theory, properly understood, causes the parameters of an econometric model to be dependent on specific policy actions and institutional structures, thereby invalidating the forecasts of empirically estimated models as policies or institutions change. Substantial changes in any of these policies or institutions may nullify the best econometric model (even when the estimates are thought to possess all the desirable statistical properties), rendering its predictions unreliable. The implications of LC are especially pernicious for economic policy modelling designed to predict the consequence of various economic policy options. Even if such models were correct and followed assiduously, the new economic policy would change their underlying parameters and undermine the very predictions upon which this policy was based. In the past two decades, many studies have discussed and tested the merits of the Lucas critique, and a consensus that econometric models cannot provide accurate or useful predictions of policy options seems to be emerging.

Like quantum mechanics, the accurate prediction of the economy poses a fundamental dilemma. If the economy, or some part of it, were completely predictable, policy-makers and/or profit-seekers would likely use such information to improve the overall economy or just one individual's slice of it. While there is nothing inherently wrong with either profiteering or macroeconomic policy, the active pursuit of either can change the economy and thereby invalidate the predictions which engendered these behaviors in the first place – recall Doestovesky's uncertainty principle in Chapter 4.

The Lucas critique is the consequence of 'rational expectations' theory that assumes optimizing economic agents fully informed about the operation of the economy and possessing unbiased knowledge about all future economic developments. Rational expectations theory is believed to turn this vicious circle, Dostoevsky's uncertainty principle, into a virtuous one. However, rational expectations has often been interpreted to imply that economic policy cannot be effective because policy shifts will be anticipated, discounted, and undermined before they are allowed to work. Thus, without any hope of beneficial intervention, the statistical study of economics is at best sterile, at worst, dead wrong. At least this is what some claim to be implications of LC. The parameters of the correct econometric model will depend on the current policy regime. If forecasts of this model are used as a basis of policy, the model's parameters will change along with the policy, making the model and the predictions that stimulated this action incorrect. No sooner do the eyes of the econometrician fall upon his parameters than they turn to dust.[2] Of what value then is the statistical analysis of economic relations?

LC assumes that rational expectation theory supplies a correct causal explanation of relevant economic phenomena (Hoover, 1994). Observable relations cannot depict the underlying causal structure because new classicals regard expectations as unobservable. Thus, fitted relations will not be invariant to policy changes that alter expectations. Estimated econometric models, according to this view, do not reflect genuine economic relations, but only some complex web of coincidental correlations among observed and unobserved variables. The problem with the Lucas critique is that it does not lead to progress in economics, and it all too easily defends the dogmatism of new classical economics (Hausman, 1992). 'And, in fact, new classicism has not been able to offer a compelling alternative device for making economic predictions to the battered but stalwart community of macromodellers' (Hoover, 1994, p. 72).

Although there is great dissonance over the effectiveness of economic policy, the applicability ofLC is widely accepted. 'It is not only formalists who are disturbed. Stanley Fischer (1988, p.302) called the effect of the Lucas critique on econometric policy evaluations and on the credibility of econometric models "devastating,". . . such models are now routinely dismissed as subject to the Lucas critique' (Mayer, 1993, p. 94). However, many seem to forget that LC is based only on a theory, 'rational expectations', a theory which itself has had numerous empirical refutations.

Despite a considerable literature on the empirical validity of LC, the findings are quite ambiguous. For every study that finds empirical support for LC, one can find another that rejects it. Furthermore, to assess the advantages of meta-analysis, this meta-analysis of LC may be compared with conventional reviews – see 'Conventional Narrative Reviews', below.

META-ANALYSIS

Meta-analysis provides an overview of some field of empirical research using, more or less, the same techniques found in the original studies. It provides an empirical framework from which to review and integrate the empirical findings on a given topic, and which can, in turn, be used to stimulate and organize replications.

– Stanley and Jarrell (1989)

A Methodology for the Quantitative Review of Empirical Literature[3]

If one views scientific progress as a monotonic accumulation of empirical knowledge based on previously developed theoretic and factual founda-tions,[4] it is imperative that we reliably and consistently evaluate and integrate the vast literature that surrounds any academic subject. Otherwise, the body of scientific knowledge will be drown in a sea of seemingly contradictory findings. Such, as least, is the state of affairs in the social sciences. And, we shall return to Babel.

The house of social science research is sadly dilapidated. It is strewn among the scree of a hundred journals and lies about in the unsightly rubble of a million dissertations.

– Glass *et al.* (1981 p.11)

Fittingly, meta-analysis was developed largely to bolster the policy relevance of social research. By the 1980s, behavioral and social research had accumulated a wealth of clashing findings on important questions (Hunter and Schmidt, 1990). How could public funding be justified when research consists largely of 'conflicting results which. . . lead to no acceptable answers to guide policy for the problems posed but instead yielded unending calls for further research, and the danger that funding agencies may increasingly view social and behavioral research as muddled, unproductive, and unscientific?' (Wolf, 1986, p.10) Enter meta-analysis.

To find the genuine message in the noise, what we need are not just summaries of the literature, such as those found in the introductory chapters of dissertations and in most literature reviews, but also *critical* reviews. When empirical tests reach results that seem irreconcilable, a critical review survey should tell us which ones to disregard. ... And even if it is not possible to weed out all the invalid evidence and to reconcile the rest, it should be possible to reduce the dissonance to a substantial extent. Meta-analysis reduces the effort required for such a critical survey and makes its results more specific.

– (Mayer, 1993, p.158)

Literature reviews are indispensable in summarizing what is known about any given subject, in identifying the remaining issues at stake, and in suggesting profitable directions for future research. However, the reviewer often impressionistically chooses which studies to include, what weights to attach to these studies, how to interpret the results of a given study, and which factors to attribute observed differences among research findings. Conventional reviews are narrative and subjective. Economists have not adopted any systematic or objective procedure for dealing with the critical issues implicit in literature reviewing. At best, conventional narrative reviews employ a form of vote-counting or 'box-scoring', often implicitly.[5] However, voting methods are known to be biased. When statistical tests have low power, voting is biased in favor of finding no significant difference (Hedges and Oklin, 1985), and low power is routinely a problem in econometric studies. When there is a genuine effect but the statistical tests used have low power in small practical samples or if the econometric models upon which they are based are misspecified, the majority of tests may very likely find no significant effect.[6] Nonetheless, it is the literature review that is most likely to provide coherence in those areas where studies report large variation in findings, such as LC. Without the insightful integration that a good review can provide, researchers are likely to squander scarce research resources pursuing unfruitful lines of inquiry.

Meta-analysis is a means to improve the process of literature reviewing. It forces the reviewer to include all studies or to make explicit any rules for the inclusion or exclusion of a study. Maximizing the coverage of the literature is an essential element of meta-analysis. In a field famous for its methodological/ideological disputes, important empirical evidence is often ignored when it does not neatly fit into the reviewer's preconceived methodological/theoretical framework – 'believing is seeing' (Demsetz, 1974, quoted in Goldfarb, 1995, p.206).

Meta-analysis attempts to explain the variation found in the literature by explicitly modelling difference in design, data, techniques, and various socio-economic factors thought to affect a researcher findings. And, if differences in methodological or technical approaches are thought to be important, these too may be modelled and their effects estimated. For example, meta-regression analysis may take the form of a standard regression equation:

$$\hat{\beta}_j = \alpha_0 + \sum_{k=1}^{K} \alpha_k Z_{kj} + \varepsilon_j \qquad j = 1,2, \ldots , L \qquad (8.1)$$

where $\hat{\beta}_j$ is the estimated regression coefficient for the *j*th study and Z_{kj}, are meta-independent (or moderator) variables designed to explain the study-to-study variation in an area of research containing *L* studies. Using such models, the unemployment rate is found to have a significant effect on the estimated size of the union wage premium (Jarrell and Stanley, 1990), the author's sex is found to affect his or her estimate of the magnitude of gender wage discrimination, and this estimate of the gender wage gap is found to be closing at a significant rate, nearly 1 percent per year (Stanley and Jarrell, 1998). Thus, research, itself, may be studied, and its results better estimated and understood. Meta-analysis offers a large and largely untapped potential for improving economics.

Needless to say, meta-analysis is no 'philosopher's stone'; it has its own problems. See Phillips and Goss (1995) and Stanley and Jarrell (1989) for a discussion of these issues. The most common criticism of meta-analysis concerns the 'file drawer' problem which results from the tendency of academic journals to publish only those studies that find a significant effect (i.e., reject some null hypothesis) (Glass *et al.*, 1981). In contrast, Goldfarb (1995) and DeLong and Lang (1992) argue for an opposite publication bias. Although meta-regression analysis is subject to this potential bias, so are conventional narrative literature reviews. However, only meta-analysis actively seeks to minimize this problem by including all studies, published and unpublished, alike.

Others assert that it is inappropriate to lump together studies which use different data sets, methods, or different auxiliary theories. However, estimating the effects of such differences is precisely the purpose of *meta-regression analysis* and its use of moderator variables. In our meta-analysis, we first test for the homogeneity of the literature. If the literature is found not to be homogeneous, then systematic differences need to be filtered out before any inference may be drawn.

Combining F-Tests of Parameter Invariance

The typical study in the empirical literature on LC involves an F-test for the constancy or invariance of regression coefficients.[7] These studies posit an econometric model of some important economic phenomenon fitted both before and after a historic shift in economic policy (e.g., the founding of the Federal Reserve banking system in 1914 or the Volcker disinflationary policy of 1979). Although several specific types of hypothesis tests are employed in this literature (including tests of superexogeneity), they are generally of the pattern set by Chow (1960) where a regression model is estimated separately before and after some policy change and compared to the fit of the model over the entire period. This heavy reliance on F-tests raises the question of how computed Fs can be statistically compared and combined.

What is required is some way to measure and evaluate the average size of the invariance, one where misspecification biases are at least 'averaged out' if not eliminated altogether. Although there is a large literature on alternative estimates of effect size (effect size measures the magnitude of the average observed effect relative to experimental variation), none are applicable to F-tests of parameter constancy or invariance. To this end, a new meta-analytic approach is offered which can summarize and combine separate F-tests.[8] My approach is based on a normal approximation to the F-distribution which is not large sample bound (Abramowitz and Stegun, 1964). Given a random variable, f, which is distributed $F(v_1, v_2)$, then V is approximately distributed $N(0, 1)$ where:

$$V = \frac{f^{1/3}(1 - 2/9v_2) - (1 - 2/9v_1)}{(2/9v_1 + f^{2/3}2/9v_2)^{1/2}} \tag{8.2}$$

(Abramowitz and Stegun, 1964, p.947).[9]

Our approach allows invariance tests from entirely different studies, employing different data sets and investigating different economic phenomena, to be measured on the same metric. Given this 'common denominator', such tests can be directly compared and combined using conventional descriptive and inferential statistics. After this conversion, even those statistical methods that assume normality (e.g., regression analysis) are appropriate.

To assess the overall parameter variability of econometric models, a simple mean, $\bar{V}$, may be calculated. Larger values of $\bar{V}$ are associated with greater average parameter variability. The Lucas critique suggests that V_i should be large or at least larger than zero, where V_i is the normal approximation to the reported F-test from the ith study and a measure of the parameter variability on a common scale. To determine whether this overall parameter variability is statistically significant, the statistic $z = \bar{V} \cdot L^{1/2}$ may be compared to 1.96 because each V_i is a standard normal variate under the null hypothesis of no effect. Alternative explanations for the variations among studies may be tested by a meta-regression analysis of V_i. The preferred process of conducting a meta-analysis may be sketched as:

1. Include all studies found in a standard database (i.e., EconLit) which contain relevant empirical tests or estimates.
2. Reduce this empirical evidence to some acceptable common denominator (i.e., V_i) and calculate summary descriptive statistics.
3. Test for the homogeneity of the empirical results. If the studies are sufficiently homogeneous, then the descriptive summary statistics provide a fair representation of this literature.
4. Otherwise, if the empirical results in a given area show excess variation, conduct a meta-regression analysis.
5. Subject the meta-regression model to extensive specification testing.
6. Check remaining error variance to determine whether all systematic variation (hence bias) has been filtered out.

Next, we apply these methods to the empirical literature on the Lucas critique.

A META-ANALYSIS OF THE LUCAS CRITIQUE

Our study began with Mayer's (1993) literature review of the empirical validity of LC, and his challenge to conduct more *critical* reviews. 'When empirical tests reach results that seem irreconcilable, a critical review survey should tell us which ones to disregard. . . . And even if it is not possible to weed out all the invalid evidence and to reconcile the rest, it should be possible to reduce the dissonance to a substantial extent' (Mayer, 1993, p.158). To his seventeen references, thirty more bibliographic entries were found in the AEA's EconLit database through any reference to 'Lucas critique' or 'parameter invariance'. The necessity of confining our focus to those studies which empirically test LC, narrows the literature to thirteen studies containing nineteen tests (see Meta-Analysis References at the end of this chapter).

Because this is such a small sample, some may wonder whether meta-analysis is needed or its results can be trusted. First, this sample represents all the empirical tests of the LC found in AEA's EconLit database and is therefore worthy of our scrutiny. To insure replicability, it would be prudent for all reviewers to use the same generally accepted database, EconLit. Otherwise, the chosen filter could unduly influence the findings of a meta-analysis. Selective filtering of the existing evidence is a genuine problem for conventional narrative reviews. Furthermore, if significant effects are uncovered in a small sample, as our study does, such effects are all the more striking and more likely, not less likely, to represent genuine effects of practical importance. Still, some may wonder whether a traditional narrative literature review may be more revealing particularly when the literature is so small. Fair enough, such a comparison is the topic of the next section.

Simple descriptive statistics: $\bar{V}$ = .88; S_v = 1.66; range = 6.12 , seem to justify Mayer's assessment that the results are mixed but with some tendency to support the Lucas critique. In fact by combining all these tests of LC, the average parameter variability, $\bar{V}$ = .88, is statistically quite significant ($z = 3.83$; $p < .001$).

However, it is no major accomplishment to obtain statistical significance by combining the results of an entire literature, even a literature containing only nineteen tests. This is especially true when there is a publication bias towards studies that report statistically significant test results (i.e., the 'file drawer problem'). More convincing would be an average effect that has a practically relevant magnitude. For an analogous problem, Cohen (1969) offered plausible definitions of small ($\leq .25\sigma$), medium ($\leq .50\sigma$), and large ($\geq 1.0\sigma$) effects (Tversky and Kahneman, 1971).[10] Of course, if we know the error loss function, practical significance may be defined accordingly. Due to the omnipresence of misspecification biases in applied econometrics, it would be prudent to require a large effect before some empirical finding is taken too seriously. In the present context, the average parameter variability is nearly large (.88σ) and sufficient to marshal genuine interest in and support for LC.[11]

The first impression made by this meta-analysis is to strengthen one's belief in the merit of Lucas's argument. Yet, first impressions can be quite misleading. Especially troublesome is the large variation observed in the literature. In a sample of nineteen, a range of 6.12 among standard normal variables seems a bit too large. This is more sharply exhibited by the standard deviation, 1.67, among these studies compared to the known standard deviation of 1.0 for each. Clearly, there is more variation among these studies than what is consistent with sampling from some homogeneous population of possible test results (χ^2 = 49.56; d.f. = 18; p<.01).[12] The implication is that there are additional factors influencing a researcher's reported test results; thus, the overall test of parameter variability may be misleading and inappropriate. Therefore, a further analysis (i.e., meta-regression analysis) of the reasons for the study-to-study variations in the reported test results is needed if we are to understand the empirical evidence of LC. Next, we turn to the variables that were *a priori* chosen to explain the variation among the tests of the Lucas critique.

All studies in this literature are based on time series data that are notoriously vulnerable to problems of nonstationarity and spurious regression, and inertia is a common dynamic structure of economic time series. Such considerations generate the *a priori* hypothesis that inertia and the associated statistical problems of nonstationarity dominate empirical tests of LC. In fact, all of the economic phenomena investigated by this literature, aggregate consumption and income, wages, interest rates, and money, have been found to possess unit roots. Thus, the form of the fitted regression model is likely to make a great difference in its validity. Although it might be preferable to categorize studies formally according to the results of tests of nonstationarity and cointegration, so few studies conduct such tests that other proxies must be found. The only, readily available, related characteristics concern whether a model uses first differences (*Diff*=1) and/or lags (*Lag*=1). When all tests of the Lucas critique are conducted on well-known nonstationary economic time series, it is essential that a study takes some action to prevent the effects of misspecification and spurious regression if its results are to have any validity. At a minimum, nonstationary variables must be differenced and/or lagged.

Because Mayer (1993) concludes 'that the Lucas critique is fully applicable to financial markets'' (p.95), we investigate whether there is a difference for monetary and financial markets (*Money* = 1) versus commodity and labor markets. Others, notably Favero and Hendry (1992) and Cuthbertson and Taylor (1990), have identified the expectations mechanism to be crucial. If an econometric model is dependent upon some assumed expectations mechanism (whether rational or adaptive), *Expect* = 1.[13]

Meta-regression analysis finds each of these hypothesized effects to be statistically significant, explaining more than two-thirds of the variation among the tests of LC. [14]

$$V_i = 4.56 - 4.12\ Diff_i - 1.91\ Lag_i + 1.67\ Expect_i + 1.55\ Money_i \qquad (8.3)$$
$$(-4.13) \qquad (-2.79) \qquad (2.62) \qquad (2.52)$$
$$n = 19 \quad \text{adj. } R^2 = .67 \quad \hat{\sigma}_e = .95$$

where the numbers reported in parentheses are t-values.[15]

Date of publication and country of data (US or other) are the only other study characteristics investigated. Goldfarb (1995) argues that there is a 'positive-then-negative publication bias' (p.209). First, economists search for 'empirical results that support strongly held priors' (p.204). However, date of publication has no effect in linear or quadratic representation, but models of the US economy have marginally larger parameter variability (t=1.61; one tail p < .10). Adding country to the above meta-regression model does not alter the significance or interpretation of any of our results. It does, of course, marginally improve the overall explanatory power of the resulting meta-regression model, adj. R^2 = 71 percent.

Ignoring nonstationarity by not differencing the data makes a great difference in one's conclusion,[16] increasing parameter variability (in the apparent support of LC) by the equivalent of 4.12 standard deviations (t = −4.13 ; p < .01). The omission of lags also strengthens the support of LC, increasing the expected parameter variability by 1.91 standard deviations (t=−2.79; p < .05). Expectation models report greater parameter variability by 1.67 standard deviations (t = 2.62; p <.05). Lastly, monetary phenomena raise parameter variability by 1.55 (t=2.52; p<.05). This meta-regression model predicts *V* to be −1.47 in non-monetary markets and .08 for monetary phenomena, assuming a nonexpectational model that uses lags and differences. Thus, the evidence for the Lucas critique dissolves when econometric models control for the well-known nonstationarity of economic time series.

It is also quite interesting to note that the unexplained variance, $\hat{\sigma}^2_e$ = .90, is of the proper magnitude demanded by the *V*'s normal approximation (χ^2 = 12.63; d.f. = 14; accept H0: σ^2_e = 1).[17] Anything smaller and with higher R^2 would be 'too good to be true'. The magnitude of remaining error variance suggests that the above meta-regression model fully accounts for all systematic variation found in the empirical literature on LC. The *a priori* selected moderator variables –*Diff*, *Lag*, *Expect* and *Money* – explain all the systematic variation found among tests of LC. Thus, a better statistical explanation of the empirical tests of the Lucas critique is implausible.

CONVENTIONAL NARRATIVE REVIEWS

How do conventional narrative reviews compare to findings from this meta-analysis of LC? Are such narratives more or less compelling or persuasive? This particular meta-analysis was undertaken because an excellent traditional review of LC (Mayer, 1993) seemed lacking, its findings too ambiguous. In his recent critique of economics, Thomas Mayer surveyed the empirical literature on LC and concludes,

> The results . . . are mixed. They suggest that the Lucas critique is fully applicable to financial markets, but that its applicability to the labour market is more problematic. All in all, while obviously valid and a major contribution to empirical science economics, . . . the Lucas critique does not tell us that the inherent endogeneity of the usual macroeconomic coefficients is necessarily more

serious than other problems that we encounter in forecasting and in giving policy
advice.

– Mayer (1993, p. 95)

Thus, even this critical review largely accepts the relevance of LC. One
advantage of meta-regression analysis is its ability to test explicitly and
more formally Mayer's hypothesis about the differential validity of LC in
various markets. Recall that $t = 2.62$; $p < .05$ for monetary and financial
markets.

It appears that Mayer's appraisal follows from a simple vote-counting.
Of the seventeen studies he reviewed, ten are assessed to be supportive of
LC while seven are judged to offer evidence against it. Even the best
narrative reviews are susceptible to the distorting power of vote-counting.
Unlike economic policy, research evaluations should not be democratic.

Ironically, in his concluding recommendations for improving the
profession, Mayer (1993) offers meta-analysis as one method that may help
(p.158). Yet, in his own review of LC, he uses the traditional, narrative
style of literature reviewing. As a result, Mayer finds ambiguity where our
meta-analysis finds considerable clarity.

In another recent study, Ericsson and Irons (1995) also attempt to
identify and review the empirical evidence of LC. They begin with 590
articles which cite Lucas (1976) and count the numbers of papers that fall
into various categories: theoretical, empirical, etc. From these they identify
fifty-four empirical or mixed articles. 'Of those, only forty-three find any
evidence for LC: less than 10 percent of the total citations' (Ericsson and
Irons, 1995, p.274). Or, to be fairer, evidence favorable to LC represents 80
percent of our empirical knowledge on the subject. However, because they
use conventional, rather than meta-analytic, methods, their assessment
reduces to a vote-count that they quickly discount or skew on
methodological grounds. That is, the majority of empirical tests of the
Lucas critique are classified as supportive, but Ericsson and Irons (1995)
dismiss them for various logical/theoretical reasons. For example, Ericsson
and Irons (1995) dismiss all empirical tests that find nonconstancy. 'Simply
put, the observed nonconstancy may arise from misspecifications other than
the one involving expectations' (p.277). Because there are no accepted
standards for narrative reviews or for counting votes, interpretations vary
greatly. Apparently, Ericsson and Irons (1995) use a minority rule to tally
LC's votes.[18]

While it is of course true that supportive evidence for LC may be a
symptom of some misspecification, it is neither fair nor persuasive to
dismiss all supportive studies without specific evidence of misspecification.
Following their exemplar, all empirical economics could likewise be

dismissed because all models and tests have the *possibility* of being misspecified. Enter the Duhem–Quine thesis (Chapter 5).

Ericsson and Irons (1995) choose to focus on what they regard as the theoretically superior test of superexogeneity. Thirty tests of superexogeneity are found, and twenty-five are classified as supporting superexogeneity and therefore rejecting LC. However, on the same page, Ericsson and Irons (1995) conclude, 'An extensive search of the literature reveals virtually no evidence demonstrating the empirical applicability of the Lucas critique' (p.301). Again, the pernicious charm of vote-counting. Even if we dismiss the first forty-three supportive studies, following Ericsson and Irons, does not five of thirty (or 17 percent) constitute *some* support? Indeed, among the set of preferred tests for superexogeneity, the support found for LC is proportionally greater than what would be expected by chance alone – 17 percent compared to the conventional 5 percent risk of a type I error, a statistically significant difference. 'In summary, the vast majority of articles citing Lucas (1976) are not concerned with testing the Lucas critique *per se*. Those that are provide scant evidence for its empirical basis' (Ericsson and Irons, 1995, p.280).

Although their criticisms of the empirical evidence for LC may, in fact, be valid, they seem biased and unconvincing. If others followed this practice, it could be used to support the prior theoretical beliefs of any reviewer. 'Believing is seeing.' Conventional narrative literature reviews makes it all too easy to dismiss unwanted evidence for some seemingly good methodological reason that no one knows applies to the actual study at hand.

Fortunately, meta-analysis permits and encourages the empirical investigation of the correct specification of each study in the empirical literature. This is precisely the reason for choosing the moderator variables concerning the use of differences and lags. Their statistical significance casts doubt on the validity of tests that make no correction for nonstationarity. Furthermore, one can incorporate evidence of proper specification directly. For example, a meta-analysis could highly weight those tests of LC which also pass at least two specification tests. Passing one is too easy, especially when one considers the low power of many specification tests. As a result of this stringent (0,1) quality weighting, only seven studies remain as valid tests of the Lucas critique, containing no excess parameter variability ($\bar{V} = -.17$; $z = -.46$) and eliminating all support for the Lucas critique.

In contrast to traditional literature reviews, meta-analysis proceeds in a systematic and less subjective manner. Recall,

1. Include all studies found in a standard database (i.e., EconLit) which contain relevant empirical tests or estimates.
2. Reduce this empirical evidence to some acceptable common denominator (i.e., V_i) and calculate summary descriptive statistics.
3. Test for the homogeneity of the empirical results. If the studies are sufficiently homogeneous, then the descriptive summary statistics provide a fair representation of this literature.
4. Otherwise, conduct a meta-regression analysis if the empirical results in a given area show excess variation.
5. Subject the meta-regression model to extensive specification testing.
6. Check remaining error variance to determine whether all systematic variation (hence bias) has been filtered out.

Note that all the above steps, with the notable exception of the first, are dictated by objective statistical criteria and standards. The exception proves the rule for a conventional acceptance of some particular database, such as EconLit. Any review, which successfully navigates all of these steps, earns some credibility and deserves to be taken seriously. It is quite possible that a conventional narrative review would come to a similar or perhaps a more insightful conclusion. However, the idiosyncratic nature of narrative reviews and their unconstrained potential for self-serving filtering engender no additional degree of plausibility beyond the reader's *a priori* disposition.

CONCLUSION

In summary, how a researcher chooses to model the economy largely determines how well the resulting econometric model holds up to policy changes. Misspecification and expectations are the major themes that emerge from this meta-analysis of LC. Misspecification (specifically, the failure to difference nonstationary time series data or to use lagged dependent variables) distorts tests of parameter invariance towards the apparent applicability of LC.

The purpose of this chapter and the next is to reveal how the existing empirical economic literature is riddled with the pernicious effects of inertia. Inertia, nonstationarity and misspecification have caused great ambiguity over the validity of the Lucas critique and Ricardian equivalence. Whether or not a model incorporates the structural components of BIH (differences and lags) makes a great difference in its findings. But econometric models that are correctly specified need not worry about the Lucas critique. Due to the importance placed on specification testing by the econometric methodology proposed here (Chapter 5), and the fact that BIH does not rest upon expectations, it is not subject to the Lucas critique.

There is nothing surprising about the sensitivity of tests of parameter invariance to model misspecification. In fact, long before Lucas's critique, parameter invariance tests were employed as tests of proper model specification. Large variation in the estimates of a model's parameters is one indication that the model omits important factors or misrepresents those that are included. Since Lucas (1976), rejecting the constancy of an econometric model's parameters carries the additionally ambiguous interpretation that the model may correctly capture the underlying economic relations at some point in time but that these relations are themselves sensitive to policy changes. Before a researcher has full license to choose one or the other of these interpretations, she must first carefully test the model's statistical specification through additional testing. A researcher is justified in using evidence of parameter variability as support for the Lucas critique only after first eliminating misspecification. Attempting to validate LC by testing the parameter constancy of the typical or even the conventionally accepted econometric model provides no substantive evidence for LC because the published econometric models are often misspecified.

The second emergent theme concerns the role of expectations. Models, which are based primarily on expectations, are more likely to find excessive parameter variability (increasing V by 1.67 standard deviations). Perhaps this too reflects the misspecification of expectations models. A similar interpretation is made by Favero and Hendry (1992) who suggest that the data used to test LC can be reconciled by realizing that 'agents do not use parametric expectations models to predict future values of decision variables' (p.299). Simple inertia models can provide the missing link (Hendry and Ericsson, 1991). Thus, empirical tests, which seemed to confirm LC, may alternatively be seen to undermine the very basis for his critique, rational expectations.

Our meta-analysis identifies how sensitive a researcher's findings on Lucas critique are to model specification. If one wishes to find support for LC, choose an expectation model of some monetary phenomenon in the US and avoid using lags or differences. Making the opposite modelling choices is likely to supply evidence in support of the econometric model's invariance. The solution to this apparent dilemma is simple. Specification testing is needed to accompany any alleged test of LC to insure that the model is otherwise well specified. If we were to apply this standard to the existing LC literature, an entirely different conclusion emerges from the conventionally accepted view. That is, if we include only those models which employ and pass at least two specification tests, excluding tests of parameter invariance themselves, only seven acceptable empirical studies remain, containing no excessive parameter variability $\bar{V} = -.17\ (z = -.46)$ nor support for LC.

Can statistical models predict the economy? Of course, if they are correctly specified. Contra Lucas, there is no fundamental reason, which itself withstands empirical scrutiny, to restrain econometric modelling from predicting the economy. Our meta-analysis explains the mixed results found in empirical tests of the Lucas critique but finds no empirical support for Lucas's critique when likely misspecifications are removed.

EMPIRICAL TESTS OF THE LUCAS CRITIQUE

Alogoskoufis, G.S. and Smith, R. (1991), 'The Phillips Curve, the Persistence of Inflation, and the Lucas Critique: Evidence from Exchange Rate Regimes,' *American Economic Review*, **81**, 1254-75.

Blanchard, O.J. (1984), 'The Lucas Critique and the Volcker Deflation,' *American Economic Review*, **74**, 211-15.

Brodin, P.A. and Nyman, R. (1992), 'Wealth Effects and Exogeneity: The Nowegian Consumption Function,' *Oxford Bulletin of Economics and Statistics*, **54**, 431-54

Cagan, P. and Feller, W. (1983), 'Tentative Lessons from Recent Disinflationary Effort,' *Brookings Papers of Economic Activity*, 603-608.

Cuthbertson, K. and Taylor, M.P. (1990), 'The Case of the Missing Money and the Lucas Critique,' *Journal of Macroeconomics*, **12**, 432-54.

Engle, R.F. and Hendry, D.F. (1993), 'Testing the Superexogeneity and Invariance in Regression Models,' *Journal of Econometrics*, **56**, 119-39.

Favero, C. and Hendry, D.F. (1992), 'Testing the Lucas Critique: A Review,' *Econometric Reviews*, **11**, 265-306.

Fischer, A.M. (1989), 'Policy Regime Changes and Monetary Expectations: Testing for Superexogeneity,' *Journal of Monetary Economics*, **24**, 423-36.

Fischer, A.M. and Peytrignet, M. (1991), 'The Lucas Critique in Light of Swiss Monetary Policy,' *Oxford Bulletin of Economics and Statistics*, **53**, 481-93.

Hendry, D.F. (1988), 'The Implications of Feedback versus Feedforward Mechanisms in Econometrics,' *Oxford Economic Papers*, **40**, 132-49.

Hurn, A.S. and Muscatelli, V.A. (1992), 'Testing Superexogeneity: The Demand for Broad Money in the UK,' *Oxford Bulletin of Economics and Statistics*, **54**, 543-556.

Perry, G.L. (1983), 'What Have We Learned about Disinflation?' *Brookings Papers of Economic Activity*, 587-602.

Taylor, J.B. (1984), 'Has the Response of Inflation to Macro-Policy Changed? Recent Changes in Macro Policy and its Effects: Some Time Series Evidence,' *American Economic Review*, **74,** 1206-10.

NOTES

1 Examples include: Stanley and Jarrell (1989), Jarrell and Stanley (1990), Vanhonacker, *et al.* (1990), Phillips (1994), Button (1995), Phillips and Goss (1995), V.K. Smith and Huang (1995), Doucouliagos (1995), Button and Kerr (1996), Baaijens *et al.* (1998), Stanley (1998), and Stanley and Jarrell (1998).

2 This is a variation of Bacharach's (1989) Orpheus effect.

3 See Stanley and Jarrell (1989) for a more extensive discussion of meta-analysis.

4 If, on the other hand, progress in economic thought is viewed as cyclical, or perhaps chaotic, the potential gains from a more systematic, analytic review of its development are even greater. Meta-analysis does not rest on any specific view of science; however, it does assume that empirical research matters.

5 Light and Smith, 1971. See Ericsson and Irons (1995), Mayer (1993), de Haan and Zelhorst (1988) and 'Conventional Narrative Reviews' of this chapter for examples of the use of voting to evaluate an empirical economic literature.

6 Although specification biases can effect subsequent testing in either direction, depending on the type of misspecification involved, they often swamp such tests. Goldfarb (1995) argues that at first there is a publication bias toward findings that are statistically significant because such findings are usually associated with the proposed theory. However, as the field matures, this positive bias may reverse itself because findings contrary to the conventional wisdom may assume a position of greater interest. In any case, this bias of vote-counting is of a different order, and it exists even when there are no publication biases.

7 Some studies employ t-tests, others χ^2 likelihood ratio tests. However, these other statistical distributions can be converted either to the F-distribution or the normal, allowing them to be incorporated in the below meta-analysis. More recently, studies have examined a model's 'superexogeneity', but this too is based on a F-test and thus poses no additional statistical problems.

8 Fisher's combined test is the conventional strategy for combining tests of significance. It focuses on the p-values and takes advantage of the fact that they are uniformly distributed and independent under the null hypothesis of no effect. However, because of its problems and bias, we choose not to use the Fisher test. See Stanley and Jarrell (1998) for an extended discussion of this issue.

9 This procedure has also been used to evaluate the evidence for Ricardian equivalence, Chapter 9, and is similar to Lipák's (1958) inverse normal method of combining independent tests.

10 Where σ^2 is a measure of the experimental, or error, variance.

11 Recall that the normal approximation to the F-distribution forces each V_i to have a unit variance and that $\bar{V} = .88$.

12 The null hypothesis for this test is H_0: $\sigma_v^2 = 1.0$.

13 Of course, other reviewers may wish to focus upon different study characteristics. Our selections were made before any study was coded or analyzed, and subsequent empirical results show a remarkable statistical fit. The empirical proof is in the pudding. Because there are so few observations it takes little model experimentation to use up all the available degrees of freedom.

14 In one study of the Phillips curve (Alogoskoufis and Smith, 1991), there is a problem in interpreting the reported parameter invariance test statistics. The authors report that their Wald tests are asymptotically normal (Alogoskoufis and Smith, 1991, p.1261). But elsewhere, the Wald test is known to have a chi-squared distribution (Greene, 1990, pp.404-5). Therefore, we treat the Wald tests as $\chi^2(1)$ and convert them to N(0,1) accordingly. If, on the other hand, the numbers reported by Alogoskoufis and Smith (1991) are considered N(0,1), we still obtain the same general results, although, of course, the specific estimates are affected.

15 Further statistical testing supports this meta-regression specification. After ordering the data by time, a Lagrange multiplier test shows no signs of autocorrelation: LM = 1.62 and d.f. = 1. Breusch-Pagan testing reveals no suggestion of heteroskedasticity using either the sample size or whether a study passed two or more specification tests: BP = .31 and d.f. = 2. Also, RESET finds no misspecification of any type: $F_{2,14} = 1.94$.

16 Only one model in one study, Blanchard (1984), failed to difference the data.

17 Whether or not the Lucas critique is valid, the normal approximation used here causes the error variance, σ_e^2, for the properly specified meta-regression model to have a unit variance, i.e., $\sigma_e^2 \geq 1$.

18 Barro (1989) and de Haan and Zelhorst (1988) all seem to use such a minority rule when evaluating Ricardian equivalence; see Chapter 9.

9. Meta-Analysis of Ricardian Equivalence: New Wine in Old Bottles*

> This argument of charging posterity with the interest of our debt, or of relieving them from a portion of such interest, is often used by otherwise well informed people, but we confess we see no weight in it.
>
> – David Ricardo (1820, p.187)

> (R)esults are all over the map, with some favoring Ricardian equivalence, and others not.
>
> – Barro (1989, p. 49)

INTRODUCTION

In recent years, there has been much discussion in the United States Congress and the popular media (not to mention the academic journals) about the US budget deficit, its effects, and possible elimination. To the clamorous cacophony of balanced budget rhetoric, Barro (1974) added a clear and reassuring note. Budget deficits do not matter; they affect neither aggregate demand nor the real interest. '(A) decrease in the government's savings (that is, a current budget deficit) leads to an offsetting increase in desired private savings, and hence to no change in desired national savings' (Barro, 1989, p.39). 'This is the so-called Ricardian-equivalence theorem which states that it is economically equivalent to maintain a balanced budget or to run a debt-financed deficit, since the substitution of debt for taxes does not affect private sector wealth and consumption' (Leiderman and Blejer, 1988, p. 2). It is the 'so-called' Ricardian equivalence theorem (RET) because David Ricardo did not believe that people are indifferent to debt financing, Buchanan's (1976) claims and the label 'Ricardian equivalence' to the contrary.

Contrary to the misattribution of 'Ricardian equivalence', David Ricardo did not believe that government debt financing was neutral (O'Driscoll, 1977, Ricardo, 1820). In an article written by David Ricardo for the Fourth Edition of the *Encyclopædia Britannica*, he clearly favored financing war expenditures through taxes over either deficit financing or deficit financing accompanied by a sinking fund to retire the accumulated debt. 'Of these three modes, we are decidedly of the opinion that the preference should be given to the first' (Ricardo, 1820, p. 186). The confusion arises from the fact that Ricardo correctly recognized the equivalence of these three modes of financing government expenditures from the perspective of present value calculus (i.e., 'point of economy'), and yet that people will not react the same to deficit financing as they do to taxes.

> In point of economy, there is no real difference in either of the modes; for twenty millions in one payment, one million per annum for ever, or 1,200,000 l. for 45 years, are precisely the same value; but people who pay the taxes never so estimate them, and therefore do not manage their private affairs accordingly. We are too apt to think, that war is burdensome only in proportion to what we are at the moment called to pay for it in taxes, without reflecting on the probable duration of such taxes.
>
> – Ricardo (1820, pp. 186-87)

Ricardo actually made the case for the nonequivalence and the inferiority of debt financing (O'Driscoll, 1977). In this Chapter, I follow the conventional nomenclature (i.e., 'Ricardian' equivalence as debt-neutrality) to avoid unnecessary confusion.

Needless to say, such a provocative proposition has attracted much discussion and empirical testing. Empirical testing, however, has had little impact on theoretical or policy discussions because the results are so mixed that they convince no one. Nonetheless, the orthodox view expressed in the economic literature seems to be that the Ricardian equivalence is a 'valid and useful proposition' (Leiderman and Blejer, 1988, p. 29).[1] Or as Barro (1989) states, 'It is easy on theoretical grounds to raise points that invalidate strict Ricardian equivalence. Nevertheless, it may still be that the Ricardian view provides a useful framework for assessing the first-order effects of fiscal policy' (p. 48).

The purpose of this chapter is much the same as the last chapter. A meta-analysis of a large number of empirical tests of Ricardian equivalence is undertaken, in the process, uncovering the importance of inertia and the applicability of BIH. I endeavor to assess the wealth of empirical research on this provocative topic and to explain its vast variation. How sensitive is the empirical support for RET to the particular model specification? Does the amount of information utilized by a statistical test affect its results? Are models which pass additional specification tests more or less critical of Ricardian equivalence? Does the weight of empirical evidence support or reject Ricardian equivalence? In contrast to the conventional assessment which gives mild support for RET, our meta-analysis finds that strong evidence against Ricardian equivalence already exists in the literature. BIH and other well-specified econometric models tend to reject RET. When adjusted for the statistical quality of a given test, the non-Ricardian effect becomes larger still.

A META-ANALYSIS OF THE RICARDIAN EQUIVALENCE THEOREM

This study began with a review of the 110 references to 'Ricardian equivalence' found on EconLit's CD-ROM, 1980-1995.[2]   From these, twenty-eight empirical studies were identified (see Meta-Analysis References at the end of this chapter). The only selective criteria used to identify these twenty-eight empirical studies were whether the study claims to test Ricardian equivalence and reports the corresponding test statistic.[3] To avoid giving undue weight to dissertations and studies of potentially lower quality, each study is counted as a single test of RET, regardless of how many tests may actually be presented. For studies reporting multiple test results, a conventional model which uses the more sophisticated econometric method is selected. When there still remains more than one test, they are averaged. Several studies report Ricardo equivalence tests for multiple countries. Of course, these multinational studies often produce mixed results. However, if each test for each country is included, the evidence against RET strengthens. In any case, giving particular studies such a disproportionate weight is questionable, whether they represent the best or the worst the field has to offer. Better weighting schemes for a study's quality, reflecting proper statistical specification and greater statistical power, are employed in following analyses.

Standardizing RET Tests: Non-Equivalent Effect Size

The standard practice for testing Ricardian equivalence is to build an econometric model of consumption expenditures or interest rates (occasionally, exchange rates) and to estimate the model with and without the restrictions implied by RET. For example, consumption is often estimated by:

$$C_t = \alpha_0 + \alpha_1 Y_t + \alpha_2 Y_{t-1} + \alpha_3 G_t + \alpha_4 W_t + \alpha_5 T x_t + \alpha_6 B_t + \alpha_7 T r_t + \varepsilon_j \qquad (9.1)$$

where C_t is private consumption expenditures in quarter t, Y_t is personal income, G_t is government expenditures, W_t is household net wealth, Tx_t is government tax revenue, B_t is government debt, and Tr_t is government transfer payments. Given this formulation of the consumption function,

RET may be interpreted as imposing the restrictions, $\alpha_5 = \alpha_6 = \alpha_7 = 0$ (Leiderman and Blejer, 1988, p. 19). Because inertia and nonstationarity dominate consumption decisions and expenditures, the estimation of equation (9.1) is likely to give spurious results. For US data, an adequate statistical characterization involves the change in the logarithm of consumption as a function of its own lag and similar percentage changes in disposable income and interest rates (Stanley, 1994). Such statistical misspecifications are a plausible explanation for the low power of many RET tests. Parameter restrictions, consistent with RET, always form the null hypothesis; thus low power will appear to give support to Ricardian equivalence. Although each researcher may choose a somewhat different model and differentially interpret the exact form of RET's parameter restrictions, the typical test of Ricardian equivalence is, nonetheless, a test of parameter restrictions.

There is also considerable variation in the type of statistical test used in RET testing. Often the traditional F-test, or t-test for a single parameter restriction, is employed. Or more recently, Wald and Lagrange multiplier (LM) tests, both of which possess χ^2-distributions, have become the popular choice. Such variation in test strategy and form presents an obstacle for the smooth integration and summary of the empirical record.

How can results of different studies using a variety of statistical tests be accurately compared and rationally accumulated and analyzed? We seek, that is, a reasonable method to compare and measure empirical results from different studies, using different data sets, employing different models and relying on different statistical testing procedures. Towards this end, non-equivalent effect size (NEES) is defined.[4]

Fortunately, useful approximations exists that can convert various statistical distributions – ts, Fs and χ^2s – to a common and meaningful metric, one which has a standard normal distribution. First, F-tests of parameter restrictions may be transformed using a normal approximation to the F-distribution which is not large sample bound (Abramowitz and Stegun, 1964) – recall Chapter 8. Given a random variable, f, which is distributed $F(v_1, v_2)$ and is used to test a model's parameter restrictions, study i's non-equivalent effect size (NEES) is:

$$N_i = \frac{f^{1/3}\,(1 - 2/9\,v_2) - (1 - 2/9\,v_1)}{(2/9\,v_1 + f^{2/3}2/9\,v_2)^{1/2}} \tag{9.2}$$

N_i has an approximate standard normal distribution, N(0,1) (Abramowitz and Stegun, 1964, p. 947). In the case of t-tests, they can be converted to

F-distributions with $v_1 = 1$ by squaring. The resulting Fs may, in turn, be further transformed by (9.2).

Similarly, Wald and LM tests, χ^2 distributions with v degrees of freedom, can be approximated by a standard normal variable:

$$N_i = \frac{(\chi^2 / v)^{1/3}-(1- 2/9v)}{(2/9v)^{1/2}} \tag{9.3}$$

(Abramowitz and Stegun, 1964). These normal approximations are so accurate that they can be used to extend standard statistical tables (e.g., Levin and Rubin, 1991). Even for small degrees of freedom, they are often accurate to $\pm.01$. In this way, all types of RET tests may be measured on the same scale, N_i.

N_i is a common metric, measuring the strength of the evidence against Ricardian equivalence or debt neutrality (i.e., non-equivalent effect size, NEES). The larger a positive N_i, the stronger the evidence against RET is. Negative values reflect a smaller than expected, assuming that RET is true, test statistic. If Ricardian equivalence is an accurate description of the effect of government deficits, NEES will be approximately zero. Given this 'common denominator', RET tests can be directly compared and combined using conventional descriptive and inferential statistics. Even those statistical methods which explicitly demand normality (e.g., regression analysis) are appropriate.

Methods[5]

To assess the overall strength of the evidence against RET, the average non-equivalent effect size, $\bar{N} = \Sigma N_i /L$, may be calculated (where L is the number of studies). To determine whether the literature contains a statistically significant non-equivalent effect, the statistic, $z = \bar{N} \cdot L^{1/2}$, may be compared to 1.96, because each N_i is a standard normal variate under the null hypothesis of RET. If Ricardian equivalence were true, $\mu_N = 0$ and $\sigma_N^2 = 1$.[6]

Results

First, simple descriptive statistics, summarizing the empirical literature on RET, provide strong evidence against Ricardian equivalence. The average non-equivalent effect size (NEES), $\bar{N}$, is 2.41 which is both statistically and practically significant (t = 6.52; rejecting H_0: $\mu_N = 0$; p<.01). Although it is no major accomplishment to obtain statistical significance by combining results over an entire literature, this value is much larger than background variation. Recall that effects of 1.0σ can be called 'large' (Chapter 8). From this perspective, Ricardian non-equivalent effects found in this literature – $\bar{N} = 2.41\sigma$ – are very large indeed.

Weighting a study's test results by obvious statistical measures of quality further increases the average NEES. $\bar{N}$ is 3.47 when a study's findings are weighted by the number of degrees of freedom on which the test is based, and it is 2.94 when weighted by the number of specification tests a study reports and passes.[7] Thus, when additional consideration is given to the amount of information available to a given study or the proper specification of the econometric model, the strength of the evidence against RET increases still.

Vote-counting or 'box-scoring',[8] the strategy used by conventional narrative reviews (often implicitly), is the least censorious method of accumulating the empirical evidence on RET. Would it not be reasonable to count the number of studies that supply evidence 'for' or 'against' Ricardian equivalence? The median NEES is 2.03, and the rule of 2 (rounding the standard normal value, 1.96, to 2.00) gives nearly a fifty–fifty percentage split between RET test results (see Figure 9.1). If, instead, each study is classified as 'for' or 'against' RET by how the authors summarize their study, we find: 61 percent against RET, 29 percent for, and 11 percent mixed. Although voting still rejects RET by a democratic rule, such mixed findings give purchase to any reviewer wishing to confirm his or her prejudices.[9]

However, voting methods are known to be biased. When statistical tests have low power, voting is biased in favor of finding no significant difference (Hedges and Oklin, 1985). Low power is routinely a problem in econometric studies and can be particularly pernicious in applications such as tests of RET, where multiple misspecification biases present a genuine danger.[10] This issue of low power and the resulting bias of voting is especially significant in reviewing tests of Ricardian equivalence where a finding of no significant difference (usually in the form of accepting certain parameter restrictions) is taken as validation of RET.

To illustrate how misleading counting statistical test outcomes can be and thereby how biased the most 'unbiased' conventional literature review is likely to be, suppose one were to dismiss all studies with findings against RET (when NEES > 1.96). Even when attention is confined to the twelve most favorable studies (100 percent of which may be construed as supporting RET), this evidence entails a strong statistical rejection of RET – $\bar{N} = .784$; $t = 3.05$; rejecting H_0: $\mu_N \le 0$; $p < .01$. Studies, leaning towards rejection but individually too weak to overcome the presumption of doubt favoring RET, may add up to strong evidence when taken together. If

Ricardian equivalence were true, NEES should be close to zero with nearly as many negative values as positive ones. Yet, far too many studies that are interpreted to support RET actually give evidence against RET, albeit at p-values higher than conventional significance levels. Given the inherent bias in favor of RET and the low statistical power of econometric tests, it is surprising that so many tests, nonetheless, find sufficient evidence to reject Ricardian equivalence.

Figure 9.1: Histogram of NEES

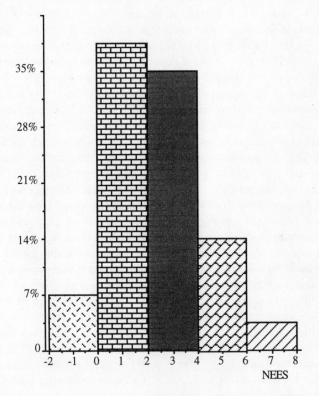

Returning to the full sample of twenty–eight studies, if Ricardian equivalence were true, both $\mu_N = 0$ and $\sigma_N^2 = 1$. The uniformly most powerful test strongly rejects this joint hypothesis ($\chi^2 = 266.88$; p<.01) (Hogg and Craig, 1970). Also, testing the unity of variance hypothesis yields a powerful rejection ($\chi^2 = 103.6$; p<.01) and indicates excess variation.

Such heterogeneity among test results demands explanation. When a meta-analysis uncovers excess variability, a comprehensive understanding of the literature requires further analysis. Meta-regression analysis is designed with precisely this purpose in mind (Stanley and Jarrell, 1989, Jarrell and Stanley, 1990).

Nine study and model characteristics are found to make a significant contribution towards understanding the large variation among tests of Ricardian equivalence.[11] See Table 9.1 for the variable definitions and Table 9.2 for the meta-regression results. Together, these variables explain nearly 83 percent of the study-to-study variation among RET test results and, of course, are statistically significant ($F_{9,17} = 9.29$; p < .01).[12] Nor is there any evidence that this meta-regression model is misspecified. After ordering the studies by year, a Lagrange multiplier test reveals no signs of autocorrelation ($\chi^2(1) = .18$). Likewise, the Breusch–Pagan tests fail to find heteroskedasticity, regardless of the choice of variables ($BP_3 = 3.61$). And, RESET uncovers no sign of generic misspecifications ($F_{2,15} = 3.16$).

Focus upon the individual effects on RET tests highlights how sensitive these tests are to modelling choice and specification. For example, all studies in this literature are based on time series data which are notoriously vulnerable to problems of nonstationarity and spurious regression.[13] Because inertia is omnipresent in economic time series, the form of the fitted regression model is likely to make a great difference to its validity. Like the meta-analysis of the Lucas critique (Chapter 8), the inclusion of a lagged dependent variable, *Lag* (t = –3.05; p < .01), and the use of differenced variables, *diff* (t = –3.98; p < .01) have a significant effect on a study's assessment of Ricardian equivalence. Again, inertia is key to understanding this empirical literature on Ricardian equivalence.

Models which are based on rational expectations, *Expect* = 1, are also more likely to support RET (t =-5.43; p < .01) and, perhaps surprisingly, so are Keynesian models (t =-1.80; one-tail p < .05). Keynesian models are identified primarily as those which use disposable income in a consumption function. Using US data (t = 2.04; one-tail p < .05), or vector autoregressive models (t = 3.06; p < .01), or models based on the permanent income hypothesis (t = 2.35; p < .05) all tend to increase NEES. Each of these econometric model specification choices has a significant effect on RET test results. On the other hand, variables measuring the year and the type of economic phenomena investigated (*Consume*) exhibit no detectable effect on RET test outcomes (see Table 9.3).

The coefficient on *Expect* has the largest magnitude and the greatest significance on Ricardian equivalence tests. New classical economists are likely to view this result as validation of Ricardian equivalence. When a study assumes rational expectations, it is much less likely to reject RET.[14]

Table 9.1: Meta-Independent Variables

df	the number of degrees of freedom available to the RET test
Year	the average year of the data that a study uses
Expect	= 1 if a study is based primarily on 'rational' expectations
Lag	= 1 if a study used a lagged dependent variable
PIH	= 1 if study used a permanent income model
Keynes	= 1 if a study used a Keynesian model with disposable income
VAR	= 1 if a study used a vector autoregressive model
Diff	= 1 if a model is expressed primarily in differences
Spec	the number of specification tests passed less those that failed
Consume	= 1 if a study investigated consumption expenditures
US	= 1 if a study used only US data

Table 9.2: Meta-Regression Results

Variable	Coefficient	t-value	p-value
Intercept	3.71	–	–
Expect	–3.73	–5.43	.0001
Diff	–1.99	–3.98	.001
df	.0058	3.42	.003
Spec	.76	3.32	.004
VAR	2.00	3.06	.007
Lag	–1.82	–3.05	.007
PIH	1.10	2.35	.031
US	.98	2.05	.057
Keynes	–1.26	–1.80	.090
Adj. R^2	.742	–	–
F	9.29	–	.0001
Standard Error	1.00	–	–
Sample Size	27	–	–

An alternative explanation for the significance of *Expect* is that expectational models are more likely to be misspecified. In Chapter 8, an econometric model's reliance on expectations is also found to be important in tests of the Lucas critique. When models with questionable specification are removed so is the empirical support for the Lucas critique.

Table 9.3: Meta-Regression Results Using All Independent Variables

Variable	Coefficient	t-value	p-value
Intercept	3.21	–	–
Expect	–3.63	–4.72	.0003
Diff	–1.77	–3.22	.006
df	.0058	3.21	.006
Spec	.67	2.74	.015
VAR	2.06	3.08	.008
Lag	–1.98	–3.17	.006
PIH	.96	1.92	.074
US	.83	1.64	.123
Keynes	–1.30	–1.70	.11
Consume	.72	1.03	.32
Year	.00114	.16	.877
Adj. R^2	.73	–	–
F	7.48	–	.0003
Standard Error	1.02	–	–
Sample Size	27	–	–

This misspecification of rational expectations thesis is confirmed by the current meta-analysis, through both the sign and significance of the coefficients on *Spec* and *df*. If RET were an accurate summary of reality, larger samples would not increase the likelihood of its rejection. Because RET is assumed true in the null hypothesis, the probability of its erroneous rejection is controlled by each study and constrained to the conventional $\alpha=.05$. However, our meta-regression reveals a strong association between the degrees of freedom available to a study and the size of the non-Ricardian effect which it uncovers, df ($t = 3.42$; $p < .01$). Such a significant relation is consistent only with the falsity of Ricardian equivalence. If RET were false, then larger degrees of freedom would increase statistical power and thereby raise the probability of its rejection. Such a statistically significant relation between df and NEES is itself a powerful testimony of the empirical inapplicability of Ricardian equivalence.

This interpretation is further corroborated by the relation of specification testing and RET test results. Some economists dismiss evidence critical to Ricardian equivalence through vague reference to problems of econometric specification (Barro, 1989, p. 49). However, more careful analysis of econometric specification rejects such a convenient rationalization. The number of specification tests that an econometric model passes increases, not decreases, the likelihood of RET's empirical rejection. On average, each additional specification test passed increases NEES by 3/4 σ (t = 3.32; p < .01).[15]

It is also quite interesting to note that the unexplained variance, $\hat{\sigma}^2_e =$ 1.00 (recall the standard error in Table 9.2), is precisely the proper magnitude demanded by the normal approximation.[16] Anything smaller or possessing a higher R^2 would be suspect. The magnitude of remaining error variance suggests that the above meta-regression model fully accounts for all systematic variation found in this empirical literature. Thus, it would be unreasonable and counterproductive to expect a better statistical explanation of the empirical tests of Ricardian equivalence.

A meta-analysis of the empirical tests of Ricardian equivalence finds strong evidence of its falsity. When considered together, the extant literature constitutes a convincing rejection of RET. Studies which subject their models to additional successful specification testing are more likely to reject RET, and the falsity of RET is further corroborated by the importance of the degrees of freedom. Only a false Ricardian equivalence is consistent with the observed positive association of *df* and NEES.

RICARDIAN EQUIVALENCE AND BEHAVIORAL INERTIA

This meta-regression analysis may also be used to predict the outcomes of Ricardian equivalence tests not yet conducted and research that might be regarded as 'best practice'. From empirical findings reported in previous chapters, we have reason to believe that the behavioral inertia model of consumption is well specified. The above estimated meta-regression coefficients (Table 9.2) predict that the BIH model employed in Chapter 6 would yield a non-Ricardian effect of approximately 2.17 (*Expect* = 0, *Diff*=1, *df* = 50, *Spec* = 3, *VAR* = 0, *Lag* = 1, *PIH* = 0, *US* = 1, *Keynes* = 1).

As a further validation of my MRA model of Ricardian equivalence, deficit spending can be incorporated into the behavioral inertia model of consumption (recall Chapter 6). The advantage of employing BIH to test Ricardian equivalence is that usual statistical misspecification may be avoided. Most of the literature on RET uses models which are clearly misspecified. For example, the majority of studies do not report the passing of any specification tests. For those studies which model consumption, most do not use disposable income, and less than one-fifth use the lags and differences found necessary in Chapter 6. Thus, embedding deficit spending into the behavioral inertia model, equation (6.9), is likely to give a valid test of Ricardian equivalence.

How will deficit spending affect consumption? In Barro's re-introduction of Ricardian equivalence, he considers and dismisses the idea that consumers might regard government bonds as net wealth. 'Government bonds are perceived as net wealth only if their value exceeds the capitalized value of the implied stream of future tax liabilities' (Barro, 1974, p. 1095). However, Ricardo gave the opposite answer to the identical issue, 'but people who pay the taxes never so estimate them, and therefore do not manage their private affairs accordingly' (Ricardo, 1820, p.186). Thus, when consumers regard government bonds as wealth and if there is a Pigou effect (i.e., a wealth effect on consumption expenditures), deficit spending becomes an independent variable in the consumption function. Because the change in the amount of government bonds outstanding is related to the size of the government's deficit, the deficit can be directly added to BIH. However, the correctly specified model, equation (6.9), is in terms of percentage changes. To be consistent, therefore, the federal deficit (which is correlated to the *change* in bond holdings) needs to be relatively measured. The percentage of GNP is the usual comparison.

Incorporating the *Def/GNP* (real federal deficit as a ratio to real GNP) into BIH gives:

$$dln\hat{C}_t = .0027 + .212 \, dlnC_{t\text{-}1} + .585 \, dlnY_t + .165 \, Def/GNP \qquad (9.4)$$
$$\phantom{dln\hat{C}_t =} (4.58) \qquad (16.16) \qquad (2.46) \qquad R^2 = .886$$
$$s = .0096 \quad h = -1.01 \qquad LM = 4.97 \qquad \text{G-Q} = 1.26 \qquad n = 55$$

Ricardian equivalence is rejected ($F_{1,51} = 6.03$, $p < .05$) by this model of consumption. Notice further that all specification tests are passed and that the t-tests for $dlnC_{t\text{-}1}$ and $dlnY_t$ are slightly improved without appreciably changing the regression coefficients. From this BIH test of RET, NEES may be calculated as 2.13, virtually the same as predicted by our MRA model, 2.17; recall Table 9.2.

However, if there is a Pigou effect, then wealth, in general and not only that portion in government bonds, belongs in the consumption function. Adding the percentage change in real private wealth, dW, does not materially affect the previous results.

$$dln\hat{C}_t = -.0032 + .159 dlnC_{t\text{-}1} + .562 dlnY_t + .274 Def/GNP + .231 dW \qquad (9.5)$$
$$\phantom{dln\hat{C}_t =} (3.27) \qquad (15.83) \qquad (3.57) \qquad (2.56)$$
$$R^2 = .899 \quad h = -.49 \qquad LM = 6.86 \qquad \text{G-Q} = 1.21 \qquad n = 55$$

Now both wealth effects are statistically significant, and Ricardian equivalence is more strikingly rejected ($F_{1,50} = 12.77$, $p < .001$). This analysis permits a further test of the government bonds as net wealth hypothesis. When deficits are treated as net wealth, the two coefficients, for *Def/GNP* and *dW*, should be roughly the same. This linear restriction ($\beta_3 = \beta_4$) is easily accepted ($F_{1,50} = .29$).

Thus, contra Barro, there is clear empirical evidence that RET is false and that bonds are treated as net wealth. Furthermore, the results from this BIH model are entirely consistent with what is found in the meta-analysis of the existing empirical literature. Models like BIH, for which there are good reasons to accept their specification, tend to reject RET, while models whose specification is suspect tend to accept Ricardian equivalence.

CONVENTIONAL NARRATIVE REVIEWS OF RICARDIAN EQUIVALENCE

> First, and foremost, the empirical evidence is extremely ambiguous. Second, the
> 'mild' version of debt neutrality seems confirmed by the data. . . .
> – Perasso (1987, p. 672)

How do conventional literature reviews evaluate the evidence on Ricardian equivalence? How do they compare to the results obtained through meta-analysis? '(R)esults are all over the map, with some favoring Ricardian equivalence, and others not' (Barro, 1989, p. 49). Although every review acknowledges that the empirical record of Ricardian equivalence is mixed and that there are serious problems of test sensitivity and model specification, five of six, nonetheless, interpret the empirical record to be consistent with RET.[17] The exception is Bernheim (1987). 'A succession of studies have established the existence of a robust short-run relationship between deficits and aggregate consumption. . . . (T)ime series evidence weighs against Ricardian equivalence . . .' (p. 291).

In contrast, Perasso (1987) summarizes his survey of this literature as:

> First, and foremost, the empirical evidence is extremely ambiguous. Second, the
> 'mild' version of debt neutrality seems confirmed by the data. . . .   (p.672).

If, as Perasso claims, the evidence is 'extremely ambiguous', how can it be said to confirm Ricardian equivalence?

Similarly, Leiderman and Blejer (1988) conclude their survey by stating that: 'the Ricardian equivalence theorem of government finance, which states that substitution of debt for taxes has no impact on private sector wealth and consumption. . . is a valid and useful proposition. . .' (p. 30). Yet, in their discussion, they identify five consumption studies which reject RET and five that do not reject RET (p. 19).

Barro (1989) uses the presence of such mixed findings on consumption and savings studies as a basis to dismiss evidence unflattering to RET (p.49). Citing problems of simultaneity and deficit endogeneity, problems which apply equally to the supportive evidence among interest rate studies that Barro embraces, he chooses to rely on anecdotal evidence of consumption and savings rather than conventional econometric tests.[18] Ironically, the problems of simultaneity and exogeneity bias which Barro uses to dismiss studies of consumption are most likely to work in favor of Ricardian equivalence, not against it. As Bernheim (1987) argues, 'Shocks to consumption may be correlated with shocks to income, which in turn raise tax revenue (lower deficits). Thus, there is a natural bias in favor of Ricardian equivalence, even in a Keynesian world' (p. 282). As demonstrated by the meta-analysis, better-specified models are more likely, not less likely, to reject RET.

Similarly, Seater (1993) relies on problems of specification and econometric methodology to discount rejections of Ricardian equivalence. 'When those problems are addressed, the aggregate consumption data almost always fail to reject Ricardian equivalence' (Seater, 1993, p. 174). Such selective interpretations allow Seater to give a favorable overall assessment of RET. 'Although tests of Ricardian equivalence do not quite give an unambiguous verdict on the proposition's validity, I think it reasonable to conclude that Ricardian equivalence is strongly supported by the data' (p. 182).

Nor does even-handed reporting of both favorable and unfavorable results provide any guarantee that the reviewer's conclusion will accurately reflect the reported results. For example, de Haan and Zelhorst(1988) summarize the empirical literature on Ricardian equivalence in a table presenting forty-nine separate tests. Yet, in spite of the fact that thirty tests (61 percent) are classified as 'falsifying' RET, the authors nonetheless infer: 'As follows from the table, the empirical evidence provides mixed support for debt neutrality theory' (p. 409). Apparently, they use a *minority* voting rule. At best, conventional, narrative reviews of empirical studies serve as vote counts. However, vote-counting is well known to be biased in favor of the null hypothesis (i.e., RET) (Hedges and Olkin, 1985). Even though all reviewers find considerable ambiguity in RET's empirical record, one might easily get the impression that it, nonetheless, supports Ricardian equivalence.

The problem with conventional, narrative literature reviews is that 'anything goes'. Some reviewers exercise great care to include studies which are both favorable and unfavorable to their favored views and to be as objective and even-handed as possible. Others seek only to persuade by selectively discussing and dismissng the literature. Potential specification problems are omnipresent; thus, some plausible excuse can always be manufactured. When reviewing an empirical literature, it seems that many economists become Bayesian, holding strong priors formed on the basis of theoretical considerations.

CONCLUSION

In summary, there already exists quite strong evidence against Ricardian equivalence in the empirical economic literature. The literature, as a whole, reflects a large and significant non-Ricardian effect. This effect is amplified when results are weighted by quality measures: degrees of freedom and the number of separate specification tests passed. Given the inherent bias in favor of RET, the non-Ricardian effects are quite ubiquitous. Even the simplest and most biased summary procedure, vote-counting, rejects Ricardian equivalence.

In addition, empirical tests of Ricardian equivalence have excess variation ($\chi^2 = 103.6$; $p < .01$). This excess variability of RET test results begs further explanation. Unsurprisingly, a meta-regression analysis (MRA) reveals great sensitivities of RET testing to model specification. Of special interest are the effects of degrees of freedom and specification testing. Our meta-regression analysis shows that passing additional specification tests tends to strengthen the evidence against RET. The strong statistical relationship between the size of the reported non-Ricardian effect and the test's degrees of freedom is consistent only with the falsity of the null hypothesis – RET. Furthermore as predicted by the behavioral inertia hypothesis, it makes a large and statistically significant difference whether a study uses lags and/or differences the data. Both meta-analyses reported here reveal the importance of inertia in different areas of empirical economic inquiry.

Conventional literature reviews of the empirical tests of Ricardian equivalence have been of little practical use. Typically, they find that the results are mixed, sensitive to model specification, and yet largely supportive of RET. On the other hand, a more inclusive and systematic meta-analysis finds a literature which is strikingly skewed towards RET's rejection. After the results of each study are quantified on a common scale, powerful evidence against Ricardian equivalence may be corroborated in several independent ways: weighted averages, vote-counting, analysis confined to studies favorable to RET, tests of variances, and the effects of both degrees of freedom and specification testing. Through meta-regression analysis, the empirical literature concerning Ricardian equivalence reveals a pattern which departs greatly from conventional wisdom. This evidence is not mixed, when taken as a whole, but is strongly inconsistent with Ricardian equivalence.

EMPIRICAL TESTS OF THE RICARDIAN EQUIVALENCE THEOREM

Ahmed, S. (1987), 'Government Spending, the Balance of Trade and the Terms of Trade in British History', *Journal of Monetary Economics*, **20**, 195-220.

Bagliano, F. (1994), 'Do Anticipated Tax Changes Matter? Further Evidence from the United Kingdom,' *Ricerche-Economiche*, **48**, 87-108.

Beck, S. (1993), 'The Ricardian Equivalence Proposition from Foreign Exchange Markets,' *Journal of International Money and Finance*, **12**, 154-169.

Bernheim, D. (1987), 'Ricardian Equivalence: An Evaluation of Theory and Evidence,' in S. Fischer (ed.) *NBER Macroeconomic Annual: 1987*, Cambridge, Mass.: MIT Press.

Boothe, P. (1989), 'Asset Returns and Government Budgets in a Small Open Economy: Empirical Evidence for Canada,' *Journal of Monetary Economics*, **23**, 65-77.

Brown, J. (1987), 'An Empirical Analysis of Time Series Consumption Behavior Under Ricardian Equivalence,' Unpublished Dissertation, Brown University.

Cadsby, C. and Frank, M. (1991), 'Experimental Tests of Ricardian Equivalence,' *Economic Inquiry*, **29**, 645-64.

Croushore, D. , Koot, R.S., Walker, D.A. (1989), 'The Effect of Government Deficits on Consumption and Interest Rates: A Two Equation Approach,' *Quarterly Journal of Business and Economics*, **28**, 85-129.

Dalamagus, B. (1992), 'How Rival Are the Ricardian Equivalence Proposition and the Fiscal Policy Potency View?' *Scottish Journal of Political Economy*, **39**, 457-76.

Dalamagus, B. (1992), 'Testing Ricardian Equivalence: A Reconsideration,' *Applied Economics*, **24**, 59-68.

Darrat, A. (1989), 'Fiscal Deficits and Long-term Interest Rates: Further Evidence from Annual Data,' *Southern Economic Journal*, **56**, 363-74.

Enders, W. and Lee, B. (1990), 'Current Account and Budget Deficits: Twins or Distant Cousins,' *Review of Economics and Business*, **72**, 373-81.

Evans, P. (1988), 'Are Consumers Ricardian? Evidence for the United States,' *Journal of Political Economy*, **96**, 983-1004.

Evans, P. (1993), 'Consumers Are Not Ricardian: Evidence from 19 Countries,' *Economic Inquiry*, **31**, 534-48.

Graham, F. (1992), 'On the Importance of the Measurement of Consumption in Tests of Ricardian Equivalence,' *Economic Letters*, **38**, 431-34.

Gupta, K. (1992), 'Ricardian Equivalence and Crowding Out in Asia,' *Applied Economics*, **24**, 19-25.

de Haan, J. and Zelhorst, D. (1988), 'The Empirical Evidence on the Ricardian Equivalence Hypothesis,' *Kredit und Kapital,* **21**, 407-21.

Haque, N. and Montiel, P. (1989) 'Consumption in Developing Countries: Tests for Liquidity Constraints and Finite Horizons,' *Review of Economics and Statistics*, **71**, 408-15.

Haug, A. (1990), 'Ricardian Equivalence, Rational Expectations, and the Permanent Income Hypothesis,' *Journal of Money, Credit, and Banking*, **22**, 305-26.

Jachi, A. (1990), 'The Ricardian Equivalence: An Empirical Examination for Six OECD Countries,' Unpublished Dissertation, Northern Illinois University.

Jung, H. Y. (1994), 'Tests of the Ricardian Equivalence Proposition,' Unpublished Dissertation, Johns Hopkins University.

Katsaitis, O. (1987), 'On the Substitutability Between Private Consumer Expenditure and Government Spending in Canada,' *Canadian Journal of Economics*, **20**, 533-43.

Khalid, A. (1993), 'Ricardian Equivalence in Developing Economies: The Evidence Re-examined,' Unpublished Dissertation, Johns Hopkins University.

Monadjimi, M. and Kearney, C. (1991), 'The Interest Rate Neutrality of Fiscal Deficits: Testing for Ricardian Equivalence and Capital Inflow,' *Journal of International Money and Finance*, **10**, 541-51.

Olekalns, N. (1989), 'Substitution between Private and Public Consumption,' *Economic Record*, **65**, 16-26.

Poterba, J. and Summers, L.H. (1987), 'Finite Lifetimes and the Effects of Budget Deficits on National Saving,' *Journal of Monetary Economics*, **20**, 369-91.

Viren, M. (1988), 'Interest Rates and Budget Deficits: Cross Country Evidence from the Period 1924-1938,' *Economic Letters*, **28**, 235-38.

Whelan, K. (1991), 'Ricardian Equivalence and the Irish Consumption Function: The Evidence Re-examined,' *Economic and Social Review,*, **22**, 229-38.

NOTES

*   From the *Southern Economic Journal,* **64**, 1998, 713-727.

1   As more fully discussed in a following section, this is also the view of most of the conventional narrative reviews.

2   More references could be found by searching all bibliographies and seminal papers. However, my search is confined to AEA's official database to maximize the replicability of the following meta-analysis.

3   Some economists may wish to discount some tests, believing them to be of a lesser quality or relevance. However, in an effort to be as objective as possible, meta-analysis must include all studies. If researchers are convinced that quality differs, weights may be attached accordingly. Weights for proper specification and statistical power are employed below. For example, some economists may question VAR models because they are not behavioral. However, the results of this meta-analysis are so robust that if all VAR models are removed, there remains a significant non-equivalent effect ($t = 5.89$; $p < .01$).

4   Effect size is a standard measure of a study's effect found in the meta-analysis literature for purposes of accumulating and analyzing the empirical record of a given area of research. In simple experimental studies, it is measured as the difference in the means of the control and experimental groups divided by some measure of the in-group standard deviation (Hedges and Olkin, 1985). NEES supplies an analogous measure for parameter restriction tests.

5   These methods are much the same as those employed in the last chapter. Also see the steps recommended for meta-analysis identified in Chapter 8.

6   Where μ_N is the true mean of NEES, and σ_N^2 is its variance.

7   The weights used here are equal to *Spec* +1, chosen so that the many studies which report no specification tests are given at least some weight. By this measure, studies which fail more specification tests than they pass receive a weight of zero, those which pass no specification tests have weight equal to one, and studies successfully employing more extensive testing are given increasingly larger weight according to the number of tests passed.

8   Light and Smith, 1971.

9   Note the examples in the next section on conventional narrative reviews.

10 For example, in the related field of 'rational expectations' and 'market efficiency', conventional testing is well know to have low power and to be insensitive to departure from rationality (Shiller, 1981b, Linter, 1981, Camerer, 1989, Summers, 1986).

11 To minimize the potential biases of specification searches, I did not employ stepwise, or any other model search algorithm. All eleven coded meta-variables were included in the meta-regression model. Two variables with no detectable explanatory power (*Year* and *Consume*) were removed. See Table 9.3 for the regression results from the more general model and notice that there are no

meaningful differences, other than the predictable improvement of statistical significance for the variables remaining in the meta-regression model.

12 These independent variables are neither mutually exclusive nor highly multicollinear. R^2 for the auxiliary regression of Xs alone is 56 prrcent.

13 One study, Cadsby and Frank (1991), is an exception because it uses experimental evidence. As a result, the explanatory variables which identify various modelling choices made by the conventional tests cannot be defined, and this study is not included in the meta-regression analysis. However, this study is included in the summary descriptive statistics.

14 However, even among studies which rely on rational expectations, there remains a large and significant non-equivalent effect size– $\bar{N}$ = 1.69; t = 2.65; p <.05.

15 A one-tail test is appropriate if we are to give the benefit of the doubt to Barro's prior hypothesis that rejection of RET is associated with misspecification. See the next section on conventional narrative reviews for a more extended discussion.

16 Whether or not RET is valid, the normal approximation used here causes the error variance, σ_e^2 in equation (9.4), for the properly specified meta-regression model to have at least a unit variance, i.e., $\sigma_e^2 \geq 1$.

17 Nearly every study provides some brief discussion of the literature; however, in the course of conducting our meta-analysis, we encountered four papers which are primarily literature reviews plus de Haan and Zelhorst (1988). De Haan and Zelhorst (1988) offer an introductory review which is so extensive and specific, covering forty-nine separate tests of RET, that it must also be considered as a literature review.

18 Relying on anecdotal evidence, or 'natural experiments', only compounds specification biases. Such causal empiricism merely increases specification biases by adding known, omitted variable biases. By selectively choosing which 'natural experiment' to report, an author is guaranteed the appearance of empirical confirmation for his views.

10. The Trouble with Testing: Bubbles, Inertia and Experience in Experimental Asset Markets[*]

Conventional economics assumes that investors possess all the necessary information to buy and sell assets in an efficient and rational manner. 'Rational' expectation theory requires that investors behave as if they know the actual mechanism, which determines prices and can forecast market prices unbiasedly. Although it is widely accepted that such knowledge is denied mere mortals, these assumptions remain an essential component of orthodox economic theory and policy advice.

It is the thesis of this chapter that market participants adopt a less demanding heuristic: *an asset is worth what someone has paid for it*. That is, inertia rather than rationality may dominate the market. Like rational expectations theory, this strategy circumvents the interesting, and extremely difficult, questions concerning what determines prices, and how. Asset traders, however, may be forgiven for avoiding these perplexing problems of price determination in an effort to get on with the practical issues of managing asset portfolios. When investors rely on market valuations, inertia forms a basis for market action without an unrealistic or impossible reliance on maximization, efficient markets, or rational expectations. If agents believe that future prices will be what they were, so they will be. Such behavior is self-fulfilling, thus self-perpetuating, a natural survivor of evolving economic institutions. Inertia is the dominant force in experimental markets (perhaps in actual markets as well), yet it remains difficult to detect by conventional empirical testing.

Speculative bubbles have a long history, their importance unquestioned. There was, for example, the Dutch tulip mania of the seventeenth century, the eighteenth century monetary experiment of John Law's Mississippi company, Japanese property prices, and various stock market booms that catastrophically crashed (e.g., 1929 and 1987). At first blush, any bubble might be considered 'irrational' because it represents, by definition, a systematic overvaluing of an asset.

If it were truly that simple, numerous conspicuous examples of bubbles in stock, real estate, and other markets would provide strong evidence of market irrationality and that would be the end of it. Unfortunately, it is never that simple. If a bubble can be expected to grow at the discount rate indefinitely, it may be deemed 'rational'. In a survey of the economics of bubbles, Camerer (1989) concludes by requesting 'more experiments in which intrinsic value and discount rates are controlled' (p.30). Experiments with inexperienced subjects readily exhibit irrational bubbles (even 'silly bubbles') where price is inversely related to fundamental value (Stanley, 1994). On the other hand, considerable research by Vernon Smith and his colleagues (Smith and Williams, 1992, Van Boening *et al.*, 1993) have found that replication can cause the bubble-crash cycle to dissipate. In these experiments, markets of inexperienced traders form irrational bubbles. But after subjects twice experience the experimental market conditions, price tracks fundamental values as rational expectations suggest (Van Boening *et al.*, 1993). However, these experimental subjects know precisely when the experiment will end and therefore the exact value of the asset at that time. Thus, it would be interesting to learn whether more realistic conditions of uncertain stopping and terminal values induce bubbles in a market of experienced traders. Because 'real' asset markets do not have terminal values, while experimental markets must, experimental design needs to insure subjects do not anchor market values to some experimentally fixed value. The purpose of this chapter is to explore whether a market of experienced traders can generate irrational bubbles and if conventional econometric tests are likely to be fooled. Along the way, I will show how inertia explains both the observed 'irrational' market behavior and the insensitivity of conventional testing.

TESTING RATIONAL BUBBLES

Obviously, prices in a 'rational' or 'efficient' market must reflect intrinsic or 'fundamental' values. An asset market composed of risk neutral, utility-maximizing investors will set prices according to the 'fundamentals'. Or,

$$P_t = \sum_{i=1}^{\infty} E(D_{t+i}|I_t) / (1 + r)^i \qquad (10.1)$$

where: P_t is the current market price

              r is the discount rate

             D_{t+i} is the dividend in period $t+i$

              I_t is the information broadly available at time t.

The right hand side of equation (10.1) is the 'fundamental' price, P^f_t.

Rationality requires the equality of market price and the discounted stream of all expected future returns – conditional, of course, on the available information. However, the above 'Euler equation' holds only if the transversality condition, $\lim_{n->\infty} [1/(1 + r)]^n E(P_{t+n}|I_t) = 0$, is also satisfied. When price is expected to grow by the discount rate, or faster, the rational market price need not closely track the 'fundamentals'. Thus, a rational bubble may foam.

However, all discrepancies between price and fundamentals cannot be deemed rational. To be rational, a bubble must grow at the discount rate. Or,

$$B_t = E(B_{t+1})/(1 + r)$$
and, because $B_{t+1} = E(B_{t+1}) + \varepsilon_{t+1}$,
$$B_{t+1} = (1 + r)B_t + \varepsilon_{t+1} \tag{10.2}$$

where $B_t = P_t - P^f_t$ (Camerer, 1989). In other words, only bubbles that are expected to grow can be rational. Equation (10.2) may be immediately interpreted as a regression model, $B_t = \alpha_0 + \alpha_1 B_{t-1} + \varepsilon_t$, with restrictions $\alpha_0 = 0$, $\alpha_1 = 1+r$, and ε_t independent of ε_{t+1}. Testing these restrictions, then, tests the rationality for observed market bubbles.

In actual markets, the researcher cannot know exactly the fundamental values but must model them as a function of investors' discount rates, levels of risk aversion, and the broad array of public information that influences the future dividends and/or prices. Experimental markets have the advantage of directly controlling fundamentals, thus enabling the researcher to know fundamental prices and the magnitude of any bubble precisely. In our experiment, any observed bubble is irrational. Subjects know that the market is finite lived (maximum $t = 15$). Therefore, the transversality condition must hold, $t \geq 16$. Differences between prices and fundamentals must be random or irrational.

EXPERIMENTAL DESIGN

For several decades, economists have employed experimental methods similar to those used by the other social sciences to simulate and to test market behavior and decision making (Smith, 1986, 1989, 1991). Although experimental analysis has revealed a great deal about price convergence and equilibrium, few studies have investigated markets that do not preclude the effects of speculative trades and hence prohibit bubbles. The design of bubble experiments is forced to impose artificial constraints. Some experiments eliminate the uncertainty concerning the future value of the dividends; others restore initial endowments after brief periods of trading and the identical experiment is repeated over and over. Smith *et al.* (1988) introduce greater realism by employing 15 trading periods and stochastic dividends. However knowledge of the exact terminal value at the end of the trading session can prematurely burst those bubbles which do form and, when combined with experience, foreordain price to converge to fundamental value. Thus, the question of whether bubbles will form in a more realistic, less restrictive, environment remains to be fully explored.

In a series of experiments conducted by Smith and Williams (1992) and Van Boening *et al.* (1993), the bubble-crash cycle is found to dissipate with experience. In these markets of experienced traders, prices converge to the rational expectations result. In our experiment, we use the same experimental design as Smith, Williams, and their colleagues and adopt their definition of experience. However, we introduce greater realism by making the timing and value of termination uncertain. Here, a double oral auction experiment with stochastic dividends and an uncertain overall length is used to investigate if speculative bubbles can develop, whether they will persist as subjects gain experience, and most importantly for the purpose of this book whether conventional empirical testing is likely to detect irrationality or mistake inertia for rationality.

Subjects

Eight undergraduate volunteers from a liberal arts college serve as market traders.[1] Subjects received different endowments of asset shares and cash (measured in 'francs': 1 f = \$.001) worth approximately \$7.00 per hour of their participation. Traders act independently, making profit by receiving dividends or by selling shares of the asset for a premium over its purchase price. Subjects were given different endowments of asset shares and cash and an instruction sheet fully revealing all relevant distributions and trading rules. Several practice-trading sessions were conducted to insure subjects fully understood the trading process and experimental conditions.

Market Design

In these experiments, there is a single asset, which receives stochastic dividends as its only source of 'intrinsic' value. Trading periods last up to five minutes. During these periods, subjects are entirely free to buy or sell. Whenever a buyer and seller agree on price, an exchange takes place. The market price is immediately recorded and displayed for all participants to see. Traders have the option of ending a session prematurely if unanimous consent is given.

A random length of the overall trading session was chosen to permit the formation of speculative bubbles in the confining context of a controlled experiment. It is well known that rational investors will not allow bubbles to form in a market where the asset has a finite life. If the value of the asset is known with certainty at some future point, say time t, rational investors will only be willing to pay the discounted terminal value at time $t-1$. Continuing a backward induction, it is easy to verify that price increases are limited and can never bubble up. Some backward induction is likely to exist even in irrational markets and would tend to anchor potential bubbles to future values when they are fully known. Even when investors hold irrational expectations, experience is likely to make them painfully aware of any certain terminal value. Such anchoring of expectations may explain why Smith *et al.* (1988) found slow convergence to the rational expectations solution (Smith and Williams, 1992) and why Van Boening *et al.* (1993) found that replication dissipates bubbles. Most of the previous experimental research remains unrealistic. A notable exception is Camerer and Weigelt (1991) who solve this problem by giving a constant probability to the asset living beyond the current trading period. However, their results are somewhat contaminated by the subjects' previous participation in an inflation experiment (Camerer, 1989). Even, irrational and shortsighted speculators would eventually learn the terminal value and feel its anchoring effects.

Unlike real asset markets, an experiment must have a finite length. To avoid artificially 'popping' a bubble, a random trading length between 7 and 15 periods was used. Our experiment is similar to that of Camerer and Weigelt (1991) but with a uniform stopping distribution. Subjects were told that the experiment would last somewhere between 7 and 15 periods, inclusively, and that there was an equal probability of ending after any period in this interval (i.e., a uniform stopping distribution). As a further safeguard, traders were told that they would receive a 'buy out' price equal to the 'intrinsic' value of the asset at the termination of the experiment. However, no specific terminal value was stated. In theory, subjects had sufficient public information to calculate the asset's intrinsic value. The randomness of actual dividends may, however, tend to obscure the fundamental value to the market participants. Thus, our experiment avoids anchoring any potential bubble to an obvious, known terminal value and does not, as a result, prematurely bust a speculative bubble before it is given a chance to form.

The entire experiment, lasting between 7 and 15 trading sessions, was repeated three times during a single evening to investigate the effects of experience. In previous experiments, twice experienced traders set prices that usually appeared to be rational.

Dividends

At the end of each trading period, an announcement was made regarding the amount of dividend that each share of the asset receives. To simulate the cyclical component of corporate earnings, subjects were informed that there would be 'good years' and 'bad years' and that the probability of each is 50 percent. The unconditional expected dividend is 180 f but dividends vary according to the distribution displayed in Table 10.1.

Table 10.1: Dividend Distributions

	'good year'		'bad year'	
	D_i	$Prob_i$	D_i	$Prob_i$
	400 f	.5	400 f	.1
	150 f	.4	150 f	.4
	0 f	.1	0 f	.5
	$E(D|G) = 260f$		$E(D|B) = 100f$	

Expectations

After each trading session except the final one, subjects were asked to record their forecast of the price they expected to prevail over the forthcoming trading session. This information permits the direct testing for the rationality of the experimental subjects' expectations.

RESULTS

Irrational Prices and Bubbles

Experiments with inexperienced subjects readily exhibit irrational, even 'silly', bubbles where price is *inversely* related to fundamental value (Van Boening *et al.*, 1993, Stanley, 1994). In our experiments, bubbles continue to form and burst even after participants gain experience (Figures 10.1 and 10.2). To conform to observational studies, bubbles and fundamentals are calculated from *ex post* rational prices, P^*. The *ex post* rational price, P^*, is computed as the sum of the discounted value of the actual future dividends received and the last observed market price for that experiment. Using the exact fundamental values, rather than *ex post* rational prices, only strengthens the evidence against rationality. With experience, market prices appear more closely associated to the fundamentals, but bubbles continue to form in markets of experienced traders.

Figure 10.1: Prices and Fundamentals

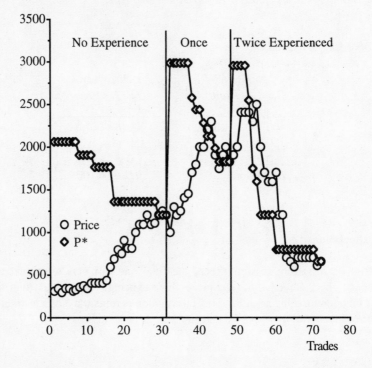

In these experiments, *any* observed *bubble* is *irrational*. Subjects knew that the market was finite lived (maximum $t = 15$). Therefore, the transversality condition must hold, for $t \geq 16$. Differences between prices and fundamentals must either be random or irrational. As illustrated in Figure 10.2, bubbles are clearly not random. There is a strong pattern in the premium subjects are willing to pay.

$$B_t = 29.9 + .93B_{t-1} \qquad R^2 = .93 \qquad (10.3)$$
$$(30.17) \qquad\qquad n = 69$$

(Numbers in the parentheses are t-values; $B_t = P_t - P^*_t$). Or, a runs tests of the experiment most favorable to rationality (twice experienced subjects) finds significant autocorrelation among price premiums ($z = -3.67$; $p < .01$), Figure 10.2. Thus, irrational speculative bubbles may continue to form in experimental markets if asset values are not artificially anchored to a known terminal value.

Figure 10.2: Bubbles

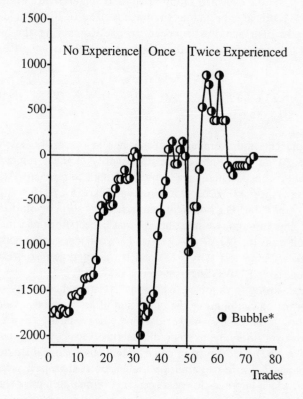

As discussed more fully below, this pattern of speculative bubbles is easily explained by inertia. It is also consistent with 'self-generating trading' and 'information mirages' (Camerer and Weigelt, 1991). When traders overreact to 'uninformative' price movements, price will respond to its own inertia and bubbles result. Below, different aspects of pricing are tested in the conventional manner, often revealing anomalies. Furthermore, each of these anomalies can be shown to be a manifestation of inertia and the insensitivity of conventional econometric tests of market rationality.

Rational Expectations

When expectations are rational,

$$P_{t+1} = \beta_0 + \beta_1 E(P_{t+1} | I_t) + \varepsilon_{t+1} \qquad (10.4)$$

Where $E(P_{t+1} | I_t)$ is the expected future price based on currently available information, I_t. Rational expectations implies that $\beta_0 = 0$, $\beta_1 = 1$, and ε_{t+1} is independently distributed with mean zero. Comparing the price expectation of the average trader to the observed average market price, we find:

$$P_t = 216.73 + .95\, P^e_t \qquad R^2 = .76 \quad \text{D-W} = 1.39 \qquad (10.5)$$
$$(.31)\quad (8.87) \qquad\qquad n = 26$$

where P^e_t represents the average price expectation before the session's trading begins. Oddly, in light of the irrationality of these prices, the hypothesis that these expectations are 'rational' cannot be rejected. Accept H_0: $\beta_0=0$, accept H_0: $\beta_1=1$, accept the joint hypothesis H_0: $\beta_0=0$ and $\beta_1=1$ ($F_{2,26}=2.57$), and the Durbin–Watson test for autocorrelation is inconclusive. Furthermore, we must accept that expectations and market prices have unit roots ($t = \{-1.77\ \&\ -.93\}$) and are cointegrated by both the modified Dickey–Fuller test ($t = -5.25$) and the cointegrating regression Durbin–Watson test (CRDW) (Engle and Yoo, 1987).

Nevertheless, strong-form testing which investigates whether any other available information can improve the prediction of price reveals evidence of irrationality. Past excess market demand (measured by the excess number of bids over offers) helps to predict market price beyond expected price alone ($t = 4.62$). However, in conventional observational studies, it is at best a haphazard affair to find a variable, other than past price or expected price, which improves forecast accuracy. Worse still, most studies do not use observed expectations from surveys but model them using whatever proxies can be invented. In these cases, strong-form testing is unavailable to the researcher, for any variable found useful in predicting price will be assumed to be a part of model that identifies expectations, making rational expectations tautologically self-fulfilling.

Nonetheless, past prices better predict current market prices than do expectations, and they explain expectations better than expectations explain future prices – see Figure 10.3.

$$P_t = 118.8 + .93\, P_{t-1} \qquad R^2 = .86 \qquad \text{D-W} = 1.48 \qquad (10.6)$$
$$(10.63) \qquad\qquad n = 21$$

$$P^e_t = 50.1 + .92 P_{t-1} \qquad R^2 = .99 \qquad \text{D-W} = 1.61 \qquad (10.7)$$
$$(39.07) \qquad\qquad n = 21$$

Figure 10.3: Prices and Expectations

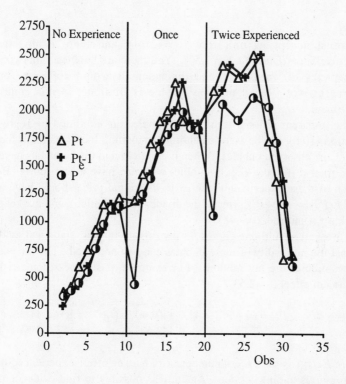

The simple explanation is inertia. Price is approximately what it was last period, and participants grow to expect next period's price to be about what it was last period. Thus, adaptive expectations and simple inertia may give the appearance of rational expectations and go undetected by conventional tests.

Rational Bubbles

Next, we focus on the bubble directly. Given the undeniable existence of bubbles (Figure 10.2), are they rational? A rational bubble must behave according to: $B_{t+1} = (1 + r) B_t + \varepsilon_t$, recall equation (10.2). Because the delay in receiving cash payments was only a matter of minutes, the discount rate, r, may be safely treated as negligible. In this case, a rational bubble will also be a random walk. The regression equation (10.3), reported below for convenience, provides no conventional evidence of irrationality.

$$B_t = 29.9 + .93 B_{t-1} \qquad\qquad R^2 = .93 \qquad\qquad (10.8)$$
$$(30.17) \qquad\qquad n = 69$$

We must accept its unit root (t = −2.14), and there is no sign of autocorrelation (Durbin's h = 1.50). Yet, there are bubbles; otherwise, the discrepancy between price and fundamentals would not be so highly autoregressive. Recall that any bubble is irrational in this controlled experiment.

The apparent rationality of these bubbles, as exhibited by regression equation (10.8), can be ascribed entirely to inertia. Inertia explains the unit root of the observed bubbles. When both prices and fundamentals have unit roots, their difference (i.e., a bubble) will also have a unit root.[2] By the design of these experiments, the *ex post* rational price should have a unit root: $E(P^*_t) = -180 + P^*_{t-1}$ (recall the dividend distribution), and market prices also have a unit root (t = −.48).

However, should one choose to investigate further, statistical evidence against the rationality of these bubbles can be uncovered. The innovations in the bubbles are not random. For example, past excess demand has a significant effect (t = 2.53).

$$dB_t = B_t - B_{t-1} = 41.0 + 10.40\,ExD_{t-1} \qquad R^2 = .11 \qquad (10.9)$$
$$(2.53) \qquad\qquad n = 57 \quad D\text{-}W = 1.88$$

where ExD_{t-1} is the excess number of bids over offers experienced during the previous trading session. Again, it is possible to find evidence of the irrational bubble if the researcher is sufficiently fortuitous to look in the right places. In observational studies, such information may be unavailable or easily overlooked by those expecting to find rationality.

Excess Volatility

In most empirical studies of market rationality, observations of expectations are typically not available to the researcher. Also, any test of a bubble presupposes that the researcher knows the true model of market fundamentals. To finesse these difficulties, tests of price volatility have become important. Market rationality implies that the market price is an unbiased forecast of the perfect foresight, or fundamental, price, and hence its variance is less than the variance of the fundamental price. Because 'rationality' requires that the market price is an unbiased estimate of fundamental price, $P^*_t = P_t + \varepsilon_t$ (where ε_t is an independent random error). Recall that observational studies must rely on the *ex post* rational prices, P^*, to measure the fundamental prices because exact fundamental values are not known as they are in experimental markets. Furthermore, the variance of ε_t must be positive. Thus counterintuitively, the variance of the fundamental price must exceed the variance of the market price.

Because simple volatility tests are fraught with potential problems (Kleidon, 1986a, 1986b), it has become accepted practice to compare the variance of differences in the *ex post* rational price, P^*, from a naïve forecast (say, past market prices) with the variance of the difference in actual price from this naïve forecast. Market rationality implies that the variance of (P^*-P^0), where P^0 is any naïve forecast, will exceed the variance of (P^*-P_t) and also the variance of (P_t-P^0) – Mankiw, Romer and Shapiro (1985). Using past market price as the naïve forecast uncovers no evidence for the irrationality of this experimental market, F= {.91 ; .04}.

The obvious explanation for the poor performance of volatility testing is again inertia. Because the market price is so strongly associated with the past price, the 'naïve forecast', there is little difference to detect. When there is considerable price inertia and past price is used as the naïve forecast, one would expect the volatility tests to confirm rationality whether or not market prices are 'rational' or related to the fundamentals.

Experience and Regression-Based Tests

Volatility tests were developed, in part, to circumvent problems in conventional regression analysis of market rationality (Shiller, 1981b). Regression tests cannot be used if the data are misaligned, and they may be biased if prices are nonstationary. However when carefully considered, regression testing can provide helpful information regarding market rationality.

Market rationality implies that price will be an unbiased forecast of the perfect foresight price,

$$P^*_t = \beta_0 + \beta_1 P_t + \varepsilon_t \qquad\qquad (10.10)$$

and $\beta_0 = 0$ and $\beta_1 = 1$. P_t and ε_t must be uncorrelated, otherwise agents could profit by buying (or selling) as P_t is unusually low (or high). The hypothesis that price will be an unbiased forecast of the *ex post* rational price is disconfirmed by our experiment in three ways.

$$P^*_t = 1315.2 + .36\, P_t \qquad R^2 = .11 \qquad (10.11)$$
$$\quad\ (8.28)\quad (3.00) \qquad\qquad n = 72 \quad \text{D-W} = .21$$

The above regression leads to the rejection of both H_0: $\beta_0 = 0$ and H_0: $\beta_1 = 1$, the joint hypothesis that $\beta_0 = 0$ and $\beta_1 = 1$ ($F_{2,72} = 19.42$; p<. 01), and the independence of the errors. Nor is there any evidence of cointegration by either the modified Dickey–Fuller t =–2.09 or CRDW.

Although regressing *ex post* prices on market prices provides the most powerful test of rationality, some readers might question whether this is an aberration of market inexperience. The effect of experience on trading is confirmed by adding experience dummies ($F_{2,68} = 15.0$; p < .01) and interactions terms ($F_{2,66} = 56.7$; p <. 01).

$$P^* = 2223.9 - .86 P_t + 1946.2 Ex1 - 2174.3 Ex2 - .17 P_t Ex1 + 1.79 P_t Ex2$$
$$\quad (-4.73)\ \ (4.53)\quad\ (-10.35)\qquad (-.57)\qquad\ (8.63)\quad (10.12)$$
$$R^2 = .77 \qquad\qquad\qquad \text{D-W} = .67$$

where *Ex1* represents the once-experienced experiment, *Ex2*, the twice-experienced experiment, and the last two terms are interactions.

To minimize the effect of inexperience on the market, we focus on the most experienced market, which again seems to confirm rationality.

$$P^* = 49.6 + .93\, P_t \qquad R^2 = .62 \quad \text{D-W} = .28 \qquad (10.13)$$
$$\quad (.21)\ \ (6.05) \qquad\qquad\qquad n = 24$$

The appearance of rationality for this twice experienced market experiment is confirmed by accepting, H_0: $\beta_0 = 0$, H_0: $\beta_1 = 1$, and the joint test of these hypotheses ($F_{2,24} = .18$). Yet, there appears to be some problem with autocorrelation. Although both market prices and *ex post* rational prices seem to have unit roots, t ={–.48, –1.99}, there is no evidence of cointegration by either the modified Dickey-Fuller t =–2.42 or CRDW – critical values are –2.99 and .78 (Engle and Yoo, 1987, MacKinnon, 1991).

The evidence that is seemingly supportive to rationality, the twice-experienced experiment, may be attributed to a spurious regression (Granger and Newbold, 1975). *Ex post* rational and market prices are not cointegrated, but they both possess unit roots and therefore are nonstationary. These are the exact conditions that give rise to spurious regressions, and this prognosis is further confirmed by the low Durbin–Watson in equation (10.13) (Granger and Newbold, 1975). Again, inertia is responsible for illusory positive results in conventional tests of rationality.

Overall, regression-based tests do correctly detect the irrationality of this market experiment. However, the same testing strategy may be used to confirm rationality among experienced traders if the researcher does not fully probe the potentially spurious nature of the estimated regression relations.

PRICE INERTIA

Finally, simple inertia, rather than optimizing behavior, explains the apparent statistical support for rationality.

$$P_t = 52.0 + .96\, P_{t-1} \qquad R^2 = .94 \qquad (10.14)$$
$$(32.74) \qquad D\text{-}W = 1.86 \quad n = 69$$

The modified Dickey–Fuller test accepts the unit root of prices (t=–1.33), and there is no sign of autocorrelation (Durbin's h= –.59).

In addition, we have shown that inertia explains:

- Why expectations may appear rational even though they are entirely based on price inertia.
- The failure of volatility testing.
- How spurious regressions may give the erroneous impression that market price is an unbiased forecast of the *ex post* rational price (in the twice-experienced market experiment).

The pivotal role played by inertia in these experiments is consistent with the behavioral inertia hypothesis. These experimental price data accept the unit root of prices along with BIH's restriction that the coefficients on lagged price and twice lagged price sum to one ($F_{1,63}$= 3.05).

When inertia is the principal force in price determination, bubbles would likely form because prices will be slow to respond to changes in the fundamentals. Confirmation of rationality in observational studies of market price may be little more than the manifestation of inertia. '*It is easy to obtain confirmation, or verifications for nearly every theory – if we look for confirmations*' (Popper, 1963, p.36)(emphasis added). Even when market behavior is 'silly' (i.e., market price strongly and inversely correlated with the fundamentals), many conventional tests will confirm its rationality (Stanley, 1994). Conventional tests have low power and often find rationality when there is nothing but inertia.

SUMMARY

First and foremost, these experimental markets quite clearly illustrate that bubbles can form in asset markets even when participants are experienced. In these experiments, experience does affect market behavior, but it does not eliminate irrational bubbles. Conventional economists will likely attribute this odd market phenomenon to the inexperience of the subjects. Although inexperience may explain some 'silly' market behavior, can we honestly say that such inexperience and naïveté does not exist in the 'real' security markets? Smith and Williams (1992) and VanBoening, *et al.* (1993) have found that replication can cause the bubble-crash cycle to dissipate, but our experiment demonstrates that uncertain stopping and terminal values permit bubbles in a market of experienced traders.

Secondly, conventional empirical tests are quite insensitive to grossly irrational pricing. Price expectations may be appear to be rational even though market prices are not. As demonstrated by this experiment, conventional empirical testing can be very insensitive to irrational pricing, especially when prices exhibit substantial inertia (Linter, 1981, Camerer, 1989, Stanley, 1994). This experiment illustrates how conventional econometric tests may misidentify self-fulfilling behavior as 'rational'.

Finally, these experimental markets show how market prices may be 'near rational' (in the sense that they are self-fulfilling) yet very 'irrational' (in the sense that they are unrelated to intrinsic value). 'Rationality', in this sense, means only that expectations tend to be self-perpetuating (i.e., Nash 'rational'). Inertia, habit, and fads are well known to be self-fulfilling behaviors, and they are sufficient to generate the observed experimental prices. Yet, this simple behavioral dynamics need not be 'rational' in the sense that it is the result of some optimizing strategy or efficient use of information. As shown in this study, inertia alone is sufficient to account for the observed patterns of price expectations and experimental market prices. Inertia causes bubbles to appear rational and conventional tests to find 'rationality' in irrational prices and expectations.

NOTES

* From the *Journal of Socio-Economics*, **26,** 1997, 611-25.
1 Student participation in economic experiments is generally accepted as long as their monetary incentives are sufficiently generous to insure behavior analogous to real market traders. The more serious limitation of this experiment is related to the modest sample sizes resulting from trading among only eight subjects. The experiment's economical size is entirely the consequence of limited financial support. However, it should be noted that the statistical results reported below are highly significant, a fact that is all the more remarkable given the handicap of the small sample sizes.
2 An exception can occur if prices and fundamentals are cointegrated. However, there is no evidence of cointegration of prices and fundamentals in this experimental study, see equation (10.11).

11.   Dénouement: What's the Difference?

In the previous chapters, a theory and methodology of economic time series are presented and derived from epistemological constraints. A broad range of empirical findings from experiments, meta-analyses, and more conventional econometric studies illustrate the advantages of this theory and econometric methodology. Consumption, inflation, prices, GNP, and the effects of deficit spending all corroborate the behavioral inertia hypothesis. The importance of inertia is found in experimental assets markets along with the empirical literature on Ricardian equivalence and the Lucas critique. The behavioral inertia hypothesis identifies the distinctive features of these challenging time series. Nonetheless, conventional economists are likely to remain skeptical of the merits of the approach offered here. An array of orthodox criticisms is easy to anticipate and may be roughly summarized as 'if it's not optimal, can it be economics?' and 'so what's new?'

IF IT'S NOT OPTIMAL, CAN IT BE ECONOMICS?

> (T)he insistence that economic phenomena be treated by a single unified theory – equilibrium theory in particular – has no general justification. Whether equilibrium theory is the best way to proceed is an empirical question; and there is little reason to reject other approaches because they cannot be a unified theory of the economic realm.
>
> – Hausman (1992, p.247)

Orthodox economics is largely defined by its commitment to methodological individualism, *i.e.*, to individual utility maximization (or the equivalent). Theories which are not derived from this 'fundamental rationality' postulate, explicitly or implicitly, are often dismissed by mainstream economists as 'noneconomics', relegated to some lesser social science. Or, they are not considered to be theory at all, because 'theory' is equated to the neoclassical equilibrium theory. Individual utility maximization and its concomitant equilibrium analysis serve as the demarcation criterion for orthodox economics.

Conventional economics is like a medieval castle. It is isolated from outside advancements and influences by defining itself to be a 'separate science' (Hausman, 1992). Defensive strategies, such as the conventional use of auxiliary hypotheses (Chapter 5), serve only to deflect criticism, thereby bringing stagnation to economics. For example, this separation of economics from other fields of inquiry has allowed orthodox economists to dogmatically defend individual utility maximization from decades of overwhelming empirical evidence of intransitivity (Hausman, 1992). Yet, to what end? Only through criticism, whether empirical or otherwise, can there be progress. It is deeply ironic that a field whose ideal of economic progress involves the free exchange of goods and services across national boundaries is so *protectionistic* when it comes the exchange of ideas across artificial disciplinary boundaries.[1]

I could point out, as many others have done before, that maximization is not possible, or even relevant, when there are genuine 'uncertainties' confronting the decision maker or when the outcomes of the decision makers' actions are profoundly interdependent (recall game theory). The knowledge of economic agents can be no better than our best knowledge. All scientific knowledge is uncertain, and other spheres of knowledge are less certain. I share the Popperian view that 'knowledge is unfathomed and unfathomable, and that we do not know what we are saying or what we are doing' (Bartley, 1989, p. 209). Humans can grasp only the finite. 'There is an infinity of unforeseeable nontrivial statements belonging to the informative content of any theory. . . . We can therefore never know or understand all the implications of any theory, or its full significance' (Popper, 1976, p. 28). The importance of inertia and caprice emerges from an understanding of these limits to human knowledge.

In contrast, orthodox optimization theory requires 'full knowledge of the data needed to succeed in this attempt' (Friedman, 1953, p.21). Take, for example, the seemingly trivial data of prices, perhaps the price of an automobile. No one possesses the requisite 'full knowledge' of prices necessary to maximize some continuous, twice-differentiable utility function. In our modern market economy, there are simply too many relevant prices for the same or substitute product varying over time and geography.[2] Furthermore, the process of collecting price information is likely to change the prices. First, time passes, and prices are dynamic. Secondly, bargaining power may be created by such a search, which may induce the salesman to offer a better deal (i.e., to lower his price). Lastly, unknowable future prices are almost always relevant to present utility maximization, because future consumption is usually a good substitute for current consumption. The very notion of what the relevant prices are or are not is uncertain. Nonetheless, prices are the simplest, most publicly available, data on the economy.

> (T)he neoclassical equilibrium economics that dominates many professional departments of economics is incompatible with the theory of objective knowledge. Such economics tends to focus on situations where all knowledge is already known to all concerned parties. Or it may even assume that all parties know in advance what they are ignorant of, and have *deliberately chosen* whatever existing ignorance they enjoy following a cost–benefit analysis of the cost of remedying it.[3]
>
> – Bartley (1989, p. 216)

However, such discussions are likely to serve little purpose. Numerous books and essays have already made this case, but 'rational maximization' remains at the core of the orthodox economist's belief system (Heilbroner, 1988). Thus, neoclassical economists are unlikely to be swayed. Talk about inertia, belief systems are notoriously stubborn.

One purpose of the approach advocated here is to make room for explanations of economic phenomena that are not explicitly based on individual utility maximization. There is no justification – philosophical, methodological or empirical – to prohibit alternative theories of economic phenomena (Hausman, 1992). My theory of behavioral inertia does not preclude conventional, neoclassical contributions. Considerations of equilibrium and maximization can form an important part of the behavioral inertia hypothesis, recall the $X_t \beta$ term. And, if it is only appearances that matter, the behavioral inertia hypothesis may be derived from an individual utility maximization problem (recall the Appendix of Chapter 3). Contrary to economic orthodoxy, satisfactory explanations of economic phenomena are entirely independent of optimal decision making.

Against the orthodox view, the perspective taken here is that considerations of individual utility maximization are irrelevant. Because there are limits to human knowledge, there is behavioral inertia in economic data. These epistemological constraints precede and preclude individual utility maximization, which requires 'full knowledge' at some level. If 'economic' analysis must be based on individual utility maximization, then it is time for a 'noneconomic' science of economic phenomena. Actual economic phenomena and events in our modern 'global' economy are simply too important to continue to be thus ignored.

SO WHAT'S NEW?

Orthodox economists are likely to point out that the use of lags and differences in econometric applications represents nothing new. Inertia has been long recognized in empirical economic research and increasingly so in theoretical economics – for example, Dixit (1989, 1992), Pindyck (1991) Drakopoulos (1994), and Conlon and Liu (1997). VAR, cointegration, error correction models and time series methods, in general, underscore the importance of time series dynamics in applied econometrics. By their very nature, time series statistical techniques broadly allow for inertia and thereby address similar issues to the behavioral inertia hypothesis. So what's new?

At the greatest level of generality, little, if anything, is 'new' in the behavioral inertia hypothesis. The significance of inertia has long been acknowledged, in physics since the seventeenth century, Galileo, and in the social sciences since the eighteenth century with Hume's *Human Nature*. No claim of the discovery of the ideas of inertia or caprice, nor their application to economics has been made in this book or is intended. The purpose of this book is to elevate their importance and encourage their wider, more explicit, use. Rather than *ad hoc* appendages of applied econometrics, inertia and caprice should be made an explicit and material part of economic theory. Would that not be 'new'? It should be pointed out that a significant number of empirical studies ignore inertia in economic time series because it has not been regarded as an economic theory. For example, among the twenty-seven econometric studies of Ricardian equivalence, twelve did not use lags, fifteen did not difference the data, and five studies did neither. Although such examples are thankfully becoming less frequent, they may still be found throughout the empirical literature. And, is it reasonable to expect further progress when inertia is antithetical to one of the dominant economic views – the new classical school?

So what's new? That behavioral inertia is a theory (or 'law') of economics as significant and as essential as the laws of supply and demand. That inertia is prior to individual utility maximization and 'rationality'. Inertia is the human, Humean response to fundamental epistemological constraints, which are applicable to all actual economic decision problems. The difference is a matter of emphasis. This book seeks to integrate various haphazard, *ad hoc*, practices into a coherent general theory of economic time series.

Some economists may also discount these econometric results because they do not use all of the most recent advances in econometric theory and estimation. True enough. However, this is not an oversight but rather an intended characteristic of my philosophical-methodological position. The conventional notion that for every potential econometric problem there is a technical solution (the more recent and more sophisticated the better) is mistaken and likely to be counterproductive. For example, the past use of technical remedies for autocorrelation (e.g., Hildreth–Lu and Cochrane–Orcutt procedures) merely masked the misspecification (nonstationarity, omitted variables, improper functional forms) which are the genuine cause of the symptom of autocorrelation found in regressions of economic time series. Such technical fixes for 'autocorrelation' do not solve inference problems; rather they worsen them. After employing the recommended technical remedy, the econometric model remains misspecified, because the underlying problems are unaffected, and generate erroneous inferences. Evidence that the error distribution is not i.i.d. is a *symptom* that we are relying upon the wrong econometric model rather than a problem that needs some remedy. These symptoms are not somehow 'fixed' by a more sophisticated estimator that incorporates some other information or variance–covariance matrix.

Nor can the most recent econometric advances avoid this 'illusion of technique' (Chapter 5). When using any of the more advanced estimation procedures (whether nonlinear, full-information maximization likelihood, GLS, or any of the latest time series techniques), the researcher can never know whether the complication treated by the chosen technique is an incidental manifestation of deeper misspecification or not. Technique is neither theory nor explanation. The pretest-specification dilemma evades all technical solution. Econometric techniques, no matter how advanced, can only treat symptoms without knowing the underlying cause. Because there are an infinite number of potential estimation procedures, the illusion of technique reinforces the dogmatic defense of conventional theory. What is needed is testable theory, theory which may be rigorously tested, not yet another technique.

Still many econometricians will discount the behavioral inertia hypothesis because it is a very simple linear regression model. The approach taken here does not eschew more sophisticated models when appropriate. However, rather than a box of tools always at the ready, alternative models need to be treated as theories to be tested and rejected when the data demand (recall Chapter 5). The simple linear form of the behavioral inertia hypothesis is used because it is all that is required to explain a broad array of economic phenomena. Furthermore, such simplicity has additional merit. Simple regression models are easier to test and therefore more susceptible to empirical criticism and falsification. Simplicity is to be prized when it reflects a theory's transparency and testability. Because the behavioral inertia hypothesis relies upon no advance in econometric technique nor advancement of mathematical analysis, it could have (and should have) been offered decades ago. If it's not new, not the most sophisticated or most rigorous theory, what good is it?

SUMMARY

The merit of an economic theory should not be measured by the sophistication of the mathematics used in its derivation or of the statistical techniques employed in its estimation. Rather it is the theory's ability to solve empirical puzzles and to explain economic phenomena which should serve as its metric. The more that can be explained with less, the better. So what does this approach accomplish?

First consider the empirical explanatory power of the behavioral inertia hypothesis. Econometric analyses of consumption prices, inflation, GNP, and the effect of deficit spending all corroborate it. And, there is the experimental evidence.

Experimental Evidence

Inertia is found to be the principal force in experimental asset markets. Prices are more closely linked to inertia than they are to the fundamentals with correlation coefficients of .97 and .33, respectively. Past prices may also be seen to drive expectations. In these markets, the observed irrational bubbles are also a function of inertia, and inertia can fully explain the misleading evidence of market rationality found by many conventional econometric tests. That inertia may be easily confused with rationality by conventional testing is an important and powerful finding which can explain many of the ambiguous and 'mixed' results found in the literature.

From this research, the importance of inertia in price determination emerges. Inertia may actually be the dominant force in a strictly empirical theory of value. In markets of inexperienced traders, value may be governed by little more than the heuristic, 'an asset is worth what someone has paid for it', because prices are unrelated, sometimes inversely related, to the 'fundamentals'. Yet, prices remain closely linked to their past, both in times series of actual prices and in experimental markets with experienced traders. Although one might hope that experienced economic agents in the 'real world' act more sensibly, can anyone deny the importance of inertia when assessing the recent high value of US stocks? Consider, in particular, the high-priced Internet companies for which there is no 'rational' expectation of any future profits. What else could be the basis for the observed prices of such stocks?

Meta-analysis

Meta-analyses of past empirical studies also disclose the consequence of inertia in empirical tests of economic hypotheses. Inertia plays a significant role in tests of both the Lucas critique and Ricardian equivalence. How an econometric model filters out, or fails to filter out, inertia makes a crucial difference in what the researcher will find. Tests of the Lucas critique are more likely to be supportive the less an econometric model resembles the behavioral inertia hypothesis, and the BIH model of consumption directly rejects Ricardian equivalence.

GNP

In addressing GNP 'paradoxical' time series structure, the behavioral inertia hypothesis distinguishes itself clearly from technical statistical approaches to economic time series. Recall that Rose (1986) identified several puzzles concerning the highly unlikely shape of GNP's time series. Of course, many different time series statistical *techniques* (e.g. ARIMA, VAR, etc.) can be used to represent GNP or any other time series, no matter how complex. There are, after all, an infinite number of parameters upon which to draw. However, it is GNP's simplicity – a simplicity that has no conventional theoretical or technical basis – that is so puzzling and yet is easily explained by the behavioral inertia hypothesis's postulated dynamics.

In particular, inertia, which is at the center of the behavioral inertia hypothesis, gives GNP its unit root, Rose's first paradox. Secondly, the low order of GNP's autoregressivity that Rose sees as paradoxical, AR(1) and AR(2), is a direct implication of the behavioral inertia hypothesis (recall the derivations in Chapters 2, 6 and 7). Finally, the behavioral inertia hypothesis unravels why both the quarterly and annual GNP time series have the same ARIMA representation, with the same autoregressive coefficients.

Consumption

The behavioral inertia hypothesis resolves the famous consumption puzzle and accounts for consumption behavior during exceptional periods – the Great Depression and the Second World War. The behavioral inertia hypothesis is well corroborated through specification testing and tests of the behavioral inertia hypothesis's restrictions. It rationalizes the ubiquitous autocorrelations and misspecifications found in many other econometric consumption models and account for both the apparent successes and failures of rival theories, *e.g.* the permanent income hypothesis and error correction models. The behavioral inertia hypothesis model of consumption also forms a well-specified basis upon which to test Ricardian equivalence, the results of which are quite closely predicted by the meta-regression model of Ricardian equivalence (Chapter 9).

Together these empirical findings constitute a strong corroboration of behavioral inertia, reminiscent of Friedman's *A Theory of the Consumption Function*. However, when combined with the well-known anomalies of the permanent income hypothesis, the behavioral inertia hypothesis may be interpreted as PIH's falsifying hypothesis. Thus a second pattern emerges from this research. the behavioral inertia hypothesis often serves as a falsifying hypothesis for accepted conventional theories.

Inflation

Similarly, an econometric analysis of prices and inflation corroborates the behavioral inertia hypothesis and becomes a falsifying hypothesis to the widely accepted natural rate hypothesis (or NAIRU or the expectations-augmented Phillips curve). Inflation embodies the same time series structure found in consumption. As in previous applications, the BIH model of inflation is corroborated by specification and restriction testing and resolves the anomalous behavior of prices during the 1970s, the Great Depression, and Western Europe since the 1970s. After inertia is filtered from price data, a clear link between inflation and the *change* in the unemployment rate is exposed. This dependence of inflation upon the change in unemployment engenders 'full hysteresis' and overturns both old Keynesian and new classical views on policy. When demand grows moderately faster than supply, a 'free lunch' of lower unemployment and lower inflation is possible (witness the US, 1997-1999).

These empirical results clearly illustrate the generality and flexibility of the behavioral inertia analysis. Not only does it fit the data well, but the behavioral inertia hypothesis also makes sense of the mixed record of empirical support and anomaly found for so many conventional economic theories.[4] In this way, it serves as a viable falsifying hypothesis for 'rationality' and a number of conventional theories. In particular, the rational expectations hypothesis – especially in its guise as efficient markets, Ricardian equivalence, the permanent income hypothesis, and the expectations-augmented Phillips curve – may be considered empirically falsified and superseded.

Of course, defenders of orthodox theory will no doubt remind us of the past supportive evidence and suggest that it is too large and diverse to be so easily dismissed. Easily dismissed? No conventional economic theory has ever been easily dismissed, or dismissed at all, for empirical considerations.

The time is long overdue for accepted economic theories to be substantively amended or overturned by some empirical findings if the scientific affectation of the economics professional is to be taken seriously.

My study reconciles how conventional econometric testing could quite easily mistake inertia for rationality. This is exactly what happened in our experimental markets. Such mistakes are all the more likely to be repeated by conventional econometric analysis where models are frequently misspecified and specification tests have low power. Evidence against 'rational expectations' is everywhere, if one is receptive to it. As seen in the literature on the Lucas critique and Ricardian equivalence, 'mixed support' evaporates when it is more carefully investigated or when evidence of proper specification is required.

Epistemological Constraints and Econometric Advance

As the laws of supply and demand are derived from budget and resource constraints,[5] the behavioral inertia hypothesis is the consequence of inescapable epistemological constraints. Hume's disproof of a justifiable induction infuses inertia into social systems. Both Dostoevsky's uncertainty principle and the Duhem–Quine thesis cause error distributions and uncertainty to be an integral part of economic theory. To solve the pretest-specification dilemma and to permit genuine empirical inquiry in economics, an econometric methodology is developed and applied. No new statistical technique can have such power.

Lastly, our meta-analysis finds that econometric applications need not be hamstrung by the variability of the parameters of its models (i.e., the Lucas critique). Empirical evidence casts doubt on the validity of the Lucas critique and thereby removes yet another threat to a genuinely empirical economics.

CONCLUSION

The behavioral inertia hypothesis provides a general framework with which to understand and to model economic time series as well as specific theories of consumption, inflation and prices. It seriously addresses Hume's critique by not assuming that economic agents know what they cannot know and, following Hume, makes custom and habit pivotal. Individual utility maximization assumes the impossible, that agents have full knowledge of all of the necessary magnitudes, or parameters of central location when rational expectations are also assumed. Without a valid inductive principle, such knowledge is impossible, and individual utility maximization is irrelevant. Instead, human economic agents must employ some imperfect heuristic as evidenced by the observed inertia of economic and financial time series.

Three general heuristic strategies are available. First, economic decision makers may behave randomly, i.e., the error term in the behavioral inertia hypothesis. From the short run individual perspective, such behavior is the very definition of 'irrational'. Yet, even random behavior may serve a useful purpose. As genetic mutations and random environmental adaptations are occasionally good for the evolution of a species, random individual behavior may lead to social and economic advance. Secondly, a sensible response to uncertainty is to follow custom and habits, i.e., inertia. Actions which were successful in the past, more or less, should remain so in the future, at least for a while. Although such an inductive disposition cannot be justified, recall Hume, it too can serve a useful evolutionary function. Like genotype or one's DNA, inertia preserves past successful decisions and adaptations. As discussed previously, learning and the growth of scientific knowledge requires some persistence. Lastly, one might try to adjust one's decisions sensibly in response to changes in circumstances, i.e., the $X_t\beta$ term in the behavioral inertia hypothesis. In this way, the more conventional forces of supply and demand may also be accommodated. The behavioral inertia hypothesis is the combination of all three heuristic approaches, and economic time series may be seen as their weighted average.

Although such heuristics do not support usual normative pronouncements of *laissez faire* policies inherent in individual utility maximization, they are empirically more defensible. So what's the difference? Explaining actual economic data and events as observed is the difference, and *vive la différence*!

Orthodox economics assumes that man is rationally stupid – full of facts, perhaps, but incapable of genuine learning. True innovation and invention, however, cannot come from human Turing machines. They flow from capricious individuals who would not make the great sacrifices required if their decisions were based upon rational calculation of self interest alone. The wish to be different, to create something new and unique, is not 'rational'; but it does have great, long run economic and evolutionary value.

Against the conventional economic view, I believe that people are intelligent, capable of genuine learning and innovation. Contrary to the orthodox view, the behavior of economic agents is dominated by inertia and caprice, both of which yield to modelling and to prediction. If our purpose is to study economic man, we have no genuine choice but to incorporate the stochastic manifestations of economic behavior into our most fundamental economic theories.

Man is not a computer.   Nor can man survive by rational calculation alone. Behavioral economic man is an intelligent panoply of hierarchy and recursion, of inertia and caprice.   People are intelligent – capable of genuine learning, of innovation, and caprice.

NOTES

1   Economists adopt a strong mercantilist policy regarding their theories and profession. Conventional economic ideas are readily exported, e.g., game theory or the economic imperialism of Gary Becker, while ideas from other disciplines are embargoed (i.e., Hausman's 'separate science'), and economists who attempt to smuggle in contraband ideas are exiled from orthodoxy and its journals, or at least heavily taxed.   Most modern economists cannot believe that the mercantilists could be so ignorant about the operation of the economy and the benefits from free trade. Yet their own attitudes are very different when they are thought to serve professional self-interests.   Perhaps seventeenth century merchants were not so unenlightened after all.

2   Neither can search theory, the orthodox response, fill this gap, for search theory assumes knowledge of the parameters of the relevant distributions.   Such parameters are themselves unknown and unknowable. Although we can always bury our ignorance a level deeper by postulating a theory of the unknown that is based upon some other entirely presumed knowledge, our full ignorance remains, though perhaps better hidden.

3   Search theory as viewed by a philosopher of science.

4   Preliminary analysis of exchange rate movements also conforms to the behavioral inertia hypothesis's pattern.

5   As is well known, the law of demand cannot be derived from individual utility maximization. However, it does follow directly from the budget constraint when consumers buy randomly (Becker, 1962).

References

Abramowitz, M. and Stegun, I.A. (eds) (1964), *Handbook of Mathematical Functions with Formulas, Graphs and Mathematical Tables*, Washington, D.C., U.S. Department of Commerce.

Akerlof, G. and Yellen, J. (1985), 'A Near-Rational Model for the Business Cycle with Wage and Price Inertia', *Quarterly Journal of Economics, Supplement*, **100**, 823-38

Akerlof, G.A., Dickens, W.T. and Perry, G.L. (1996), 'The Macroeconomics of Low Inflation', *Brookings Papers on Economic Activity*, **1**, 1-59.

Alogoskoufis, G. and Smith, R. (1991), 'On Error Correction Models, Specification, Interpretation, Estimation', *Journal of Economic Surveys*, **5**, 97-128.

Armstrong, J. S. (1984), 'Forecasting with Econometric Methods: Folklore versus Fact.' pp. 19-34, in S. Makridakis (ed.), *The Forecasting Accuracy of Major Time Series Methods*, New York, Wiley.

Baaijens, S.R., Nijkamp, P. and VanMonfort, K. (1998), 'Explanatory Meta-Analysis for the Comparison and Transfer of Regional Tourist Income Multipliers', *Regional Studies*, **32**, 839-849.

Bacharach, M. (1989), 'Expecting and Affecting', *Oxford Economic Papers* **41**, 339-355.

Banerjee, A., *et al.* (1986), 'Exploring Equilibrium Relationships in Econometrics Through Static Models: Some Monte Carlo Evidence', *Oxford Bulletin of Economics and Statistics*, **48**, 253-277.

Barrett, W. (1958), *Irrational Man*, New York, Doubleday.

Barro, R.J. (1974), 'Are Government Bonds Net Wealth', *Journal of Political Economy*, **82**, 1095-1117.

Barro, R.J. (1978), 'Unanticipated Money, Output, and the Price Level in the United States', *Journal of Political Economy*, **27**, 1-26.

Barro, R.J. (1989), 'The Ricardian Approach to Budget Deficits', *Journal of Economic Perspectives*, 37-54.

Bartley, W.W. (1989), 'Unfathomed Knowledge in a Bottle', in F. D'Agostino and I.C. Jarvie (eds) *Freedom and Rationality: Essays in Honor of John Watkins, Boston Studies in the Philosophy of Science.* Dordrecht, Kluwer Academic Press.

Baumol, W.J. (1991), 'Towards a Newer Economics: The Future Lies Ahead!' *Economic Journal,* **101**, 1-8.

Becker, G.S. (1962), 'Irrational Behavior and Economic Theory', *Journal of Political Economy,* **60**, 1-13.

Bernheim, D. (1987), 'Ricardian Equivalence: An Evaluation of Theory and Evidence', in S. Fischer (ed.) *NBER Macroeconomic Annual: 1987,* Cambridge, Mass., MIT Press.

Binmore, K. (1987), 'Modeling Rational Players: Part I', *Economics and Philosophy,* **3**, 179-214.

Binmore, K. (1988), 'Modeling Rational Players: Part II', *Economics and Philosophy,* **4**, 9-55.

Blanchard, O.J. (1981), 'What is Left of the Multiplier Accelerator?' *American Economic Review Papers and Proceedings,* **71**, 150-154.

Blanchard, O.J. (1984), 'The Lucas Critique and the Volcker Deflation,' *American Economic Review,* **74**, 211-15.

Blanchard, O. J. and Katz, L.F. (1997), 'What We know and What We Don't Know About the Natural Rate of Unemployment', *Journal of Economic Perspectives,* **11**, 51-72.

Blaug, M. (1980), *The Methodology of Economics: Or How Economists Explain,* Cambridge, Cambridge University Press.

Blaug, M. (1992), *The Methodology of Economics: Or How Economists Explain,* 2nd ed. Cambridge, Cambridge University Press.

Boland, L.A. (1979), 'A Critique of Friedman's Critics, *Journal of Economic Literature,* **17**, 503-522.

Boland, L.A. (1982), *The Foundations of Economic Method,* London, George Allen & Urwin.

Brown, J. (1987), 'An Empirical Analysis of Time Series Consumption Behavior Under Ricardian Equivalence', Unpublished Dissertation, Brown University.

Buchanan, J.M. (1976), 'Barro on the Ricardian Equivalence Theorem', *Journal of Political Economy,* **84**, 337-49.

Bunting, D. (1989), 'The Consumption Function Paradox', *Journal of Post Keynesian Economics,* **11**, 347-59.

Bush, R. and Mosteller, F. (1955), *Stochastic Models for Learning,* New York, John Wiley and Sons.

Button, K.J. (1995), 'What Can Meta-Analysis Tell Us About the Implications of Transport?' *Regional Studies,* **29**, 507-17.

Button, K.J. and Kerr, J. (1996), 'The Effectiveness of Traffic Restraint Policies: A Simple Meta-Regression Model', *International Journal of Transport Economics,* **23**, 213-225.

Cadsby, C. and Frank, M. (1991), 'Experimental Tests of Ricardian Equivalence', *Economic Inquiry,* **29**, 645-64.

Caldwell, B. (1982), *Beyond Positivism: Economic Methodology in the Twentieth Century.* London, George Allen & Unwin.

Caldwell, B. (1994), 'Two Proposals for the Recovery of Economics Practice', in R.E. Backhouse (ed.) *New Direction in Economic Methodology,* London, Routledge.

Camerer, C. (1989), 'Bubbles and Fads in Asset Prices', *Journal of Economic Surveys,* **3**, 3-41.

Camerer, C. and Weigelt, K. (1991), Information Mirages in Experimental Asset Markets. *Journal of Business,* **64**, 463-493.

Campbell, D.T. (1974), 'Evolutionary Epistemology', pp. 413-463 in P.A. Schillp (ed.) *The Philosophy of Karl Popper,* LaSalle, Open Court.

Campbell, D.T. (1987), 'Blind Variation and Selective Retention in Creative Thought as in Other Knowledge Processes', pp. 91-114 in G. Radnitzky and W.W.Bartley (eds) *Evolutionary Epistemology, Theory of Rationality, and the Sociology of Knowledge,* La Salle, Open Court.

Campbell, J. and Deaton, A. (1989), 'Why is Consumption so Smooth?' *Review of Economic Studies,* **56**, 357-74.

Campbell, J. and Mankiw, N.G. (1990), 'Permanent Income, Current Income, and Consumption', *Journal of Business and Economic Statistics,* **8**, 265-79.

Carlson, J.A. (1977a), 'A Study of Price Forecasts', *Annals of Economics and Social Measuremen*t, **6**, 749-54.

Carlson, J.A. (1977b), 'Short-Term Interest Rates As Predictors of Inflation: Comment', *American Economic Review,* **67**, 469-75.

Chirinko, R.S. (1988), 'Business Tax Policy, the Lucas Critique, and Lessons from the 1980's', *American Economic Review,* **78**, 206-210.

Chow, G.C. (1960), 'Tests for Equality between Sets of Coefficients in Two Linear Regressions', *Econometrica,* **28**, 532-553.

Christ, C.F. (1951), 'A Test of an Econometric Model of the United States, 1921-1947', pp. 35-107, in *Conference on Business Cycles,* New York, National Bureau of Economic Research.

Christiano, L.J., Eichenbaum, M. and Marshall, D. (1991), 'Permanent Income Hypothesis Revisited', *Econometrica,* **59**, 397-423.

Cohen, J. (1969), *Statistical Power Analysis in the Behavioral Sciences,* New York, Academic Press.

Conlon, J.R. and Liu, C.Y. (1997), 'Can More Frequent Changes Lead to Price Inertia? Nonneutralities in a State-Dependent Pricing Context', *International Economic Review*, **38**, 893-914.

Cooper, R.L. (1972), 'The Predictive Performance of Quarterly Econometric Models of the United States'. pp.813-926, in B.G. Hickman (ed.), *Econometric Models of Cyclical Behavior*, New York, Columbia University Press.

Copas, J.B. (1983), 'Regression, Prediction and Shrinkage', *Journal of the Royal Statistical Society, B*, **45**, 311-54.

Cross, R. (1982), 'The Duhem–Quine Thesis, Lakatos and the Appraisal of Theories in Macroeconomics', *The Economic Journal*, **90**, 320-340.

Cushing, M.J. (1991), 'Under-Sensitivity and Under-Volatility in Aggregate Consumption Expenditures', *Journal of Macroeconomics*, **13**, 1-24.

Cuthbertson, K. and Taylor, M.P. (1990), 'The Case of the Missing Money and the Lucas Critique,' *Journal of Macroeconomics,* **12**, 432-54.

Darnell, A.C. and Evans, J.L. (1990), *The Limits of Econometrics*, Aldershot, Hants, Edward Elgar.

Darrat, A. (1989), 'Fiscal Deficits and Long-term Interest Rates: Further Evidence from Annual Data', *Southern Economic Journal*, **56**, 363-74.

Davidson, J.E.H., Hendry, D.F., Srba, F. and Yeo, S. (1978), 'Econometric Modelling of the Aggregate Time-Series Relationship between Consumers' Expenditures and Income in the United Kingdom', *Economic Journal*, **88**, 661-692.

Davidson, R. and MacKinnon, J.G.(1981), 'Several Tests for Model Specification in the Presence of Alternative Hypotheses', *Econometrica* **49**, 781-793.

Davidson, R. and MacKinnon, J.G. (1985), 'Heteroskedasticity-Robust Tests in Regression Directions', *Annals de l'INSEE,* **59/60**, 183-218.

Davidson, R. and MacKinnon, J.G.(1990), 'Specification Tests Based on Artificial Regressions', *Journal of the American Statistical Association* **85**, 220-227.

Deaton, A.S. (1987), 'Life-Cycle Models of Consumption: Is the Evidence Consistent with the Theory?' in T.F. Bewley (ed.) *Advances in Econometrics: Fifth World Congress*, vol. 2. Cambridge, Cambridge University Press.

Dewey, J. (1960), *On Experience Nature and Freedom*, New York, Liberal Arts Press.

Dixit, A. (1989), 'Entry and Exit Decisions Under Uncertainty', *Journal of Political Economy,* **97**, 620-38.

Dixit, A. (1992), 'Investment and Hysteresis', *Journal of Economic Perspectives,* **6**, 107-132.

Dornbusch, R. and Fisher, S. (1990), *Macroeconomics*, New York, McGraw- Hill.

Dostoevsky, F.(1864; 1956), 'Notes from Underground', pp. 52-82 in W. Kaufmann (ed.) *Existentialism from Dostoevsky to Sartre*, New York, World Publishing.

Doucouliagos, C. (1995), 'Worker Participation in Labor-Managed and Participatory Capitalist Firms: A Meta-Analysis', *Industrial and Labor Relations Review*, **49**, 58-77.

Dow, S.C. (1997), 'Mainstream Economic Methodlogy', *Cambridge Journal of Economics*, **31**, 73-93.

Drakopoulos, S.A. (1994), 'Hierarchical Choice in Economics', *Journal of Economics Surveys* , **8**, 133-53.

Duesenberry, J.S. (1949), *Income, Savings and the Theory of Consumer Behavior*, Cambridge, Mass., Harvard University Press.

Duhem, P.(1906: 1954), *The Aim and Structure of Physical Theory*, Princeton, Princeton University Press.

Enders, W. and Lee, B. (1990), 'Current Account and Budget Deficits: Twins or Distant Cousins', *Review of Economics and Business,* **72**, 373-81.

Engle, R.F. and Granger, C.W.J. (1987), 'Co-integration and Error Correction: Representation, Estimation ands Testing', *Econometrica,* **55**, 251-76.

Engle, R.F. and Yoo, B.S. (1987), 'Forecasting and Testing in Co-integrated Systems', *Journal of Econometrics,* **35**, 143-59.

Engle, R.F. and Yoo, B.S. (1991), 'Cointegrated Economic Time Series: An Overview with New Results', in R.F. Engle and C.W.J. Granger (eds.) *Long-Run Economic Relationships: Reading in Cotintegration,* Oxford, Oxford University Press, 237-66.

Epstein, L and Zin, S. (1989), 'Substitution, Risk Aversion, and the Temporal Behavior of Consumption and Asset Returns: A Theoretical Framework', *Econometrica*, **57**, 937-969.

Epstein, L and Zin, S. (1991), 'Substitution, Risk Aversion, and the Temporal Behavior of Consumption and Asset Returns: An Empirical Analysis', *Journal of Political Economy,* **99**, 263-286.

Ericsson, N.R. and Irons, J.S. (1995), 'The Lucas Critique in Practice: Theory Without Measurement', in K. Hoover (ed.) *Macroeconometrics: Developments, Tensions, and Prospects*, Boston, Kluwer.

Estes, W. (1954), 'Individual Behavior in Uncertain Situations: An Interpretation in Terms of Statistical Association Theory', in R. Thrall *et al.* (eds.) *Decision Processes,* New York, John Wiley and Sons.

Etzioni, A. (1987), 'On Thoughtless Rationality (Rules of Thumb)', *Kyklos,* **40**, 496-514.

Favero, C. and Hendry, D.F. (1992), 'Testing the Lucas Critique: A Review,' *Econometric Reviews,* **11**, 265-306.

Figlewski, S. and Wachtel, P. (1981), 'The Formation of Inflationary Expectations', *Review of Economics and Statistics*, **63**, 1-10.

Fischer, S. (1988), 'Recent Developments in Macroeconomics', *Economic Journal,* **98,** 294-339.

Flavin, M. (1981), 'The Adjustment of Consumption to Changing Expectations about Future Income', *Journal of Political Economy*, **89**, 974-1009.

Flew, A. (1988), 'Introduction', *David Hume*, LaSalle, Open Court.

Fogelin, R.J. (1985), *Hume's Skepticism in the Treatise of Human Nature*, London, Routledge & Kegan Paul.

Foster, J. (1987), *Evolutionary Macroeconomics*, London, Allen & Unwin.

Friedman, M. (1953), 'The Methodology of Positive Economics', *Essays in Positive Economics*, Chicago, University of Chicago Press.

Friedman, M. (1957), *A Theory of the Consumption Function*, Princeton, Princeton University Press.

Friedman, M. (1968), 'The Role of Monetary Policy', *American Economic Review*, **58**, 1-17.

Frisch, H. (1983), *Theories of Inflation*, Cambridge, Cambridge University Press.

Fuhrer, J.C. (1992), 'Do Consumers Behave as the Life-Cycle/Permanent-Income Theory of Consumption Predicts?' *New England Economic Review*, September/October, 3-14.

Galbraith, J. K. (1997), 'Time to Ditch the NAIRU', *Journal of Economic Perspectives*, **11**, 93-108.

Gilbert, C.L. (1990), 'Professor Hendry's Econmetric Methodology', in C.W.J. Granger (ed.) *Modelling Economic Series: Readings in Econometric Methodology*, Oxford, Oxford University Press, 279-303.

Giles, J. and Giles, D. (1993), 'Pre-Test Estimation and Testing in Econometrics: Recent Developments', *Journal of Economic Surveys*, **7**, 145-97.

Glass, G.V., McGaw, B. and Smith, M.L. (1981), *Meta-Analysis in Social Research*, Beverly Hills, Sage.

Goldfarb, R.S. (1995), 'The Economist-as-Audience Needs a Methodology of Plausible Inference', *The Journal of Economic Methodology, ***2**, 201-222.

Gordon, R. J. (1977), 'The Theory of Domestic Inflation', *American Economic Review, Papers and Proceedings*, **67**, 128-34.

Gordon, R. J. (1982), 'Price Inertia and Policy Ineffectiveness in the United States' *Journal of Political Economy*, **90**, 1087-1117.

Gordon, R. J. (1989), 'Hysteresis in History: Was There Ever a Phillips Curve?' *American Economic Review , Papers and Proceedings*, **79**, 220-25.

Gordon, R. J. (1997), 'The Time-Varying NAIRU and its Implications for Economic Policy', *Journal of Economic Perspectives*, **11**, 11-32.

Granger, C.W.J. (1986), 'Developments in the Study of Cointegrated Economic Variables', *Oxford Bulletin of Economics and Statistics*, **48**, 213-228.

Granger, C.W.J. (1991), 'Some Recent Generalizations of Cointegration and the Analysis of Long-Run Relationships', in R.F. Engle and C.W.J. Granger (eds.) *Long-Run Economic Relationships: Reading in Cointegration,* Oxford, Oxford University Press, 277-87.

Granger, C.W.J. and Newbold, P. (1975), 'Spurious Regressions in Econometrics', *Journal of Econometrics*, **31**, 111-20.

Greene, W.H. (1990), *Econometric Analysis*, New York, Macmillan.

Griffiths, W.E., Hill R.C. and Judge, G.C. (1993), *Learning and Practicing Econometrics*, New York, John Wiley and Sons.

Grunberg, E. (1966), 'The Meaning and Scope of External Boundaries in Economics.' *The Structure of Economic Science: Essays in Methodology*, edited by S.R. Krupp, 148-65. Englewood Cliffs, N.J., Prentice-Hall.

Gujarati, D.N. (1988). *Basic Econometrics*, 2nd ed. New York, McGraw-Hill.

de Haan, J. and Zelhorst, D. (1988), 'The Empirical Evidence on the Ricardian Equivalence Hypothesis', *Kredit and Kapital,* **21**, 407-21.

Hadjimathheau, G. (1987), *Consumer Economics after Keynes: Theory and Evidence of the Consumption Function,* Brighton, Wheatsheaf.

Hahn, F.H. (1991), 'The Next Hundred Years', *Economic Journal ,* **101**, 47-50.

Hall, R.E. (1978), 'Stochastic Implications of the Life Cycle-Permanent Income Hypothesis: Theory and Evidence', *Journal of Political Economy,* **86**, 971-987.

Hall, S.G. (1986), 'An Application of the Granger and Engle Two-Step Estimation Procedure to United Kingdom Aggregate Wage Data', *Oxford Bulletin of Economics and Statistics*, **48**, 229-239.

Hausman, D. (1992), *The Inexact and Separate Science of Economics*, Cambridge, Cambridge University Press.

Hausman, J.A. (1978), 'Specification Tests in Econometrics', *Econometrica*, **46**, 1251-71.

Hedges L.V. and Olkin I. (1985), *Statistical Methods for Meta-Analysis,* Orlando, Academic Press.

Heilbroner, R. L. (1988), *Beyond the Veil of Economics*: Essays in the Worldly Philosophy, New York, W.W. Norton.

Hendry, D.F. (1986), 'Econometric Modelling with Cointegrated Variables', *Oxford Bulletin of Economics and Statistics*, **48**, 210-212.

Hendry, D.F., Pagan, A.R., and Sargan, J.D. (1984), 'Dynamic Specification', in Z. Giliches and M.D. Intriligator, *Handbook of Econometrics*, vol II. Amsterdam: North-Holland, 1023-1100.

Hendry, D.F. and Ericsson, N.R. (1991), 'Modeling the Demand for Narrow Money in the United Kingdom and the United States', *European Economic Review*, **35**, 833-886.

Hillier, J.H. (1991), 'On Multiple Diagnostic Procedures for the Linear Model', *Journal of Econometrics*, **47**, 47-66.

Hofstadter, D.R.(1979), *Gödel, Escher, Bach: An Eternal Golden Braid*, New York, Basic Books.

Hogg, R.V. and Craig, A.T. (1970), *Introduction to Mathematical Statistics*, 3rd ed. London, Macmillan.

Hoover, K.D. (1990), 'The Logic of Causal Inference: Econometrics and the Conditional Analysis of Causation', *Economics and Philosophy*, **6,** 207-234.

Hoover, K.D. (1994), 'Econometrics as Observation, The Lucas Critique and the Nature of Econometric Inference', *The Journal of Economic Methodology*, **1**, 65-80.

Hume, D. (1739:1978), *Treatise on Human Nature*, L.A. Selby-Bigge (ed.), text revised with notes by P.H. Nidditch. Oxford, Oxford University Press.

Hume, D. (1777:1902), *Enquiries Concerning the Human Understanding and Concerning the Principles of Morals*, L.A. Selby-Bigge (ed.). Oxford, Oxford University Press.

Hunter, J.E. and Schmidt, F.L. (1990), *Methods of Meta-Analysis: Correcting Error and Bias in Research Findings*, Newbury Park, Sage Publications.

Jarrell, S. B. and Stanley, T.D. (1990), 'A Meta-Analysis of the Union–Nonunion Wage Gap', *Industrial and Labor Relations Review*, **44**, 54-67.

Johnston, J. (1991), 'Econometrics: Retrospect and Prospect', *Economic Journal*, **101**, 51-56.

Judge, G. and Bock, C. (1978), *The Statistical Implications of Pre-test and Stein-Rule Estimators in Econometrics*, Amsterdam, North-Holland.

Judge, G. *et al.* (1985), *The Theory and Practice of Econometrics,* New York, John Wiley.

Kahn, G.A. (1996), 'New Estimates of the U.S. Economy's Potential Growth Rate', *Contemporary Economic Policy*, **14,** 1-16.

Katzner, D.W. (1993), 'Some Notes on the Role of History and the Definition of Hysteresis and Related Concepts in Economic Analysis', *Journal of Post Keynesian Economics*, **15**, 323-345.

Kaufmann, W. (1956), 'Existentialism from Dostoevsky to Sartre', pp. 11-51 in W. Kaufmann (ed.) *Existentialism from Dostoevsky to Sartre*, New York, World Publishing.

Keynes, J.N. (1891:1955), *The Scope and Method of Political Economy*, New York, Kelley & Millman.

King, D.A. (1982), 'Accuracy of the Quarterly GNP Estimates', *Business Economics*, **17**, 9-15.

King, R.G. , Stock, J. H. and Watson, M.W. (1995), 'Temporal Instability of the Unemployment–Inflation Relationship', *Economic Perspectives of the Federal Reserve Bank of Chicago*, **19**, 2-12.

Kleidon, A.W. (1986a), 'Bias in Small Sample Tests of Stock Price Rationality', *Journal of Business* , **59**, 237-61.

Kleidon, A.W. (1986b), 'Anomalies in Financial Economics: Blueprint for Change?' *Journal of Business*, **59**, S469-99.

Klein, L.R. and Kosobud, R.F. (1961), 'Some Econometrics of Growth: Great Ratios in Economics', *Quarterly Journal of Economics*, **75**, 173-98.

Kmenta, J. (1971), *Elements of Econometrics,* New York, Macmillan.

Knight, F. (1940), 'What is "Truth" in Economics?' *Journal of Political Economy,* **48**, 1-32.

Kuhn, T.S. (1962), *The Structure of Scientific Revolutions*, Chicago, University of Chicago Press.

Lakatos, I. (1970), 'Falsification and the Methodology of Scientific Research Programmes', in I. Lakatos and A. Musgrave (eds) *Criticism and the Growth of Knowledge*, Cambridge, Cambridge University Press.

Lakatos, I. and Musgrave, A. (eds) (1970), *Criticism and the Growth of Knowledge*, Cambridge, Cambridge University Press.

Latsis, S.J. (1976), 'A Research Programme in Economics', in S.J. Latsis (ed.), *Method and Appraisal in Economics*, Cambridge, Cambridge University Press.

Lawson, T. (1994), 'Why are so many Economists so Opposed to Methodology?' *Journal of Economic Methodology,* **1**, 105-133.

Leamer, E. (1983), 'Let's Take the Con out of Econometrics', *American Economic Review*, **73**, 31-43.

Leamer, E. and Leonard, H. (1983), 'Reporting the Fragility of Regression Estimates', *Review of Economics and Statistics,* **65**, 306-317.

Lee, B. (1991), 'On the Rationality of Forecasts', *Review of Economics and Statistics*, **73**, 365-70.

Leiderman, L. and Blejer, M. I. (1988), 'Modeling and Testing Ricardian Equivalence', *International Monetary Fund Staff Papers*, **35,** 1-35.

LeRoy, S.F. (1989),'Efficient Captial Markets and Martingales', *Journal of Economic Literature*, **27**, 1583-1621.

Levin, R.I.. and Rubin, D.S. (1991), *Statistics for Management,* Englewood Cliffs, Prentice-Hall.

Lichtenstein, S. and Slovic, P. (1971), 'Reversals of Preference in Bids and Choices in Gambling Decision', *Journal of Experimental Psychology*, **89**, 46-55.

Light, R.J. and Smith, P.V. (1971), 'Accumulating Evidence: Procedures for Resolving Contradictions Among Different Research Studies', *Harvard Educational Review*, **41**, 429-471.

Lilien, G.L. (1974), 'Application of a Modified Linear Learning Model of Buyer Behavior', *Journal of Marketing Research*, **11**, 279-85.

Linter, J. (1981), 'The Use of Volatility Measures in Assessing Market Efficiency: Comment.' *Journal of Finance*, **36**, 307-11.

Lipák, T. (1958), 'On the Combination of Independent Tests', *Magyar Tudományos Akadémia Mathematikai Kutató Intezetenek Kolemenyei,* **3**, 1971-77.

Lipsey, R.G. (1960), 'The Relation Between Unemployment and the Rate of Change of Money Wage Rate in the United Kingdom, 1862-1957: A Further Analysis', *Economica,* **27**,456-87.

De Long, B. and Lang, K. (1992), 'Are All Economic Hypothesis False?' *Journal of Political Economy,* **100**, 1257-72.

Lovell, M.C. (1986), 'Tests of the Rational Expectations Hypothesis', *American Economic Review*, **76**, 110-124.

Lucas, R.E. jr. (1976), 'Economic Policy Evaluation: A Critique', in K. Brunner and A.H. Meltzer (eds) *The Phillips Curve and Labour Markets*, Amsterdam, North-Holland.

Machina, M. (1987), 'Choice Under Uncertainty: Problems Solved or Unsolved', *Journal of Economic Perspectives*, **1**, 121-154.

MacKinnon, J. (1991), 'Critical Values for Cointegration Tests', in R.F. Engle and C.W.J. Granger (eds), *Long-Run Economic Relationships: Reading in Cointegration*, Oxford, Oxford University Press.

Makridakis, S. and Hibon, M. (1984), 'Accuracy of Forecasting: An Empirical Investigation (with Discussion).' pp. 35-71, in S. Makridakis (ed.), *The Forecasting Accuracy of Major Time Series Methods*, New York, Wiley.

Malinvaud, E. (1966), *Statistical Methods of Econometrics*, Chicago, Rand McNally.

Malinvaud, E. (1980), *Statistical Methods of Econometrics*, 3rd ed., Amsterdam, North Holland.

Malinvaud, E. (1991), 'The Next Fifty Years', *Economic Journal,* **101**, 64-68.

Mankiw, N.G. (1981), 'The Permanent Income Hypothesis and the Real Interest Rate', *Economics Letters*, **7**, 307-311.

Mankiw, N., Romer, G. and Shapiro, M.D., (1985), 'An Unbiased Reexamination of Stock Market Volatility', *Journal of Finance*, **40**, 677-87.

March, J.G. (1992), 'The War is Over and the Victors Have Lost', *Journal of Socio-Economics*, **21**, 261-7.

Mayer, T. (1993), *Truth versus Precision in Economics*, Aldershot, Hants, Edward Elgar.

Mayo, D. (1981), 'Testing Statistical Testing', in J.C. Pitt (ed.), *Philosophy in Economics*, Dordrecht, D. Reidel.

McCloskey, D.N. (1983), 'The Rhetoric of Economics', *The Journal of Economic Literature,* **21**, 481-517.

Merton, R.C. (1987), 'On the Current State of the Stock Market Rationality Hypothesis'. in R. Dornbusch, *et al.* (eds) *Macroeconomics and Finance: Essays in Honor of Franco Modigliani,* Cambridge, Mass., MIT Press.

Miller, D. (1996), 'What Use is Empirical Confirmation?' *Economics and Philosophy*, **12**, 197-206.

Mirowski, P. (1988), *Against Mechanism*, Totawa, Rowman and Littlefield.

Mirowski, P.(1989a), 'The Probabilities Counter-Revolution, Or How Stochastic Concepts Came to Neoclassical Economic Theory', *Oxford Economic Papers*, **41**, 217-235.

Mirowski, P.(1989b), *More Heat than Light: Economics as Social Physics, Physics as Nature's Economics,* Cambridge, Cambridge University Press.

Mirowski, P.(1989c), 'Tis a Pity Econometrics Isn't an Empirical Endeavor: Mandelbrot, Chaos, and the Noah and Joseph Effects', *Richerche Economiche*, **43**, 76-99.

Mises, L. (1949), *Human Action: A Treatise on Economics*, New Haven, Yale University Press.

Mises, L. (1960), *Epistemological Problems of Economics,* Princeton, van Nostrand.

Modigliani, F. (1949), 'Fluctuations in the Saving–Income Ratio: A Problem in Economic Forecasting', *Studies in Income and Wealth,* **11**, New York, NBER, 371-441.

Morey, M.J. (1984), 'The Statistical Implications of Preliminary Specification Error Testing', *Journal of Econometrics,* **25**, 63-72.

Morgan, M.S. (1988), 'Finding a Satisfactory Empirical Model, in N. de Marchi (ed.) *The Popperian Legacy in Economics*, Cambridge, Cambridge University Press.

Mullineaux, D.J. (1978), 'On Testing for Rationality: Another Look at the Livington Price Expectations Data', *Journal of Political Economy*, **86**, 329-36.

Muscatelli, V.A. and Hurn, S. (1992), 'Cointegration and Dynamic Time Series Models', *Journal of Economic Surveys*, **6**, 1-43.

Muth, J.F. (1961), 'Rational Expectations and the Theory of Price Movements', *Econometrica*, **29**, 315-335.

Nakamura, A. and Nakamura, M. (1981), 'On the Relationship among Several Specification Error Tests Presented by Durbin, Wu, and Hausman', *Econometrica*, **49**, 1583-1588.

Naylor, T.H. *et al.* (1972), 'Box–Jenkins Methods: An Alternative to Econometric Forecasting', *International Statistics Review*, **40**, 123-137.

Nelson, C.R. and Plosser, C. (1982), 'Trends and Random Walks in Macroeconomic Time Series: Some Evidence and Implications', *Journal of Monetary Economics*, **10**, 139-162.

O'Driscoll, G.P. (1977), 'The Ricardian Nonequivalence Theorem', *Journal of Political Economy*, **85**, 207-210.

Okun, A. (1962), 'Potential GNP: Its Measurement and Significance', *Proceedings of the American Statistical Association*, 98-116.

Ormerod, P. (1997), *The Death of Economics*. New York, John Wiley & Sons.

Orszag, J.M. and Staroselsky, I. (1993), 'Aggregate Consumption Behavior and the Permanent Income Hypothesis', *Economics Letters*, **41**, 145-7.

Pant, P.N. and Starbuck, W.H. (1990), 'Innocents in the Forest: Forecasting and Research Methods', *Journal of Management*, **16**, 433-460.

Perasso, G. (1987). 'The Ricardian Equivalence Theorem and the Consumption Function: A Survey of the Literature', *Rivista Internazionale di Scienze Economichi e Commerciali*, **34**, 649-74.

Pesaran, M.H. (1982), 'On the Comprehensive Method of Testing Non-Nested Regression Models', *Journal of Econometrics*, **18**, 263-74.

Pesaran, M.H. and Deaton, A.S.(1978), 'Testing Non-nested Nonlinear Regression Models', *Econometrica*, **46**, 677-694.

Peters, S. and Smith, R.J. (1991), 'Distributional Specification Tests Against Semiparametric Alternatives', *Journal of Econometrics*, **47**, 175-94.

Pheby, J. (1988), *Methodology of Economics: A Critical Introduction*, London, Macmillan.

Phillips, A.W. (1958), 'The Relation Between Unemployment and the Rate of Change of Money Wage Rate in the United Kingdom, 1861-1957', *Economica*, **25**, 283-99.

Phillips, J.M. (1994), 'Farmer Education and Farmer Efficiency: A Meta-Analysis', *Economic Development and Cultural Change*, **42**, 149-165.

Phillips, J.M. and Goss, E.P. (1995), 'The Effect of State and Local Taxes on Economic Development: A Meta-Analysis', *Southern Economic Journal*, **62**, 320-333.

Pindyck, R.S. (1991), 'Irreversibility, Uncertainty, and Investment', *Journal of Economic Literature*, **16**, 3-29.

Plott, C.R. (1982), 'Industrial Organization Theory and Experimental Economics', *Journal of Economic Literature*, **20**, 1485-1527.

Plott, C.R. (1986), 'Laboratory Experiments in Economics: The Implications of Post-Price Institutions', *Science*, **9**, 732-8.

Plott, C.R. and Sunder, S. (1982), 'Efficiency of Experimental Security Markets with Insider Information: An Application of Rational Expectations Models', *Journal of Political Economy*, **90**, 663-698.

Podkaminer, L. (1998), 'Inflationary Effects of High Nominal Interest Rates', *Journal of Post Keynesian Economics*, **20**, 583-96.

Poirier, D.J. (1988), 'Frequentist and Subjectivist Perspectives on the Problems of Model Building in Economics', *Journal of Economic Perspectives*, **6**, 120-170.

Popper, K.R. (1959), *The Logic of Scientific Discovery*, New York, Basic Books.

Popper, K.R. (1963), *Conjectures and Refutations: The Growth of Scientific Knowledge*, New York, Basic Books.

Popper, K.R. (1972), *Objective Knowledge: An Evolutionary Approach,* London, Oxford University Press.

Popper, K.R. (1976), *Unended Quest*, La Salle, Open Court.

Popper, K.R. (1982), *Quantum Theory and the Schism in Physics*, Totowa, Rowman and Littlefield.

Popper, K.R. (1994), *The Myth of the Framework: In Defence of Science and Rationality*, London, Routledge.

Powell, J.L. (1984), 'Least Absolute Deviations Estimation for the Censored Regression Model', *Journal of Econometrics*, **25**, 303-25.

Powell, J.L. (1986), 'Symmetrically Trimmed Least Squares Estimation for Tobit Models', *Econometrica*, **54**, 1435-60.

Prigogine, I. and Stengers, I. (1984), *Order Out of Chaos: Man's New Dialogue with Nature*, New York, Bantam Books.

Quah, D. (1990), 'Permanent and Transitory Movements in Labor Income: An Explanation for "Excess Smoothness" in Consumption', *Journal of Political Economy*, **98**, 449-475.

Quine, W.V.O. (1953:1963), *From a Logical Point of View*, Harper & Row.

Radnitzky, G. and Bartley, W.W. (eds.) (1987), *Evolutionary Epistemology, Theory of Rationality, and the Sociology of Knowledge*, La Salle, Open Court.

Ramsey, J.B. (1969), 'Tests for Specification Errors in Classical Linear Least Squares Regression Analysis', *Journal of the Royal Statistical Society B*, **31**, 350-371.

Ramsey, J.B. (1974), 'Classical Models of Selection through Specification Error Tests', in P. Zarembka (ed.), *Frontiers of Econometrics*, New York, Academic Press.

Ramsey, J.B. and Kmenta, J. (1980), 'Problems and Issues in Evaluating Econometric Models', in J. Kmenta and J. Ramsey (eds.), *Evaluation of Econometric Models*, New York, Academic Press.

Redman, D.A. (1994), 'Karl Popper's Theory of Science and Econometrics: The Rise and Decline of Social Engineering', *Journal of Economic Issues*, **28**, 67-99.

Resnick, R. and Halliday, D. (1966), *Physics*, New York, John Wiley & Sons.

Ricardo, D. (1820: 1951), 'Funding System: An Article in the Supplement to the Fourth, Fifth, and Sixth Editions of the Encyclopædia Britannica', reprinted in P. Sraffa (ed.) *The Works and Correspondence of David Ricardo*, vol 4, Cambridge, Cambridge University Press. 149-200.

Robbins, L. (1962), *An Essay on the Nature and Significance of Economic Science*, London, Macmillan.

Robinson, P.M. (1988), 'Root-N-Consistent Semiparametric Regression', *Econmetrica*, **56**, 931-54.

Rose, A. K. (1986), 'Four Paradoxes in GNP', *Economics Letters*, **22**, 137-141.

Salmon, W.C. (1966), *The Foundations of Scientific Inference*, Pittsburgh, University of Pittsburgh Press.

Santomero, A. and Seater, J.J. (1978), 'The Inflation–Unemployment Trade-off: A Critique of the Literature', *Journal of Economic Literature*, **16**, 499-544.

Sawyer, K.R., Beed, C. and Sankey, H. (1997), 'Underdetermination in Economics. The Duhem–Quine Thesis', *Economics and Philosophy*, **13**, 1-23.

Seater, J.J. (1993), 'Ricardian Equivalence', *Journal of Economic Literature*, **31**, 142-190.

Sen, A.K. (1979), 'Rational Fools: A Critique of the Behavioral Foundations of Economic Theory', pp. 87-109 in F. Hahn and M. Hollis (eds) *Philosophy and Economic Theory*, Oxford, Oxford University Press.

Shapiro, M.D. (1984), 'The Permanent Income Hypothesis and the Real Interest Rate: Some Evidence from Panel Data', *Economics Letters*, 14, 93-100.

Shiller, R.J. (1981a), 'Do Stock Prices Move Too Much to be Justified by Subsequent Changes in Dividends?' *American Economic Review*, 71, 421-36.

Shiller, R.J. (1981b), 'The Use of Volatility Measures in Assessing Market Efficiency', *Journal of Finance*, 36, 291-304.

Shiller, R.J. (1984), 'Stock Prices and Social Dynamics', *Brookings Papers on Economic Activity*, 2, 457-498.

Smith, V.K. and Huang, J.C. (1995), 'Can Market Value Air Quality? A Meta-Analysis of Hedonic Property Value Models', *Journal of Political Economy*, 103, 209-225.

Smith, V.L. (1986), 'Experimental Methods in the Political Economy of Exchange', *Science*, 234, 167-173.

Smith, V.L. (1989), 'Theory, Experiment and Economics', *Journal of Economic Perspectives*, 3, 151-169.

Smith, V.L. (1991), *Papers in Experimental Economics*, Cambridge, Cambridge University Press.

Smith, V.L. (1994), 'Economics in the Laboratory', *Journal of Economic Perspectives*, 8, 113-131.

Smith, V.L. and Williams, A. (1992), 'Experimental Market Economics', *Scientific American*, 267, 116-121.

Smith, V.L., Suchanek, G. and Williams, A. (1988), 'Bubbles, Crashes and Endogenous Expectations in Experimental Spot Asset Markets', *Econometrica*, 56, 1119-51.

Spanos, A. (1986), *Statistical Foundations of Econometric Modelling*, Cambridge, Cambridge University Press.

Spanos, A. (1989), 'Early Empirical Findings on the Consumption Function, Stylized Facts or Fiction: a Retrospective View', *Oxford Economic Papers*, 41, 150-169.

Spanos, A. (1990), 'Toward a Unifying Methodological Framework for Econometric Modelling', in C.W.J. Granger (ed.) *Modelling Economic Series: Readings in Econometric Methodology*, Oxford, Oxford University Press, 335-364.

Srinivasan, V. and Kesavan, R. (1976), 'An Alternate Interpretation of the Linear Learning Model of Brand Choice', *Journal of Consumer Research*, 3, 76-83.

Staiger, D. , Stock, J. H. and Watson, M.W. (1997), 'The NAIRU, Unemployment and Monetary Policy', *Journal of Economic Perspectives*, 11, 33-52.

Stanley, T.D. (1982), 'A Search for the Growth of Economic Knowledge: Popper and Methodological Progress', unpublished Ph.D. Dissertation, Purdue University.

Stanley, T.D. (1985), 'Positive Economics and Its Instrumental Defence', *Economica*, **52**, 305-319.

Stanley, T.D. (1986a), 'Stein-Rule Least Squares Estimation: A Heuristic for Fallible Data', *Economics Letters*, **20**, 147-150.

Stanley, T.D. (1986b), 'Recursive Economic Knowledge: Hierarchy, Maximization, and Behavioral Economics', *Journal of Behavioral Economics*, **15**, 85-99.

Stanley, T.D. (1988), 'Forecasting from Fallible Data: Correcting Prediction Bias with Stein-Rule Least Squares', *Journal of Forecasting*, **7**, 103-113.

Stanley, T.D. (1989), 'Galton, Stein, and Empirical Bayes: Artifacts and Connections', *Statistica*, XLIX(4), 1-13.

Stanley, T.D. (1991), 'Criticizing Maximization and Avoiding the Ultra-Empirical Trap' in R. Frantz, H. Singh, and J. Gerber (eds.) *Handbook of Behavioral Economics,* vol. 2A, Greenwich, Conn., JAI Press, 35-51.

Stanley, T.D. (1993), 'Ain't Misbehavin' –Capricious Consumption or Permanent Income?' *Journal of Post Keynesian Economics*, **16**, 249-267.

Stanley, T.D. (1994), 'Silly Bubbles and the Insensitivity of Rationality Testing: An Experimental Illustration', *Journal of Economic Psychology*, **15**, 601-620.

Stanley, T.D. (1998), 'New Wine in Old Bottles: A Meta-Analysis of Ricardian Equivalence', *Southern Economic Journal,* **64**, 713-727.

Stanley, T.D. and Jarrell, S.B. (1989), 'Meta-Regression Analysis: A Quantitative Method of Literature Surveys', *Journal of Economic Surveys*, **3**, 161-170.

Stanley, T.D. and Jarrell, S. B. (1998), 'Gender Wage Discrimination Bias? A Meta-Analysis', *Journal of Human Resources*, **33**, 947-973.

Stiglitz, J.E. (1991), 'The Determinants of Growth', *Economic Journal*, **101**, 134-41.

Stiglitz, J.E. (1997), 'Reflections of the Natural Rate Hypothesis', *Journal of Economic Perspectives* , **11**, 3-10.

Stock, J.H. (1987), 'Asymptotic Properties of Least Squares Estimators of Cointegrating Vectors', *Econometrics,* **55**, 1035-56.

Stock, J.H. (1988), 'A Reexamination of Friedman's Consumption Puzzle', *Journal of Business and Economic Statistics*, **6**, 401-407.

Stock, J.H. and Watson, M.W. (1986), 'Does GNP have a Unit Root?' *Economics Letters*, **22**, 147-151.

Stock, J.H. and Watson, M.W. (1988), 'Variable Trends in Economic Time Series', *Journal of Economic Perspectives,* **2**, 147-174.

Summers, L.H., (1986), 'Does the Stock Market Rationally Reflect Fundamental Values?' *Journal of Finance,* **41**, 591-601.

Takayama, A. (1985), *Mathematical Economics,* 2nd ed. Cambridge, Cambridge University Press.

Theil, H.(1971), *Principles of Econometrics*, New York, John Wiley.

Thomas, J.J. (1989), 'The Early Economic History of the Consumption Function', *Oxford Economic Papers*, **41**, 131-149.

Thursby, J.G. (1979), 'Alternative Specification Error Tests: A Comparative Study', *Journal of the American Statistical Association,* **74,** 222-225

Thursby, J.G. (1981), 'A Test Strategy for Discriminating between Autocorrelation and Misspecification in Regression Analysis', *Review of Economics and Statistics*, **63**, 117- 143.

Thursby, J.G. and Schmidt, P. (1977), 'Some Properties of Tests for Specification Error in a Linear Regression Model', *Journal of the American Statistical Association,* **72**, 635-641.

Tobin J. (1987), 'Okun, Arthur M.' in J Eatwell, M. Millgate, and P. Newman (eds.) *The New Palgrave: A Dictionary of Economics*, London, Macmillan Press.

Tversky, A. and Kahneman, D. (1971), 'Belief in the Law of Small Numbers', *Psychological Bulletin,* **2**, 105-110.

Tversky, A., Slovic, P. and Kahneman, D. (1990), 'The Causes of Preference Reversal', *American Economic Review*, **80**, 204-217.

Van Boening, M.V., Williams, A.W., and LaMaster, S. (1993), 'Price Bubbles and Crashes in Experimental Call Markets', *Economics Letters,* **41**,179-85.

Vanhonacker, W.R., Lehmann, D.R., and Sultan, F. (1990), 'Combining Related and Sparse Data in Linear Regression Models', *Journal of Business and Economic Statistics*, **8**, 327-335.

White, H. (1980), 'A Heteroskedasticity-Consistent Covariance Matrix Estimator and a Direct test of Heteroskedasticity', *Econometrica,* **50**, 1-26.

White, H.(1982), 'Maximum Likelihood Estimation of Misspecified Models', *Econometrica*, **50**, 1- 25.

White, H. (1989), *Estimation, Inference and Specification Analysis.* Cambridge, Cambridge University Press.

Wierenga, B. (1974), *An Investigation of Brand Choice Processes*, Rotterdam, Rotterdam University Press.

Wilcox, J.A. (1990), 'Nominal Interest Rates Effects on Real Consumer Expenditure', *Business Economics,* **25**, 31-37.

Wolf, F.M. (1986), *Meta-Analysis: Quantitative Methods for Research Synthesis,* Beverly Hills, Sage Publications.

Wooldridge, J.M. (1991), 'On the Application of Robust, Regression Based Diagnostics to Models of Conditional Variances', *Journal of Econometrics*, **47**, 5-46.

Index